PENGUIN BOOKS

The Penguin Portuguese Phrasebook

Jill Norman enjoys exploring language, speaks several
languages and has travelled widely. Jill also created the
Penguin Cookery Library in the 1960s and 1970s, bringing
many first-class authors to the list. She has written several
award-winning books on food and cookery, and is a leading
authority on the use of herbs and spices. She is the literary
trustee of the Elizabeth David estate, and was Mrs David's
publisher for many years.

Natália Pinazza was born and raised in São Paulo, Brazil,
and has studied and researched languages, literature and
indigenous cultures at the Universities of São Paulo (Brazil),
Bath (United Kingdom) and Ottawa (Canada). She has a
PhD in Argentine and Brazilian Culture from the University
of Bath, and was nominated by the Brazilian government
as the candidate for the UNESCO Keizo Obuchi Fellowship
Awards.

D0838455

THE PENGUIN
PORTUGUESE
PHRASEBOOK

Fourth Edition

Jill Norman,
Antonio de Figueiredo,
Natália Pinazza

PENGUIN BOOKS

PENGUIN BOOKS

Published by the Penguin Group
Penguin Books Ltd, 80 Strand, London WC2R ORL, England
Penguin Group (USA) Inc., 375 Hudson Street, New York, New York 10014, USA
Penguin Group (Canada), 90 Eglinton Avenue East, Suite 700, Toronto, Ontario, Canada M4P 2Y3
(a division of Pearson Penguin Canada Inc.)
Penguin Ireland, 25 St Stephen's Green, Dublin 2, Ireland (a division of Penguin Books Ltd)
Penguin Group (Australia), 707 Collins Street, Melbourne, Victoria 3008, Australia
(a division of Pearson Australia Group Pty Ltd)
Penguin Books India Pvt Ltd, 11 Community Centre, Panchsheel Park, New Delhi – 110 017, India
Penguin Group (NZ), 67 Apollo Drive, Rosedale, Auckland 0632, New Zealand
(a division of Pearson New Zealand Ltd)
Penguin Books (South Africa) (Pty) Ltd, Block D, Rosebank Office Park,
181 Jan Smuts Avenue, Parktown North, Gauteng 2193, South Africa

Penguin Books Ltd, Registered Offices: 80 Strand, London WC2R ORL, England

www.penguin.com

First edition 1971
Second edition 1979
Third edition 1988
This revised and updated edition published 2014
001

Set in 9/12pt TheSans and TheSerif
Typeset by Jouve (UK), Milton Keynes
Printed in England by Clays Ltd, St Ives plc

ISBN: 978–0–141–39482–4

www.greenpenguin.co.uk

CONTENTS

INTRODUCTION

This series of phrasebooks includes words and phrases essential to travellers of all kinds: the business traveller; the holidaymaker, whether travelling alone, with a group or the family; and the owner of a house, an apartment or a time-share. For easy use the phrases are arranged in sections which deal with specific situations and needs.

The main focus of the book is Portuguese as spoken in Brazil; some words and the pronunciation of the language are different from European Portuguese. Many people in Portugal are familiar with Brazilian Portuguese, whereas relatively few Brazilians are aware of Portuguese as spoken in Portugal, so if you are visiting Portugal you will be able to speak and be understood.

Pronunciation is given for each phrase and for all words in the extensive vocabulary. See pp. xi–xvii for the pronunciation guide which should be read carefully before starting to use the book. It includes notes to explain the differences in pronunciation between Portuguese spoken in Portugal and in Brazil.

Some of the Portuguese phrases are marked with an asterisk* – these give an indication of the kind of reply you might get to your questions, and of questions you may be asked in turn.

For those who would like to know a little more about the Portuguese language, the main points of its grammar are covered at the end of the book (pp. 234–243).

We have added new words and phrases to take into account recent social and technological developments. However, there is a tendency to use original English words; terms such as 'stress', 'freezer', 'piercing', 'shopping centre', 'fitness' are still better known than their Portuguese equivalents. But you will always be rewarded for, and helped in, your efforts to speak Portuguese.

PRONUNCIATION

The pronunciation guide is intended for people with no knowledge of Portuguese. As far as possible the system is based on English pronunciation. However, Portuguese has a more complex system of sounds than English. This means that complete accuracy will sometimes be lost for the sake of simplicity, but the reader should be able to understand Portuguese pronunciation, and to be understood after reading this section carefully. Each phrase and each word in the vocabulary is given with a pronunciation guide.

The pronunciation used throughout the book is Brazilian; if the pronunciation of certain sounds is different in Portugal this is shown below.

Vowels

a as **a** in father	symbol **ah**	fábrica (**fah**-bree-ka) – factory
as **a** in about or as **u** in put	symbol **a**	amigo (a-**mee**-goo) – friend
e, **è** as **e** in bet	symbol **e**, **eh**	serra (**soh**-ha) – mountain
e, **ê** as **ay** in stay or as **ey** in they	symbol **e**, **ey**, **ay**, **ai**	fazer (fa-**zair**) – to do

e, i as e in open or as i in bit (occurs only in an unstressed syllable). In Brazil final e can have the sound of e or ee. In Portugal it is almost silent.	symbol e	antes (a^n-tes) – before carne (kar-ne) *B* (karn) *P* – meat
i as i in machine	symbol ee	bicicleta (bee-see-kle-ta) – bicycle
before a, e, o or u in unstressed syllables i resembles y in yes	symbol y, ee	férias (fe-ryas) – holiday
o as o in olive	symbol o	bola (bo-la) – ball
o, ou, ô, final oa as o in so, most	symbol oh	ôvo (oh-voo) – egg
o as oo in boot (used in most unstressed syllables)	symbol oo	dormir (door-meer) – to sleep
final o can be emphasized and pronounced as oo		como (ko-mo or ko-moo) – how
u as u in rule or oo in boot	symbol oo	usar (oo-zar) – to use
before a, e, i, and after o the u sound resembles w in wet	symbol w	água (a-gwa) – water

Double Vowels

The following double vowels – **ei, éi, éu** – do not have special sounds. They are very close to the sounds of the separate parts as listed above and the same symbols are used.

e.g. céu – sky (seh-oo).

The double vowels below are pronounced as shown

ai as **ie** in tie	symbol **i, ie, y**	pai (pie) – father
au as **ow** in how	symbol **ow**	causa (**kow**-za) – cause
oi, ói as **oi** in oil or **oy** in boy	symbol **oy**	lençois (**lay**^{n}-soyss) – sheets

Nasals

These sounds should be made through the nose, but without pronouncing the 'n'. Nasalization is shown in spelling by a tilde (~) over the vowel, or by an **m** at the end of a word, or by **m** or **n** before a consonant.

ã, am, an	symbol **a^n**	maçã (ma-sa^n) – apple
ẽ, em, en	symbol **ay^n e^n**	cento (**se**^{n}-too) – hundred
im, in	symbol **ee^n**	cinco (**see**^{n}-koo) – five
õ, om, on	symbol **o^n**	bom (bo^n) – good
um, un	symbol **oo^n**	um (oo^n) – one
ão	symbol **ow^n**	pão (pow^n) – bread

| ãe. ãi | symbol y^n | mãe (my^n) – mother |
| Õe | symbol oy^n | limões (lee-**moy**^{n}s) – lemons |

Consonants

b, f, l, m, p, q, t, v are pronounced as in English, but note the following:

c before a, o, u or a consonant is pronounced **k**	symbol **k**	casa (**kah**-za) – house
c before e, i and ç are pronounced **s**	symbol **s**	certo (**sair**-too) – certain
ch is pronounced **sh** as in ship	symbol **sh**	chave (**shah**-ve) – key
d is softer than in English. When followed by **i** and sometimes **e** it is often pronounced as **j** in Brazilian Portuguese	symbol **j/d**	dia (**jee**-ah) – day cidade (see-**da**-jee) – city
g before a, o, u is pronounced **g** as in got; **gu** in combinations gue and gui the u is not pronounced; its purpose is to keep the **g** hard, as above	symbol **g**	garfo (**gahr**-foo) – fork guia (**gee**-a) – guide

g before e, i is pronounced as s in pleasure	symbol zh	gente (zhe^{n}t) P (zhe^n-te) B – people
h is always silent		hotel (o-**tew**)
j is pronounced as s in pleasure	symbol zh	laranja (lar-a^n-zha) – orange
l is pronounced as w at the end of a word in Brazil	symbol w	Brasil (**brah**-zeew) metal (me-**tow**)
lh is like lli in million	symbol ly	toalha (too-a-lya) – towel
nh is like ni in onion	symbol ny	vinho (**vee**-nyoo) – wine
r has two sounds as h in hot	symbol h	carro (**ka**-ho) – car Rio de Janeiro (**hee**-o je zha-**ne**-ro)
as r in later	symbol r	caro (**ka**-roo) – expensive
s. ss at the beginning of a word or after a consonant is pronounced s. In Portugal final s is pronounced sh	symbol s	saber (sa-**bair**) – to know
s between two vowels is pronounced z	symbol z	mesa (me-za) – table
s in pleasure	symbol zh	luz (loozh) – light
In Brazil t can be pronounced as ch when it comes before unstressed e or i or at the end of a word		tipo (**chee**-poo) – type elefante (eh-leh-fa^n-chee) – elephant

x is pronounced s at the end of a word or when ex is followed by a consonant	symbol s	excelente (es-say-le^{n}t) P (es-say-le^n-te) B – excellent
as z when ex is followed by a vowel	symbol z	exato (ez-a-too) – exact
as ch when between vowels or a nasal and a vowel	symbol ch	enxame (e^n-cha-me) – swarm
as s between two vowels	symbol s	auxílio (ow-see-lyoo) – help
and occasionally as ks in imported words	symbol ks	táxi (tak-see) – taxi
z is pronounced as z	symbol z	azul (az-ool) – blue
and sometimes as s in pleasure	symbol zh	luz (loozh) – light

Stress

Words ending in the single vowels **a, e, i, o, u** or in **m** or **s** are stressed on the last syllable but one: **fa**lo – I speak; **ca**sas – houses; ves**ti**do – dress.

In other words the stress usually falls on the last syllable: fa**lar** – to speak; ma**çã** – apple; na**ção** – nation; ani**mal** – animal. Note that nasal vowels and double vowels at the end of a word carry stress. Exceptions to these rules are shown by a written accent: ca**fé**.

Stressed syllables are printed in **bold type** in the pronunciation guide.

The Portuguese Alphabet

A	á	H	agá	O	ó or ô	V	vê
B	bê	I	i	P	pê	W	dáblio
C	cê	J	jota	Q	quê	X	xis
D	dê	K	ká or kápa	R	érre	Y	ípsilon
E	é or ê	L	ele	S	ésse	Z	zê
F	efe	M	eme	T	tê		
G	gê or ghê	N	ene	U	u		

ESSENTIALS

First Things

Key Phrases

Yes	**Sim**	Seeⁿ
No	**Não**	Nowⁿ
OK	**OK**	OK
Please	**Por favor**	Poor fa-**vor**
Thank you	**Obrigado (m)/ Obrigada (f)**	O-bree-**ga**-do (a)
You're welcome	**De nada**	De **na**-da
Sorry	**Desculpe**	Des-**kool**-pe

Greetings

Key Phrases

Good morning/ good day	**Bom dia**	Buⁿ **Jee**-a
Good afternoon	**Boa tarde**	Bo-a **tar**-je

Good evening/ good night	Boa noite	Bo-a no-ee-te
Hello	Olá	Oh-la
Hello (when answering the phone)	Alô	A-loh
Hi	Oi	Oh-ee
Goodbye	Tchau	Chow

How are you?	Como está? / Como vai?	Ko-moo es-ta/Ko-moo vy
How is it going?/ Are you all right?	Tudo bom? /Tudo bem?	Too-doh bo^n /Too-doh be^n
Fine, thank you	Muito bem, obrigado (a)	Mwee too bay^n o-bree-ga-doo (a)
See you soon/ See you later	Até logo/ Até mais	A-te lo-goo/A-te ma-ees
Have a good journey	Boa viagem	Bo-a vee-a-zhay^n
Have a good time	Aproveite	Apro-vey-teh
Good luck/All the best	Boa sorte/ Tudo de bom	Bo-a sor-te/Too-doh je bo^n

Polite Phrases

Key Phrases

Sorry/Excuse me	**Me desculpe/ Com licença**	Me jes-**kool**-pe/**Ko**ⁿ lee-se ⁿ-sa
That's all right (*in reply to* Excuse me)	**Está bem**	Es-ta beⁿ
With pleasure	**Com prazer**	Koⁿ pra-**zayr**
Not at all/don't mention it	**De nada**	Je **na**-da
Is everything all right?	**Está tudo bem?**	Es-ta **too**-doh beⁿ
It's all right	**Tudo bem**	**Too**-doh beⁿ
Thanks for your help	**Obrigado(a) pela sua ajuda**	Ob-ree-**ga**-doo(a) **pe**-la **soo**-a a-**zhoo**-da

Don't worry	**Não se preocupe**	Nowⁿ se pray-o-**koo**-pe
It's a pity	**Que pena**	Kay **pe**-na
It doesn't matter	**Não importa**	Nowⁿ eeⁿ-**por**-ta
I beg your pardon?	**O quê/Como disse?**	Oo ke/ko-moo **jees**-se
Am I disturbing you?	**Estou incomodando?**	**Es**-toh eeⁿ koo mo daⁿ-doo
I'm sorry to have troubled you	**Desculpe o incomodo**	Des-**kool**-pe oh eeⁿ-koo-mo doo
Good/That's fine	**Bem/Está bem**	Beⁿ/es-ta beⁿ

Language Problems

Key Phrases

Do you speak English?	**Fala inglês?**	**Fa**-la eeⁿ-**glayss**
Does anybody here speak English?	**Há aqui alguém que fale inglês?**	Ah a-**kee** al-**ge**ⁿ ke **fa**-le eeⁿ-**glayss**
I don't speak (much) Portuguese	**Não falo (muito bem) português**	Nowⁿ **fa**-loo (**mwee**-to beⁿ) poor-too-**gayss**
I don't understand	**Não entendo/ compreendo**	Nowⁿ ayⁿ-**tay**ⁿ-doo/ koⁿ-pre-**ay**ⁿ-doo
Would you say that again, please?	**Pode repetir, por favor?**	**Po**-je he-**pe**-teer poor fa-**vor**
Please write it down	**Por favor, escreva num papel**	Poor fa-**vor** es-kre-**va** nooⁿ pa-**pel**

I'm English/American	**Sou inglês (inglesa)/ americano (americana)**	So eeⁿ-**glayss** (eeⁿ-**glay**-za)/a-me-ree-**ka**-no (a-me-ree-**ka**-na)
I speak a little Portuguese	**Eu falo um pouco de português**	**Ay**-oo **fa**-loo ooⁿ **poh**-koo je poor-too-**gayss**
Do you understand (me)?	**Você (me) entende?**	**Vo**-seh (me) eⁿ-**te**ⁿ-je
Please speak slowly	**Fale devagar por favor**	**Fa**-le je-**va**-gar poor fa-**vor**
What does that mean?	**O que isso quer dizer?**	Oo ke **ees**-soo ker jee-**zayr**
Can you translate this for me?	**Pode me traduzir isto?**	**Po**-je me tra-doo-**zeer ees**-to

What do you call this in Portuguese?	**Como se chama isto em português?**	**Ko**-moo se **sha**-ma ees-too ay^n poor-too-**gayss**
How do you say that in Portuguese?	**Como você fala isso em português?**	**Ko**-moo vo-seh **fa**-la ees-so ay^n poor-too-**gayss**
Please show me the word in the book	**Por favor me mostre a palavra no livro**	Poor fa-**vor** me **mos**-tre a pa-**la**-vra noo **lee**-vroo

Questions

Key Phrases

Who?	**Quem?**	Kay^n
Where Is/are . . . ?	**Onde está/estão . . . ?**	O^n-je es-ta/estow^n
When?	**Quando?**	**Kwa**^{n}-doo
How?	**Como?**	**Ko**-moo
How many?	**Quanto/Quantos?**	**Kwa**^{n}-too/ **Kwa**^{n}-toos
How much is/are . . . ?	**Quanto é/são . . . ?**	**Kwa**^{n}-too eh/sow^n
Why?	**Porquê?**	**Poor**-kay
Is/Are there . . . ?	**Há . . . ?/ Tem . . . ?**	Ah /Te^n

How long?	**Quanto tempo?**	**Kwa**^{n}-too **tay**^{n} poo
How far?	**Qual é a distância?**	Kwnl eh a **jees**-ta^n -see-a
What's that?	**O que é aquilo?**	Oo ke eh a-**kee**-loo
What do you want?	**O que deseja?**	Oo ke de-**ze**-zha
What must I do?	**O que devo fazer?**	Oo ke de-vo fa-**zer**

Do you have . . . ?	**Tem . . . ?**	Te^n
Have you seen . . . ?	**Viu . . . ?**	Vee-**oo**
Where can I find . . . ?	**Onde posso encontrar . . . ?**	O^n-je **pos**-soo ay^n-ko^n-**trar**
What is the matter?	**Que se passa?**	Ke se **pas**-sa
Can I help you?	***Posso ajudá-lo?**	**Pos**-soo a-zhoo-**da**-loo
Can you help me?	**Pode me ajudar?**	**Po**-je me a-zhoo-**dar**
Can you tell/give/ show me?	**Pode me dizer/me dar/ me mostrar?**	**Po**-je me jee-**zayr**/ me **dar**/ me moos-**trar**

Useful Statements

Key Phrases

I want . . .	**Quero . . .**	**Ke**-roo
I don't want . . .	**Não quero . . .**	Now^n **ke**-roo
I need . . .	**Preciso . . .**	Pre-**see**-zoo
Here is/are . . .	**Aqui está/ estão . . .**	A-**kee** es-**ta**/ es-**tow**^{n}
I know	**Eu sei**	**Ay**-oo **say**
I don't know	**Eu não sei**	**Ay**-oo now^n **say**
It's urgent	**É urgente**	Eh oor-**zhay**^{n}-te

It is. . . .	**É . . .**	Eh
It isn't . . .	**Não é . . .**	Now^n eh
I have . . .	**Eu tenho . . .**	**Ay**-oo **te**-nyoo

I don't have . . .	Eu não tenho . . .	Ay-oo now^n te-nyoo
I would like . . .	Eu gostaria . . .	Ay-oo gos-ta-ree-a
I like it/I don't like it	Gosto disto/ Não gosto disto	Gos-too jees-too/ Now^n gos-too jees-too
It's cheap	É barato	Eh ba-ra-too
It's (too) expensive	É caro	Eh ka-roo
That's all	É tudo	Eh too-doo
I didn't know	Não sabia	Now^n sa-bee-a
I think so	Penso que sim	Pe^n-soo ke see^n
I'm hungry/thirsty	Estou com fome/ sede	Es-toh ko^n fo-me/say-je
I'm tired	Estou cansado (a)	Es-toh ka^n-sa-doo (a)
I'm in a hurry	Estou com pressa	Es-toh ko^n pre-sa
I'm ready	Estou pronto (a)	Es-toh pro^n-too (a)
Leave me alone	Deixe-me por favor	De-she-me poor fa-vor
Go away	Vá embora	Va e^n-bo-ra
I'm lost	Estou perdido (a)	Es-toh per-jee-doo (a)
We are looking for . . .	Estamos procurando . . .	Es-ta-moos pro-koo-ra^n-doo
Just a minute	*Um minuto/ minutinho	Oo^n mee-noo-to/mee-noo-tee nyo
This way/follow me	*Por aqui/siga-me	Poor a kee/see-ga-me
Take a seat	*Sente-se	Se^n te se
Come in!	*Entre	E^n-tre

You are mistaken	**Está enganado (a)**	Es-**ta** ay^n-ga-**na**-doo (a)
You're right	**Você tem razão**	**Vo**-seh te^n ha-**zow**^{n}
You're wrong	**Você não tem razão**	**Vo**-seh now^n te^n ha-zow^n
It's important	**É importante**	Eh ee^n-poor-**ta**^{n}-te

SIGNS AND PUBLIC NOTICES[1]

Aberto das . . . às . . .	Open from . . . to . . .
Água potável	Drinking water
Alfândega	Customs
Aluga-se	To let/to hire
Alugam-se quartos	Room to let
Aperte/toque a campainha	Ring the bell
Assento/poltrona	Seat
Aterrissar/aterrar	To land
Banco	Bank
Banheiros	Toilets
Caixa	Checkout, till
Cavalheiros/Homens	Gentlemen/Men
Cinto de segurança	Seat belt
Conexão / troca de avião	Connection
Correios	Post office
Cuidado	Caution
Descolar	To take off
Delegacia de Polícia	Police station

1. See also Road Signs (p. 46) and Signs to Look for at Airports and Stations (p. 15).

Dê preferência	Yield/give way
Direção proibida	No entry
É proibida a entrada	No admission
É proibido fumar	No smoking
Elevador	Lift, elevator
Empurre	Push
Entrada	Entrance
Entrada gratuita	Admission free
Esgotado	Sold out
Fechado	Closed
Guia	Guide
Hospital	Hospital
(Não) há vagas/ disponibilidade	(No) vacancies
Informação	Information
Intérprete	Interpreter
Livre/ vago	Free, vacant
Local para retirar ou reclamar a perda de bagagem	Bagagge claim
Mantenha-se à direita	Keep right
Multa	Fine /penalty
Não tem mais lugar	Sold out, house full
Não tocar	Do not touch
Ocupado	Occupied, engaged
Particular	Private

Páre	Stop
Pede-se para não ...	You are requested not to ...
Pedestres	Pedestrians
Perigo	Danger
Polícia	Police
Portão de embarque	Departure gate
Proibido ... sob multa de ... reais	It is forbidden to ... Penalty ... (R$) reais
Pronto-Socorro	First-aid centre/emergency room
Puxe	Pull
Reservado	Reserved
Saída	Exit
Saída de emergência	Emergency exit
Semáforo	Traffic lights
Sentido proibido	Do not enter
Senhoras	Ladies
Sentido de circulação de via ou pista/Sentido único	One-way street
Promoção/ liquidação	Sale
Vende-se	For sale
Vire à esquerda	Turn left
Vire à direita	Turn right
Vôo cancelado	Cancelled flight
Vôo lotado	Overbooked flight
Visto	Visa

GETTING AROUND

Arrival

Key Phrases		
I've lost my passport. I must have dropped it on the plane	**Eu perdi meu passaporte. Devo ter deixado cair no avião**	Ay-oo **pair**-jee **may**-oo pas-sa-**por**-teh. De-vo tair de-**sha**-doo ka-eer no a-vee-**ow**^{n}
My luggage has not arrived	**Minhas bagagens não chegaram**	**Mee**-nyas ba-**ga**-zhay^n now^n she-ga-**ra**^{n}
My luggage is damaged	**Minhas bagagens estão danificadas**	**Mee**-nyas ba-**ga**-zhay^{n}s es-**tow**^{n} da-nee-fee-**ka**-das
Is there an ATM/ currency exchange?	**Há um caixa eletrônico / casa de câmbio?**	Ah oo^n kay-sha e-le-**tro**-nee-eko/**ka**-sa je ka^n-bee-oo
Is there a bus/train into the town?	**Há algum ônibus/ trem para a cidade?**	Ah al-**goo**^{n} oh-nee-boos/ tre^n **pa**-ra a see-**da**-je
How can I get to . . . ?	**Como é que posso ir para . . . ?**	Ko-moo eh ke **pos**-soo eer **pa**-ha

Passports

Your passport, please	*Seu passaporte, por favor	Say-oo pas-sa-por-te poor fa-vor
Are you together/with a group?	*Estão juntos/com um grupo?	Es-low zhoon-toos/kon oon groo-poo
I'm travelling alone	Estou viajando sozinho (a)	Es-to vee-a-zhan-doo so-zee-nyoo (a)
I'm travelling with my wife/my husband/a friend	Estou viajando com a minha esposa/meu marido/um amigo	Es-to vee-a-zhan-doo kon a mee-nya es-po-za/kon me-oo ma-ree-do/oon a mee-goo
I'm here on business/on holiday	Venho a negócios/de férias	Vay-nyoo a ne-go-see-oos/de fe-ree-as
What is your address in . . . ?	*Qual é o seu endereço em . . . ?	Kwal eh oo see-oo en-dee-re-so en
How long are you staying here?	*Quanto tempo ficará aqui?	Kwan-too tayn-poo fee-ka-ra a-kee

Customs

Customs	*Alfândega	Al-fan-de-ga
Nothing to declare	*Nada a declarar	Na-da a de-kla-rar
Goods to declare	*Artigos a declarar	Ar-tee-goos a de-kla-rar
Which is your luggage?	*Qual é a sua bagagem?	Kwal eh a soo-a ba-ga-zhayn
Do you have any more luggage?	*Tem mais bagagem?	Ten ma-ees ba-ga-zhayn
This is (all) my luggage	Esta é (toda) a minha bagagem	Es-ta eh (to-da) a mee-nya ba-ga-zhayn

Have you anything to declare?	*Tem algo a declarar?	Te^n al-goo a de-kla-rar
I have only my personal things in it	Tenho somente as minhas coisas pessoais	Te^n-nyoo so-me^n-te as mee-nyas ko-ee-zas pe-soo-a-ees
Open your bag, please	*Abra a mala, por favor	A-bra a ma-la poor fa-vor
Can I shut my case now?	Já posso fechar a mala?	Zha pos-soo fe-shar a ma-la

Luggage

Luggage	bagagem	ba-ga-zhay^n
Backpack	mochila	mo-shee-la
Suitcase	mala	ma-la
Luggage storage	guarda-volumes	gwar-da vo-loo-mes
My luggage has not arrived	Minhas bagages não chegaram	Mee-nyas ba-ga-zhay^n now^n she-ga-ra^n
My luggage is damaged	A minha bagagem está danificada	A mee-nya ba-ga-zhay^n es-ta da-nee-fee-ka-da
One suitcase is missing	Falta uma das malas	Fal-ta oo-ma das ma-las
Are there any luggage trolleys?	Há carrinhos de bagagem?	Ah ka-hee-nyoos de ba-ga-zhay^n
Where is the left-luggage office?	Onde é o balcão de depósito de bagagem?	O^n-je eh oo bal-kow^n je de-po-zee-too je ba-ga-zhay^n

Moving on

Porter	Carregador de bagagem	Ka-he-ga-**dor** deh ba-**ga**-zhay^n
Would you take these bags to a taxi/the bus	Pode levar esta bagagem para o taxi/ônibus	Po-de le-**var** ess-ta ba-ga-zhay^n **pa**-ra oo **tak**-see/**oh**-nee-boos
What's the price for each piece of luggage?	Qual é o preço por cada mala?	Kwal eh oo **pray**-soo poor ka-da **ma**-la
I shall take this myself	Eu levo esta	**Ay**-oo le-voo ess-ta
That's not mine	Essa não é minha	Es-sa now^n eh **mee**-nya
How much do I owe you?	Quanto lhe devo?	Kwa^n-too lye **day**-voo
Where is the information bureau?	Onde fica o balcão de informações?	O^n- je **fee**-ka oh bal-kow^n je een-foor-ma-soy^{n}s
Is there a bus/train to the town centre?	Há um ônibus/trem para o centro da cidade?	Ah oo^n **oh**-nee-boos/tre^n pa-ra a see-**da**-je

Signs to Look for at Airports and Stations

Arrivals	Chegadas
Booking office/Tickets	Bilheteira/Bilhetes
Buses	Ônibus

Connections	**Conexões**
Departures	**Partidas**
Exchange	**Câmbio**
Gentlemen	**Cavalheiros/Senhores**
(Travel) Information	**Informação (de viagem)**
Internet access	**Acesso à internet**
Ladies	**Senhoras**
Left luggage	**Depósito de bagagem (consigna)**
Lost property	**Seção de achados e perdidos**
Luggage lockers	**Caixas de bagagem**
Newsstand	**Banca de jornal**
No smoking	**É proibido fumar**
Platform	**Plataforma**
Refreshments/snack bar	**Bar/lanchonete**
Reservations	**Reservas**
Suburban trains	**Trens suburbanos**
Taxi rank	**Ponto de táxis**
Tickets	**Bilhetes**
Tourist office	**Posto de informação turística**
Underground	**Metrô**
Waiting room	**Sala de espera**

By Air

Key Phrases

What is the baggage allowance?	Qual é o limite de bagagem?	Kwal eh oo lee-mee-te je ba-ga-zheⁿ
I'd like to change my reservation	Eu gostaria de mudar minha reserva	Ay-oo gos-ta-ree-a je moo-dar mee-nya he-zer-va
Can I check in online?	Posso fazer o check-in online?	Pos-so fa-zair oo check-in online
I have only hand luggage	Eu só tenho bagagem de mão	Ay-oo so te-nyoo ba-ga-zheⁿ je mowⁿ
Flight to ... has been delayed/ cancelled	O vôo para ... está atrasado/foi cancelado	Oo voo pa-ra es-ta a-tra-za-do/foy kaⁿ-se-la-doo

Where's the airline office?	Onde são os escritórios da companhia aérea	Oⁿ-je sowⁿ oos es-kree-to-ree-oos da koⁿ-pa-nyee-a ay-ree-a
I'd like to book two seats on the plane to ...	Quero fazer duas reservas de vôo para ...	Ke-roo fa-zair do-es he-zer-vas je voo pa-ra
What is the cheapest price?	Qual é o mais barato?	Kwal eh oo ma-ees ba-ra-too
First class	Primeira classe	Pree-may-ra klas-se
Business class	Classe executiva	Klas-se e-se-koo-tee-va
Economy	Classe econômica	Klas-se e-ko-no-mee-ka

How long is the flight?	Qual é a duração do vôo?	Kwal eh a doo-ra-sow[n] do voo
I'd like an aisle/window seat	Eu quero ficar no corredor/na janela	Ay-oo ke-ro fee-kar noo ko-he-dor/na zha ne-la
I'd like to order a vegetarian/special meal	Eu gostaria de pedir uma refeição vegetariana/especial	Ay-oo gos-ta-ree-a je pe-jeer oo-ma re-fe-sow[n] ve-zhe-ta-hee-a-na/es-pe-syaw
Is there a flight to...?	Há algum vôo para...?	Ah al-goo[n] voo pa-ra
What is the flight number?	Qual é o número do vôo?	Kwal eh oo noo-me-roo do voo
When does the plane leave/arrive?	A que horas parte/chega o avião?	A ke o-ras par-te/shay-ga oo a-vee-ow[n]
When's the next plane?	A que horas é o próximo avião?	A ke o-ras eh oo pro-see-moo a-vee-ow[n]
Is there a coach to the airport/town?	Há ônibus para o aeroporto/para a cidade?	Ah oh-nee-boos pa-ra oo a-e-ro-port-too/pa-ra a see-da-je
Which airport does the flight leave from?	De que aeroporto sai o vôo?	Je ke ay-ro-por-too sy oo voo
Terminal	Terminal	Ter-mee-naw
Where are the check-in desks for...?	Onde ficam os balcões de check-in para...?	On-je fee-ka[n] os bal-soy[n]s je check-in pa-ra
When must I check in?	Quando devo fazer o check-in?	Kwa[n]-doo de-vo fa-zair oo check-in

Please cancel my reservation to . . .	Quero cancelar a minha reserva para . . .	Ke-roo kaⁿ-se-lar a mee-nya he-zer-va pa-ra
I'd like to change my reservation	Quero mudar a minha reserva	Ke-roo moo-dar a mee-nya he-zer-va
Can I change my ticket?	Posso trocar o meu bilhete?	Pos-soo troo-kar oo may-oo bee-lyay-te
Will it cost more?	Ficará mais caro?	Fee-ka-ra ma-ees ka-roo
I've booked a wheelchair to take me to the plane	Eu reservei uma cadeira de rodas para me levar ao avião	Ay-oo he-zer-vey oo-ma ka-dey-ra je ho-das pa-ra me le-var ow a-vee owⁿ
You will have to pay for excess baggage	Você terá de pagar por excesso de bagagem	Vo-seh te-ra je pa-gar poor es-say-soo je ba-ga-zhayⁿ
The plane leaves from gate . . .	O avião parte do portão . . .	Oo a-vee-owⁿ par-te do por-towⁿ
I've lost my boarding pass	Perdi meu cartão de embarque	Pair-jee may-oo kar-towⁿ je eⁿ-bar-kay

By Boat/Ferry

Key Phrases

Is there a boat/(car) ferry from here to...?	Há barco/balsa de aqui para...?	Ah **bar**-koo/**bal**-sa de a-**kee** pa-ra
When does the next boat leave?	A que horas sai o próximo barco?	A ke **o**-ras sy oo **pro**-see-moo **bar**-koo
I'd like a one-way/ return ticket	Eu gostaria de um bilhete de ida/ ida e volta	Ay-oo gos-ta-ree-a je ooⁿ bee-lye-te je ee-da / ee-da eh **vol**-ta

Where is the port?	Onde fica o porto?	Oⁿ-je **fee**-ka oo **por**-too
How long does the crossing take?	Quanto tempo leva para atravessar?	Kwaⁿ-too **tay**ⁿ-poo **le**-va pa-ra a-tra-**ver**-sar
How often do the boats leave?	De quanto em quanto tempo saem os barcos?	Je **kwa**ⁿ-too ayn **kwa**ⁿ-too **tay**ⁿ-poo syⁿ oos **bar**-koos
Does the boat call at...?	O barco pára em...?	Oo **bar**-koo **pa**-ra eⁿ
What does it cost for...	Quanto custa para...?	**Kwa**ⁿ– too **koos**-ta **pa**-ra
a bicycle?	uma bicicleta?	oo-ma bee-see-**kle**-ta
a child?	uma criança?	oo-ma kree-**a**ⁿ-sa
a motorcycle?	uma moto?	oo-ma **moh**-toh
Can I book a...	Posso reservar	**Pos**-soo he-zer-**var**
single cabin?	uma cabine individual?	oo-ma ka-bee-ne eeⁿ-jee-vee-doo-**aw**

a first-class cabin?	uma cabine de primeira classe?	oo-ma ka-bee-ne je pre-may-ra klas-se
a second-class cabin?	uma cabine de segunda classe?	oo-ma ka-bee-ne je se-goon-da klas-se
How many berths are there in the cabin?	Quantas camas há nesta cabine?	Kwan-tas ka-mas ah nays-ta ka-bee-ne
When must we go on board?	A que horas temos que estar a bordo?	A ke o-ras te-mos ke es-tar a bor-doo
When do we dock?	A que horas atracamos?	A ke o-ras a-tra-ka-moos
How long do we stay in port?	Quanto tempo ficamos no porto?	Kwan-too tayn poo fee-ka moos noo por-too
Where are the toilets?	Onde ficam os banheiros?	On-je fee-kan os ba-nyer-oos
I feel seasick	Eu sinto enjôo	Ay oo seen-too en-zhoo
life jacket	colete salva-vidas	ko-le-te sal-va vee-das
lifeboat	barco salva-vidas	bar-koo sal-va vee-das

By Bus or Coach

Key Phrases

| Where can I buy a bus ticket? | Onde posso comprar um bilhete de ônibus? | On je pos-soo kon prar oon bee-lye-te je oh nee-boos |
| Do I pay the driver? | Pago o motorista? | Pa-goo oo mo-to-rees-ta |

When's the next bus?	Quando passa o próximo ônibus?	Kwa^n-doo **pas**-sa oo **pro**-see-moo **oh**-nee-boos
Where can I get a bus to ... ?	Onde posso pegar um ônibus para ... ?	O^n-je **pos**-soo pe-**gar** oo^n **oh**-nee-boos **pa**-ra
Where do I get off?	Onde devo descer?	O^n-je **de**-vo des-ser

Where's the bus station?	Onde fica a estação de ônibus?	O^n-je **fee**-ka a es-ta-**sow**^{n} je **oh**-nee-boos
Bus stop	Ponto de ônibus	Po^n-too je **oh**-nee-boos
Request stop	Parada facultativa	Pa-**ra**-da fa-kool-ta-**tee**-va
I'd like to reserve a seat at the front of the coach/bus	Gostaria de reservar um assento na parte da frente do ônibus	Gos-ta-**ree**-a je he-zer-**var** oo^n as-**se**^{n}-too na **par**-te da **fre**^{n}-te doo **oh**-nee-boos
What is the fare?	Qual é a tarifa?	Kwal eh a ta-**ree**-fa
Is there a daily/ weekly ticket?	Há um bilhete diário/semanal?	Ah oo^n bee-**lye**-te jee-a-ree-oo/se-ma-**naw**
I bought my ticket online	Eu comprei o bilhete online	**Ay**-oo ko^n-**prey** oo bee-**lye**-te online
When does the coach/bus leave?	A que horas parte o ônibus?	A ke **o**-ras **par**-te oo **oh**-nee-boos
When does the coach/bus get to ... ?	A que horas o ônibus chega em ... ?	A ke **o**-ras oo **oh**-nee-boos **she**-ga e^n
What stops does it make?	Em que pontos pára?	Ay^n ke **po**^{n}-toos **pah**-ra
How long is the journey?	Quanto tempo é a viagem?	Kwa^n-too **tay**^{n}-poo eh a vee-a-**zhay**^{n}
When's the next bus?	A que horas é o próximo ônibus?	A ke **o**-ras eh oo **pro**-see-moo **oh**-nee-boos

How often do the buses run?	De quanto em quanto tempo passa o ônibus?	Je kwaⁿ-too ayⁿ kwaⁿ-too tayⁿ-poo pas-sa oo oh-nee-boos
What time is the last bus?	A que horas é o último ônibus?	A ke o-ras e oo ool-tee-moo oh-nee-boos
Does this bus go to the ...	Este ônibus vai para ...	Es-te oh-nee-boos vy pa-ra
beach?	a praia?	a pry-a
station?	a estação?	a es-ta-sowⁿ
town centre?	o centro da cidade?	oo sayⁿ-troo da see-da-je
Do you go near ... ?	Este ônibus passa perto de ... ?	Es-te oh-nee-boos pas-sa per-too je
Where can I get a bus to ... ?	Onde posso tomar o ônibus para ... ?	Oⁿ-je pos-soo too-mar oo oh-nee-boos pa-ra
Which bus goes to ... ?	Que ônibus vai a ... ?	Ke oh-nee-boos vy a
I'd like to go to ...	Quero ir a ...	Ke-roo eer a
Where do I get off?	Onde tenho que descer/ sair?	Oⁿ-je te-nyoo ke des-ser /sa-eer
The bus to ... stops over there	*O ônibus para ... pára ali	Oo oh-nee-boos pa-ra ... pah-ra a lee
You must take number ...	*Tem de tomar o número ...	Teⁿ Je too-mar oo noo-me-roo
You get off at the next stop	*Desça no próximo ponto	Des-sa noo pro-see-mo poⁿ to
The buses run every ten minutes/every hour	*Os ônibus passam de dez em dez minutos/de hora em hora	Os oh-nee-boos pas-saⁿ je des ayⁿ des mee-noo-toos/je o-ra ayⁿ o-ra

By Taxi

Key Phrases

Please get me a taxi	**Por favor me arranje um táxi**	Poor fa-**vor** me a-ra^n-**zhe** oo^n **tak**-see
Where can I find a taxi?	**Onde posso arranjar um táxi?**	O^n-je **pos**-soo a-ran-**zhar** oo^n **tak**-see
Please wait for me	**Por favor me espere**	Poor fa-**vor** me es-**pe**-re
Stop here	**Páre aqui**	**Pa**-re a-**kee**

I'd like to book a taxi for tomorrow at . . . (*time*)	**Gostaria de agendar um táxi para amanhã às . . . (hora)**	Gos-ta-**ree**-a je a-ge^n-**dar** oo^n **tak**-see **pa**-ra a-**ma**-nya as
Are you free?	**Está livre?**	Es-**ta lee**-vre
Please turn on the meter	**Por favor, ligue o taxímetro**	Poor fa-**vor lee**-ge oo tak-**see**-me-troo
Please take me to . . .	**Por favor me leve para . . .**	Poor fa-**vor** me **le**-ve **pa**-ra
the city centre	**o centro da cidade**	oo **sen**-troo dah see-**da**-je
the hotel	**o hotel**	oo o-**tel**
the station	**a estação**	ah es-ta-**sow**^{n}
this address	**este endereço**	**es**-te e^n-de-**re**-soo
Can you hurry? I'm late	**Pode ir mais depressa por favor, estou atrasado**	**Po**-je eer ma-ees de-**pres**-sa poor fa-**vor** es-**to** a-tra-**za**-doo

Please wait for me	**Espere aqui, por favor**	Es-**pe**-re a-**kee** poor fa-**vor**
Stop here	**Pare aqui**	**Pa**-re a-**kee**
Is it far?	**É longe?**	Eh lo^n-zhe
How much do you charge by the hour/ for the day?	**Quanto você cobra por hora/por dia?**	**Kwa**^{n}-too vo-seh **ko**-bra poor **o**-ra/poor **jee**-a
How much will you charge to take me to ... ?	**Quanto você cobrará para me levar até ... ?**	**Kwa**^{n}-too vo-seh **ko**-bra-**rah** pa-ra me le-**var** ah-**teh**
How much is it?	**Quanto custa?**	**Kwa**^{n} too **koos**-ta
That's too much	**É muito caro**	Eh **mwee**-too **ka**-roo
I'd like a receipt, please	**Pode me dar um recibo, por favor**	**Po**-je me dar oo^n he-**see**-boo poor fa-**vor**

By Train

Key Phrases

Where's the railway station/main station?	**Onde é a estação de trem/estação principal?**	**O**^{n}-je eh a es ta **sow**^{n} je tre^n/es-ta-**sow**^{n} **pree**^{n}-see-**paw**
What's the cheapest fare to ... ?	**Qual é a tarifa mais barata para ... ?**	Kwal eh a ta-**ree**-fa ma-ees ba-**ra**-ta pa-ra
Is there a day return?	**Tem um bilhete de um dia?**	Te^n oo^n bee-**lye**-te je oo^n **jee**-a
Where do I change?	**Onde posso mudar?**	**O**^{n}-je **pos**-soo moo-**dar**

What station is this?	Que estação é esta?	Ke es-ta-sow[n] eh es-ta
Where is the ticket office?	Onde é a bilheteira?	O[n]-je eh a bee-lye-tay-ra
Do you have a timetable, please?	Tem um horário, por favor?	Te[n] oo[n] o-ra-ree-oo poor fa-vor
What's the cheapest fare to . . . ?	Qual é a tarifa mais barata para . . . ?	Kwal eh a ta-ree-fa ma-ees ba-ra-ta
How much is it first class to . . . ?	Quanto custa um bilhete de primeira classe para . . . ?	Kwa[n]-too koos-ta oo[n] bee-lye-te je pree-may-ra klas-se pa-ra
A second-class single to . . .	Um bilhete de segunda classe para . . .	Oo[n] bee-lye-te de se-goo[n]-da klas-se pa-ra
Single/one way	Ida	Ee-da
A return to . . .	Um bilhete de ida e volta para . . .	Oo[n] bee-lye-te je ee-da ee vol-ta pa-ra
When are you coming back?	*Quando volta?	Kwa[n]-doo vol-ta
Is there a special fare for children?	Há uma tarifa especial para crianças?	Ah oo-ma ta-ree-fa es-pe-see-aw pa-ra kree-a[n]-sas
How old is he/she?	*Que idade tem ele/ela?	Ke ee-da-je te[n] e-le/e-la
How long is this ticket valid?	Por quanto tempo este bilhete é válido?	Poor kwa[n]-to tay[n]-poo es-te bee-lye-te eh va-lee-do
Is there a supplementary charge?	Há alguma cobrança suplementar?	Ah al-goo-ma ko-bra[n]-sa soo-ple-may[n]-tar

Do I need to reserve a seat?	**Preciso reservar um assento?**	Pre-**see**-zoo he-zer-**var** oo^n as-**se**^{n}-too
I'd like a window seat/sleeper	**Quero um assento na janela/no vagão leito**	Ke-roo oo^n as-**se**^{n}-too na zha-ne-la/noo va-**gow**^{n} ley-too
Is it an express or a local train?	**É um trem expresso ou local?**	Eh oo^n tre^n es-**pres**-soo oo lo-**kaw**
Is there an earlier/ later train?	**Há um trem que sai mais cedo/mais tarde?**	Ah oo^n tre^n ke sy **ma**-ees **say**-doo/ma-ees tar-je
Is there a restaurant car on the train?	**Há carruagem restaurante?**	Ah ka-roo a-**zhay**^{n} res-tow-ra^n-te
When does it get to . . . ?	**Quando chega em . . . ?**	Kwa^n-doo she-ga e^n
Does the train stop at . . . ?	**O trem pára em . . . ?**	Oh tre^n **pa**-ra e^n
I'd like to make a motorail reservation to . . .	**Quero fazer uma reserva na automotora para . . .**	Ke-roo fa-**zayr** oo-ma he-zer-va na ow-to-moo-**to**-ra **pa**-ra

Changing

Is there a through train to . . . ?	**Há trem direto para . . . ?**	Ah tre^n jee-**re**-too pa-ra
Do I have to change?	**Tenho que mudar?**	Te-nyoo ke moo-**dar**
Where do I change?	**Onde mudo?**	O^n-je moo-doo
Excuse me, what station is this?	**Me desculpe, que estação é esta?**	Me des-**kool**-pe ke es-ta-**sow**^{n} eh es-ta
Is this where I change for . . . ?	**É aqui que eu mudo para . . . ?**	Eh a-**kee** ke ay-oo moo-doo **pa**-ra

When is there a connection to . . . ?	Quando terá uma conexão para . . . ?	Kwa^n-doo te-**ra** oo-ma ko-ne-**sow**^{n} pa-ra
When does the train from . . . get in?	A que horas chega o trem que vem de . . . ?	A ke **o**-ras **shay**-ga oo tre^n ke vay^n de
Is the train late?	O trem está atrasado?	Oo tre^n es-**ta** a-tra-**za**-doo
From which platform does the train to . . . leave?	De que plataforma sai o trem para . . . ?	Je ke pla-ta-**for**-ma sy oo tre^n **pa**-ra
Change at . . . and take the local train	*Mude em . . . e tome o trem local	**Moo**-de e^n . . . ee **to**-me oo tre^n lo-**kaw**

Departure

When does the train leave?	A que horas parte o trem?	A ke **o**-ras **par**-te oo tre^n
Which platform does the train to . . . leave from?	De que plataforma sai o trem para . . . ?	Je ke pla-ta-**for**-ma sy oo tre^n **pa**-ra
Is this the train for . . . ?	É este o trem para . . . ?	Eh **es**-te oo tre^n **pa**-ra
There will be a delay of . . .	*Haverá uma demora de . . .	A-ve-**ra** oo-ma de-**mo**-ra je

On the train

We have reserved seats	Temos lugares reservados	**Tay**-moos loo-**ga**-res he-zer-**va**-doos
Is this seat free?	Este lugar está livre?	**Es**-te loo-**gar** es-**ta** **lee**-vre
This seat is taken	Este lugar está ocupado	**Es**-te loo-**gar** es-**ta** o-koo-**pa**-doo

Restaurant car	Carruagem restaurante	Ka-hoo-a-**zhay**ⁿ res-tow-ra**ⁿ**-te
Where is the sleeping car?	Onde é a carruagem com beliches para dormir?	Oⁿ-je eh a ka-hoo-a-**zhay**ⁿ koⁿ be-lee-shes **pa**-ra door-**meer**
Which is my sleeper?	Qual é a minha cabine?	Kwal eh a **mee**-nya ka-bee-ne
Could you wake me at . . . please?	Pode me acordar às . . . por favor?	**Po**-je me a-kor-**dar** as . . . poor fa-**vor**
The heating is too high/low	O aquecimento está muito alto/baixo	Oo a-ke-see-**may**ⁿ-too es-ta mwee-too al-too/**by**-shoo
I can't open/close the window	Não posso abrir/fechar a janela	Nowⁿ **pos**-soo a **breer**/fe-**shar** a zha-ne-la
What station is this?	Que estação é esta?	Ke es-ta-**sow**ⁿ eh es-ta
How long do we stop here?	Quanto tempo paramos aqui?	**Kwa**ⁿ-too **tay**ⁿ-poo pa-ra-moos a-**kee**

By Underground

Key Phrases

Where is the nearest underground station?	Qual é a estação de metrô mais perto?	Kwal eh a es-ta-**sow**ⁿ je me-troo ma-ees **per**-too
Does this train go to . . . ?	Este metrô vai para . . . ?	Es-te me-**troo** vy **pa**-ra
Have you a map of the underground?	Tem um mapa do metrô?	Teⁿ ooⁿ **ma**-pa do me-troo

Is there a daily/ weekly ticket?	Tem um bilhete para o dia/ a semana?	Te^n oo^n bee-**lye**-te **pa**-ra oo **jee**-a /a ase-**ma**-na
Can I use it on the bus too?	Posso usar no ônibus também?	Po-soo oo-**zar** noo **oh**-ne-boos ta^n-**be**^{n}
Which line goes to …?	Que linha vai para …?	Ke **lee**-nya vy **pa**-ra
Where do I change for …?	Onde mudo para …?	O^n-je **moo**-doo **pa**-ra
Is the next station …?	A próxima estação é …?	A **pro**-see-ma es-ta-sow^n eh
What station is this?	Que estação é esta?	Ke es-ta-**sow**^{n} eh **es**-ta

By Car[1]

Key Phrases

Do you have a road map?	Tem um mapa rodoviário?	Te^n oo^n **ma**-pa ho-do-vee-a-ree-oo
Where is the nearest car park/garage?	Onde fica o estacionamento/ a garagem mais próximos?	O^n-je **fee**-ka oo es-ta-syo-na-**me**^{n}-to/a ga-ra-**zhe**^{n} ma-es **pro**-see-moos
May I see your driving licence and passport, please?	*Posso ver a sua carteira de motorista e passaporte, por favor?	**Pos**-soo ver a **soo**-a kar-**tey**-ra je mo-to-**rees**-ta e pas-sa-**por**-te poor fa-**vor**

1. See also directions (p. 48) and road signs (p. 46).

(How long) can I park here?	**(Por quanto tempo) posso estacionar aqui?**	(Poor kwaⁿ-too tayⁿ-poo) pos-soo es-ta-see-oo-**nar** a-**kee**
Have you any change for the meter?	**Tem algum troco para o parquímetrô?**	Teⁿ al-**gooⁿ tro**-koo pa-ra oo par-**kee**-me-troo
How far is the next petrol station?	**Daqui a quanto tempo fica o próximo posto de gasolina?**	Da-**kee** a kwaⁿ-too teⁿ-poo **fee**-ka oo **pro**-see-moo **pos**-to je ga-so-**lee**-na
You were speeding	***Você estava em alta velocidade***	Vo-seh es-**ta**-va eⁿ **al**-ta ve-lo-see-**da**-je
Is this your car?	***É este o seu carro?***	Eh es-te oo se-oo **ka**-hoo
speed limit	***limite de velocidade***	**lee**-mee te je ve-loo-see-**da**-je
pedestrian precinct	***precinto de pedestres***	pre-**seeⁿ**-too je pe-**des** tres

Car rental

Where can I hire a car?	**Onde posso alugar um carro?**	Oⁿ-je pos soo a-loo-**gar** ooⁿ **ka**-ho
I'd like to hire a large/small car	**Eu gostaria de alugar um carro grande/pequeno**	Ay-oo gos-**ta**-ree a je a loo-**gar** ooⁿ **ka**-ho graⁿ-je/pe-**ke**-noo
I'd like an automatic/a manual vehicle	**Quero alugar um automático/carro de marcha**	Ke-**rôo** a-loo-**gar** ooⁿ ow-too-ma-**tee**-koo/**ka**-ho je **mar**-sha
I'd like a car with a sun roof/air conditioning	**Eu gostaria de um carro com teto solar/ar condicionado**	Ay-oo gos-**ta ree**-a je ooⁿ **ka**-ho koⁿ **te**-too so-**lar**/ar koⁿ-jee-syo-**na**-doo

Does the car have a GPS system/CD player?	**O carro tem GPS/ CD player?**	Oo **ka**-ho te^n Ge Pe Esse/ Ce De player
Can we rent a baby/ child seat?	**Podemos alugar um bebê-conforto/ cadeirinha?**	Po-**de**-moos a-loo-**gar** oo^n be-**be**-ko^n-**for**-too/ka-dey-**ree**-nya
What kind of fuel does it take?	**Que tipo de combustível esse carro consome?**	Ke **tee**-poo je ko^n-boos-**tee**-vel **es**-se **ka**-ho ko^n-so-me
Is there a weekend/ midweek rate?	**Há uma tarifa de fim de semana/de meio da semana?**	Ah oo-ma ta-**ree**-fa je fee^n je se-**ma**-na/je **may**-ee-oo da se-**ma**-na
I need it for two days/a week	**Preciso por dois dias/uma semana**	Pre-**see**-zoo poor **do**-ees **jee**-as/**oo**-ma se-**ma**-na
How much is it by the day/week?	**Quanto custa por dia/semana?**	**Kwa**^{n}-too **koos**-ta por **jee**-a /se-**ma**-na
Does that include unlimited mileage?	**Inclui quilometragem ilimitada?**	Ee^n-kloo-**ee** kee-lo-me-tra-**zhe**^{n} ee-lee-mee-**ta**-da
The charge per kilometre is . . .	***A tarifa por quilômetro é . . .**	A ta-**ree**-fa poor kee-**lo**-me-troo eh
Do you want comprehensive insurance?	***Você quer um seguro completo?**	**Vo**-seh ker oo^n se-**goo**-hoo ko^n-**ple**-too
You have to pay the first . . . reais/euros	***Você deve pagar de caução . . . reais/ euros**	**Vo**-seh **de**-ve pa-**gar** je kow-**sow**^{n} . . . he-**ay**-ees/ **ay**-oo-ros
I will pay by credit card	**Pago com cartão de crédito**	**Pa**-goo ko^n kar-**tow**^{n} je **kre**-jee-too

You must return the car with a full tank	*Você deve devolver o carro com tanque completo	Vo-seh de-ve de-vol-ver oo ka-ho kon tan-ke kon-ple-too
May I see your driving licence and passport?	*Posso ver a sua carta/carteira de motorista e seu passaporte?	Pos-soo vayr a soo-a kar-ta kar-tey-ra je mo-to-rees-ta e se-oo pas-sa-por-te
Sign here, please	*Assine aqui, por favor	As-see-ne a-kee poor fa-vor
Can I return it to your office in . . . ?	Posso devolver na sua filial em . . . ?	Pos-soo de-vol-ver na soo-a fee-lee-aw en
Could you show me the controls/lights?	Pode me mostrar o controle/as luzes?	Po-je me moos-trar oo kon-tro- le /as loo-zes
The car is scratched/dented here	O carro está riscado/amassado aqui	Oo ka-ho es-ta hees-ka-doo/a-mas-sa-doo a-kee

At a garage or petrol station

Fill it up, please	Complete o tanque, por favor	Kon-ple-te oo tan-ke poor fa-vor
It's a diesel engine	É um carro a diesel	Eh oon ka ho ah jee-sel
Please check the oil and the water	Verifique o óleo e a água, por favor	Ve ree fee-ke oo o-lee-oo ee ah a-gwa poor fa-vor
Could you check the brake/transmission fluid?	Pode verificar o líquido dos freios/da transmissão?	Po-je ve-ree-fee-kar oo lee-kee-doo dos frey-os/da tranzh-mee-sown
Would you clean the windscreen, please?	Pode limpar o pára-brisas, por favor?	Po-je leen-par oo pa-ra-bree-zas poor fa-vor
The oil needs changing	O óleo necessita ser mudado	Oo o-lee-oo ne-se-see-ta sayr moo-da-doo

Check the tyre pressure, please	**Verifique a calibragem dos pneus, por favor**	Ve-ree-**fee**-ke ah ka-lee-bra-zhe[n] dos **pney**-oos poor fa-**vor**
Please wash the car	**Lave o carro, por favor**	**La**-ve oo ka-hoo poor fa-**vor**
Can I garage the car here?	**Posso guardar o carro aqui?**	**Pos**-soo gwar-**dar** oo ka-ho a-**kee**
What time does the garage close?	**A que horas fecha a garagem?**	A ke **o**-ras **fay**-ee-sha a ga-**ra**-zhay[n]
Where are the toilets?	**Onde ficam os banheiros?**	**O**[n]-je **fee**-ka[n] oos ba-**nyer**-oos
Please pay at the cash desk	**Por favor, pague no caixa**	Poor fa-**vor** **pa**-ghe noo **ka**-ee-sha

Problems and repairs

I've run out of petrol	**Eu estou sem gasolina**	**Ay**-oo **es**-toh se[n] ga-soo-**lee**-na
I've locked the keys in the car	**Tranquei as chaves no carro**	Tra[n]-**kay** as **sha**-ves noo **ka**-ho
I've lost my keys	**Perdi as chaves**	Per-**jee** as **sha**-ves
The lock is broken/jammed	**A fechadura está quebrada/emperrada**	Ah fe-sha-**doo**-ra es-**ta** ke-**bra**-da /e[n]-pe-**ha**-da
My car has broken down	**O meu carro está quebrado**	Oo **may**-oo **ka**-hoo es-**ta** ke-**bra**-do
Could you give me a lift to a garage?	**Pode me dar uma carona até à oficina?**	**Po**-je me dar **oo**-ma ka-**ro**-na ah-te ah o-fee-**see**-na

May I use your phone?	Posso usar o telefone?	Pos-soo oo-zar oo te-le-fo-ne
Where is there a ... agent?	Há aqui uma agência ... ?	Ah a-kee oo-ma a-zhay^n-see-a
Do you have a breakdown service?	Há serviço de conserto de emergência?	Ah ser-vee-soo je kon-ser-too je ee-mer-zhay^n-see-a
Is there a mechanic?	Há um mecânico?	Ah oo^n me-ka-nee-koo
Can you send someone to look at it/tow it away?	Pode mandar alguém para o ver/ rebocar?	Po-je ma^n-dar al-gay^n pa-ra oo vayr/he-boo-kar
It is an automatic	É um automático	Eh oo^n ow-too-ma-tee-koo
Where are you?	*Onde está / estão?	O^n-je es-ta / es-tow^n
Where is your car?	*Onde está o carro?	O^n-je es-ta oo ka-ho
I am on the road from ... to ... near kilometre post ...	Estou na estrada de ... a ... ao quilómetro ...	Es-to na es-tra-da je ... a ... a-oo kee-lo-me-troo
How long will you be?	Quanto tempo demora?	Kwa^n-too tay^n-poo de mo-ra
This tyre is flat; can you mend it?	O pneu está furado, pode consertar?	Oo pnay-oo es-ta foo-ra-do po-je ko^n-ser-tar
The exhaust is broken	O tubo de escape está partido	Oo too-boo je es-ka-pe es-ta par-tee-doo
The windscreen wiper does not work	O limpador de pára-brisas não funciona	Oo lee^n-pa-dor je pa-ra- bree zas now^n foo^n-see-o-na
The valve/radiator is leaking	A válvula/o radiador está vazando	A val-voo-la /oo ra-jee-a-dor es-ta va-za^n-doo

My car won't start	**O meu carro não dá partida**	Oo **may**-oo **ka**-ho now[n] dah par-**tee**-da
It's not running properly	**Não anda bem**	Now[n] a[n]-da bay[n]
The engine is overheating/firing badly	**O motor está demasiado quente/ funciona mal**	Oo moo-**tor** es-ta de-ma-zee-a-doo kay[n]-te/ foo[n]-see-**o**-na mal
There's a petrol/oil leak	**Perde gasolina/óleo**	**Per**-je ga-zoo-**lee**-na/o-lee-oo
There's a smell of petrol/rubber	**Cheira a gasolina/ borracha**	**Shay**-ee-ra a ga-zoo-**lee**-na/boo-**ha**-sha
There's a rattle/ squeak	**Há um ruído/chiado**	Ah oo[n] roo-**ee**-doo/ shee-a-do
Something is wrong with …	**Há algo que não está bem …**	Ah **al**-goo ke now[n] es-ta bay[n]
my car	**no meu carro**	noo **may**-oo **ka**-ho
the brakes	**nos freios**	noos **frey**-oos
the clutch	**na embreagem**	na e[n]-bray-a-zhay[n]
the engine	**no motor**	noo moo-**tor**
the gearbox	**na caixa de câmbio**	na kay-sha je **ka**[n]-bee-oo
the lights	**nas luzes**	nas **loo**-zes
the steering	**na direção**	na jee-re-**sow**[n]
The carburettor needs adjusting	**O carburador precisa de um ajuste**	Oo kar-boo-ra-**dor** pre-**see**-za je oo[n] a-**zhoos**-te
Can you repair it?	**Pode consertá-lo?**	**Po**-je ko[n]-seh-**ta**-lo

How long will it take to repair?	Quanto tempo demora para consertá-lo?	Kwan-too tayn-poo de-mo-ra pa-ra kon-ser-ta-lo
What will it cost?	Quanto custará?	Kwan-too koos-ta-ra
When can I pick the car up?	Quando posso ir buscar o carro?	Kwan-doo pos-soo eer boos-kar oo ka-ho
I need it ...	Preciso dele ...	Pre-see-zoo day-le
as soon as possible	o mais cedo possível	oo ma-ees say-doo poos-see-vel
in the morning	pela manhã	pe-la ma-nyan
in three hours	dentro de três horas	dayn-troo je trays o-ras
It will take two days	*Demorará dois dias	De-moo-ra-ra do-ees jee-as
We can repair it temporarily	*Podemos consertá-lo provisoriamente	Po-de-mos kon-ser-ta-lo proo-vee-zo-ree-a-mayn-te
We haven't the right spares	*Não tomos as peças sobresselentes necessárias	Nown tay-moos as pes-sas soo-bre-se-layn-les ne-se-sa-ree-as
We have to send for the spares	*Temos que pedir as peças sobresselentes	Tay-moos ke pe-jeer as pes-sas soo-bres-se-layn-les
You will need a new ...	*Vai precisar de um novo ... /uma nova	Vy pre-see-zar je oon no-voo/oo-ma no-va
Could I have an itemised bill, please?	Pode dar uma fatura detalhada, por favor?	Po-je dar oo-ma fa-too-ra de-ta-lya-da poor fa-vor

Parts of a car and other useful words

accelerate (to)	acelerar	a-se-le-**rar**
accelerator	o acelerador	a-se-le-ra-**dor**
aerial	a antena	a^n-**te**-na
air pump	a bomba de ar	bo^n-ba de ar
alarm	o alarme	a-**lar**-me
alternator	o alternador	al-ter-na-**dor**
anti-freeze	o anti-congelante	a^n-tee-ko^n-zhe-**la**^{n}-te
automatic transmission	a transmissão automática	tra^{n}zh-mees-**sow**^{n} ow-too-**ma**-tee-ka
axle	o eixo	ay-ee-**shoo**
battery	a bateria	ba-te-**ree**-a
bonnet	a capota	ka-**po**-ta
boot/trunk	a mala	**ma**-la
brake	o breque/ o freio do carro	**bre**-ke/ **frey**-oo do **ka**-ho
brake lights	as luzes de freio	**loo**-zes je **frey**-oo
brake lining	os compressores	ko^n-pres-**so**-res
breakdown	o enguiço/ a avaria	e^n-**ghee**-soo / a-va-**ree**-a
bulb	a luz/lâmpada	loos/**la**^{n}-pa-da
bumper	o pára-choque	pa-ra-**sho**-ke
carburettor	o carburador	kar-boo-ra-**dor**
clutch	a embreagem	e^n-bree-**a**-zhay^n

cooling system	o sistema de arrefecimento	sees-**tay**-ma de a-he-fe-see-**may**ⁿ-too
crank-shaft	a manivela	ma-nee-**ve**-la
cylinder	o cilindro	see-**lee**ⁿ-droo
dip stick	o indicador de nível de óleo	eeⁿ-jee-ka-**dor** je nee-vel je o-lee-oo
distilled water	a água distilada	a-gwa dee-stee-**la**-da
distributor	o distribuidor	jees-tree-boo-ee-**dor**
door	a porta	**por**-ta
door handle	a maçaneta da porta	ma-sa-**ne**-ta da **por**-ta
drive (to)	dirigir	jee-ree-**zheer**
dynamo	o dínamo	jee-na-moo
engine	o motor	moo-tor
exhaust	o escapamento	es-ka-pa-**me**ⁿ-too
fan	o ventilador	vayⁿ-tee-la-**dor**
fanbelt	as correias de ventiladores	koo-**ray**-ee-as je vayⁿ-tee-la-**dor**-es
(oil) filter	o filtro	feel-troo
foglamp	o farol de neblina	fa-**rol** je ne-blee-na
fusebox	a caixa dos fusíveis	kay-sha doos foo-**zee**-vay-ees
gasket	a gaxeta	ga-**she**-ta
gearbox	a caixa de câmbio	kay-sha je kaⁿ-bee-oo
gear-lever	a alavanca de câmbio	a-la-**va**ⁿ-ka je **ka**ⁿ-bee-oo

gears	as marchas	**mar**-shas
grease (to)	lubrificar	loo-bree-fee-**kar**
handbrake	o breque de mão	**bre**-ke je mow[n]
heater	o aquecedor	a-ke-se-**dor**
horn	a buzina	boo-**zee**-na
hose	a mangueira	ma[n]-**gay**-ee-ra
ignition	a ignição	eeg-nee-**sow**[n]
ignition key	a chave de ignição	**sha**-ve je eeg-nee-**sow**[n]
indicator	a seta	**se**-ta
jack	o macaco	ma-**ka**-ko
key	a chave	**sha**-ve
lights	os faróis	fa-**roy**-ees
headlights	os faróis dianteiros	fa-**roy**-ees jee-a[n]-**tey**-roos
parking lights	os faróis de estacionamento	fa-**roy**-ees je es-ta-see-oo-na-**may**[n]-too
rear lights	os faróis traseiros	fa-**roy**-ees tra-**sey**-roos
reversing lights	os indicadores de marcha atrás	ee[n]-jee-ka-**do**-res je **mar**-sha a-**tras**
side lights	os faróis laterais	fa-**roy**-ees la-te-**rais**
lock	a trava	**tra**-va
mirror	o espelho	es-**pay**-lyoo
number plate	a placa do carro	**pla**-ka do **ka**-ho
nut	a porca	**por**-ka

oil	o óleo	o-lee-oo
pedal	o pedal	pe-daw
petrol	a gasolina	ga-zoo-lee-na
piston	o pistão	pees-tow^n
plug	o plugue	ploo-ghe
points	os pontos/pontas	po^n-toos/po^n-tas
(fuel/water) pump	a bomba	bo^n-ba
puncture	o furo	foo-roo
radiator	o radiador	ha-jee a dor
rear view mirror	o retrovisor	re-troo-vee-sor
reverse (to)	dar a marcha ré	dar a mar-sha heh
reverse gear	a marcha ré	a mar-sha heh
roof	o teto	te-too
screwdriver	a chave de parafusos	sha-ve je pa-ra-foo-zoos
seat	o assento	as-sé^n too
seatbelt	o cinto de segurança	see^n-too je se-goo-ra^n-sa
shock absorber	o amortecedor	a-mor te-se-dor
silencer	o silenciador	see-len-see-a-dor
spanner	a chave inglesa	sha ve ee^n-glay-za
spares	os sobresselentes	soo-bres-se-lay^n-tes
spark plug	a vela de ignição	ve-la je eeg-nee-sow^n
speed	a velocidade	ve-lo-see-da-je
speedometer	o conta-quilômetros	ko^n-ta kee-lo-me troos

spring	a mola	**mo**-la
stall (to)	afogar	a-**fo**-gar
starter	a chave de partida/ o motor de arranque	**sha**-ve je par-**tee**-da/ moo-**tor** je a-**ha**ⁿ-ke
steering	a direção	jee-re-**sow**ⁿ
steering wheel	o volante	vo-**la**ⁿ-te
sunroof	o teto solar	**te**-too so-**lar**
suspension	a suspensão	soos-peⁿ-**sow**ⁿ
(petrol) tank	o tanque (de gasolina)	**ta**ⁿ-ke (je ga-zo-**lee**-na)
tappets	os tuchos de válvula	**too**-shos je **val**-voo-la
transmission	a transmissão	traⁿzh-mee-**sow**ⁿ
(spare) tyre	o (estepe) pneu	(es-**te**-pe) **pnay**-oo
valve	a válvula	**val**-voo-la
warning light	a luz de advertência	loosh je ad-vayr-**te**ⁿ-see-a
wheel	a roda	**ro**-da
back	de trás	je **tras**
front	da frente	da **fray**ⁿ-te
spare	sobresselente	soo-bres-se-**lay**ⁿ-te
window	a janela	zha-**ne**-la
windscreen	o pára-brisas	pa-ra-**bree**-zas
windscreen washer	o lavador de pára-brisas	la-va-**dor** je pa-ra-**bree**-zas
windscreen wiper	o limpador de pára-brisas	leeⁿ-pa-**dor** je pa-ra-**bree**-zas

By Bike or Moped[1]

Key Phrases

Where can I hire a . . .	Onde posso alugar uma . . .	On-je pos-soo a-loo-gar oo-ma
bicycle?	bicicleta?	bee-see-kle-ta
moped?	bicicleta motorizada?	bee-see-kle-ta moo-tor-ee-za-da
motorbike?	motocicleta?	mo-to-see-kle-ta
mountain bike?	bicicleta de montanha?	bee-see-kle-ta je mon-ta-nya
Is it obligatory to wear a helmet?	É obrigatório usar capacete?	Eh o-bree-ga to-ree-oo oo-zar ka-pa-se-te
Do you repair bicycles?	Conserta bicicletas?	Kon-ser-ta bee-see-kle-tas

What does it cost per day/week?	Quanto custa por dia/semana?	Kwan-too koos-ta por jee-a /se-ma-na
I'd like a lock, please	Eu gostaria de um cadeado, por favor	Ay-oo gos-ta-ree-a je oon ka-je-a-doo poor fa-vor
Where is the cycle shop?	Onde é a loja de bicicletas?	On-je eh a lo-zha de bee-see-kle-tas
The brake isn't working	O breque não funciona	Oo bre-ke nown foon-sse o na
The tyre is punctured	O pneu está furado	Oo pnay-oo es-ta foo-ra-doo

1. See also directions (p. 48) and road signs (p. 46).

The gears need adjusting	As marchas precisam de ajuste	As **mar**-shas pre-**see**-za[a] je a-**zhoos**-te
The saddle is too high/too low	O selim está muito alto/muito baixo	Oo se-lee[n] es-**ta** mwee-too al-too/**mwee**-too by-shoo
Could you straighten the wheel?	Pode endireitar a roda?	Po-je ay[n]-jee-ray-ee-**tar** a **ho**-da
The handlebars are loose	Os guidões estão soltos	Oos ghee-**doy**[n]s es-**tow**[n] **sol**-tos
Could you lend me a spanner?	Pode emprestar uma chave inglesa?	Po-je ay[n]-pres-**tar** oo-ma sha-ve ee[n]-**glay**-za
Can I take my bike on the boat/train?	Posso levar minha bicicleta no barco/trem?	**Pos**-soo le-**var** mee-nya bee-see-**kle**-ta no **bar**-koo /tre[n]

Parts of a bicycle and other useful words

basket	a cesta	**ses**-ta
bell	a campaínha	ka[n]-pa-**ee**-nya
brake, front	o breque da frente	**bre**-ke da **fray**[n]-te
brake, rear	o breque de trás	**bre**-ke je tras
brake cable	o cabo do breque	**ka**-boo doo **bre**-ke
brake lever	a alavanca do breque	a-la-**va**[n]-ka do **bre**-ke
bulb	a lâmpada	**la**[n]-pa-da
chain	a corrente	ko-**he**[n] -te

child's seat	a cadeirinha infantil	ka-dey-**ree**-nya ee^n-fa^n-**teew**
dynamo	o dynamo	**dee**-na-moo
fork	o garfo	**gar**-foo
frame	o quadro	**kwa**-droo
gear cable	o cabo de marcha	**ka**-boo je **mar**-sha
gear lever	o cabo de mudanças	**ka**-boo je moo-**da**^{n}-sas
gears	as mudanças	moo-**da**^{n}-sas
handlebars	os guidões	ghee-**doy**^{n}s
helmet	o capacete	ka-pa-**se**-te
high-visibility jacket	a jaqueta de alta visibilidade	zha-**ke**-ta je **al**-ta vee-zee-bee-lee-**da**-je
inner tube	o tubo interior	**too**-boo ee^n-te-ree-**or**
light – front	a lanterna da frente	lan-**ter**-na da **fray**^{n}-te
rear	de trás	je tras
mudguard	o guarda-lamas	**qwar**-da la-mas
pannier	a bolsa para bicicletas	**bol**-sa pa-ra bee-see-**kle**-tas
pedal	o pedal	pe-**dow**
pump	a bomba de ar	**bo**^{n}-ba je ar
puncture	o furo	**foo**-roo
puncture repair kit	o kit de reparo e remendo para furos	kit je he-**pa**-roo e he-**me**^{n}-do pa-ra **foo** roos
reflector	o reflector	he-**flek**-tor

rim	o aro	a-roo
saddle	a sela	se-la
spoke	o raio	ha-ee-oo
suspension	a suspensão	soos-pe^n-sow^n
tyre	o pneu	pnay-oo
valve	a válvula	val-voo-la
wheel	a roda	ho-da

Road Signs

Acenda os faróis da frente	Headlights on
Anel rodoviário	Ring road
Área com desmoronamento	Falling rocks
Área de pedestres	Pedestrians only
Conserve-se à direita	Keep right
Cuidado	Caution
Curva (acentuada)	Bend (sharp)
Declive acentuado	Steep hill
Dê a preferência	Give way
Desvio	Diversion
Diminua a velocidade	Reduce speed
Estacionamento regulamentado	Restricted parking
Estrada cortada	Road blocked/closed

Faixa de ônibus	Bus lane
Limite de velocidade	Speed limit
Luzes	Lights on
Obras	Roadworks ahead
Obrigatório o uso de cartão	Parking disc required
Páre	Stop
Passagem de nível	Level crossing
Perigo	Danger
Pista escorregadia	Slippery surface
Piso irregular/perigoso	Uneven (dangerous) surface
Proibido estacionar	No parking
Proibido ultrapassar	No overtaking
Projeção de cascalho	Loose chippings
Saída (para caminhão)	Exit (for lorries)
Saliência/ Lombada	Speed bump
Semáforo	Traffic lights
Sentido proibido	No entry
Sentido único	One-way (street)
Siga pela faixa	Get in lane
Velocidade máxima permitida	Maximum speed

Directions

Key Phrases

Where is . . . ?	**Onde é . . . ?**	O^n-je eh
How do I get to . . . ?	**Como se vai para . . . ?**	**Ko**-moo se vy **pa**-ra
How many kilometres?	**Quantos quilómetros?**	**Kwa^n**-toos kee-**lo**-me-troos
Please show me on the map	**Por favor me mostre no mapa**	Poor fa-**vor** me mos-**tree** no **ma**-pa
You are going the wrong way	***Você está no caminho errado**	**Vo**-seh es-**ta** no ka-**mee**-nyo er-**ra**-doo

Excuse me, could you tell me . . .	**Com licença, pode me dizer . . . ?**	Ko^n lee-**se^n**-sa **po**-je me jee-**zayr**
How far is it to . . . ?	**A que distância fica . . . ?**	A ke jees-**ta^n**-see-a **fee**-ka
How do we get on to the motorway to . . . ?	**Como se vai para a autostrada de . . . ?**	**Ko**-moo se vy **pa**-ra a ow-to-es-**tra**-da je
Which is the best road to . . . ?	**Qual é o melhor caminho para . . . ?**	Kwal eh oo me-**lyor** ka-mee-nyoo **pa**-ra
Is there a scenic route to . . . ?	**Há alguma rota cênica para . . . ?**	Ah al-**goo**-ma **ro**-ta se^n-nee-ka **pa**-ra
Where does this road lead to?	**Para onde vai esta estrada?**	**Pa**-ra o^n-je vy **es**-ta es-**tra**-da
Is it a good road?	**É uma boa estrada?**	Eh **oo**-ma **bo**-a es-**tra**-da

Is it a motorway?	**É uma autostrada?**	Eh **oo**-ma ow-to-es-**tra**-da
Is there a toll?	**Há pedágio?**	Ah pe-**da**-gee-oo
Is the tunnel open?	**O túnel está aberto?**	Oo **too**-nel es-**ta** a-**ber**-too
Will we get to ... by evening?	**Chegaremos a ... antes de anoitecer?**	She-ga-**re**-mos a ... an-tes de a-noy-**te**-ser
Where are we now?	**Onde estamos agora?**	O^n-je es-**ta**-moos a-**go**-ra
What is the name of this place?	**Qual é o nome deste lugar?**	Kwal eh oo **no**-me dayst loo-**gar**
I'm lost	**Estou perdido**	Es-**toh** per-jee-doo
It's that way	***É por ali**	Eh poor a-lee
It isn't far	***Não é longe**	Now^n eh **lo**^{n}-zhe
It's on the square	***Fica na praça**	**Fee**-ka na **pra**-sa
It's at the end of this street	***É no final desta rua**	Eh no fee-**nal** des-ta **roo**-a
There is one in the pedestrian area	***Há um na área de pedestres**	Ah oo^n na **a**-rea je pe-**des**-tres
Follow this road for five kilometres	***Siga nessa estrada por cinco quilómetros**	See ga **nes**-sa es-**tra**-da por **see**^{n}-koo kee-lo-me-tros
Go straight on	***Siga em frente**	**See**-ga e^n **fre**^{n}-te
Turn right at the crossing	***Vire à direita no cruzamento**	**Vee**-re ah jee-**rei**- ta noo kroo-za **me**^{n}-too
Take the second road on the left	***Vire na segunda rua à esquerda**	**Vee**-re na se **goo**^{n}-da **roo**-a ah es-**kayr**-da

Turn right at the traffic-lights	*Vire à direita no semáforo	**Vee**-re ah jee-**ray**-ee-ta no se-**ma**-fo-ro
Turn left after the bridge	*Vire à esquerda depois da ponte	**Vee**-re ah es-**kayr**-da de-**po**-ees da **po**ⁿte
The best road is the . . .	*A melhor estrada é a . . .	A me-**lyor** es-**tra**-da eh a
Take the . . . to . . . and ask again	*Tome a . . . e pergunte novamente	**To**-me a . . . ee per-**goo**ⁿ-te no-va-**may**ⁿ-te
Take junction 10/the exit for . . .	*Pegue o entrocamento 10/ saída para . . .	Pe-ghe oo eⁿ-**tro**ⁿ-ka-meⁿ-too des/sa-**ee**-da **pa**-ra
one-way system	sentido único	sayⁿ-**tee**-doo **oo**-nee-koo
north	norte	**nor**-te
south	sul	sool
east	oriente/leste	o-ree-**ay**ⁿ-te /**les**-te
west	ocidente/oeste	o-see-**day**ⁿte /**oo**-es-te

ACCOMMODATION[1]

campsite	a área de acampamento	a-rea je a-kaⁿ-pa-meⁿ-too
cottage	a casa de campo	ka-za je kaⁿ-poo
country inn	a pousada/ o hotel fazenda	po-za-da/ o-tew fa-zeⁿ da
guest-house	a pensão	peⁿ-sowⁿ
youth hostel	o albergue da juventude	al-ber-ghe da zhoo-věⁿ-too-de
Rooms to let/ vacancies	*Alugam-se quartos/ há quartos vagos	A-loo-gowⁿ-se kwar-toos/ah kwar-toos va-goos
No vacancies	Sem vagas/ disponibilidade	Seⁿ va-gas/jee-spo-nee-bee-lee-da-je
No camping	Probido acampar	Pro-ee bee-doo a-kaⁿ-par
Can you show me on the map where the hotel is?	Pode me mostrar no mapa onde fica o hotel?	Po je me mos-trar no ma-pa oⁿ -je fee-ka o o-tew
Is it in the centre?	Fica no centro?	Fee-ka no seⁿ-tró
Is it near a bus stop?	Fica perto de um ponto de ônibus?	Fee-ka per to je ooⁿ poⁿ-to de ôh nee-boos
Is it on a train/metro route?	Fica em uma rota de trem/metrô?	Fee-ka eⁿ oo-ma ho-ta je traⁿ /me trôn

1. In Portugal, in addition to privately owned hotels and guest-houses, there are state-owned hotels called **pousadas**. **Estalagens** are small hotels.

Checking In

Key Phrases

Have you a room for the night?	**Tem um quarto para esta noite?**	Te^n oo^n **kwar**-too **pa**-ra es-ta **no**-ee-te
I've reserved a room; my name is . . .	**Tenho um quarto reservado; o meu nome é . . .**	Te-nyoo oo^n **kwar**-too he-zer-**va**-doo; oo **may**-oo **no**-me eh
How much is the room per night?	**Quanto custa o quarto por noite?**	**Kwa**^{n}-too **koos**-ta oo **kwar**-too poor **no**-ee-te
Does the hotel have wi-fi?	**O hotel tem wi-fi?**	Oo o-**tew** te^n wi-fi
Is there a lift/elevator?	**Tem elevador?**	Te^n ee-le-va-**dor**

Can you suggest . . .	**Você poderia me sugerir . . .**	**Vo**-seh po-de-**ree**-a me soo-**je**-reer
a moderately priced hotel?	**um hotel de preço moderado?**	oo^n o-**tew** je **pre**-so mo-de-**ra**-do
an inexpensive hotel?	**um hotel barato?**	oo^n o-**tew** ba-**ra**-too
another good hotel?	**um outro hotel bom?**	oo^n **o**-tro o-**tew** bo^n
Is there an internet connection in the rooms?	**Tem acesso à internet nos quartos?**	Te^n a-**se**-so a internet noos **kwar**-toos
Yes, it's free/it costs . . . reais/ euros per hour	***Sim, é de graça/ custa . . . reais/ euros por hora**	See^n eh je **gra**-sa/**koo**-sta . . . he-**ay**-ees /ay-oo-ros poor **o**-ra

Does the hotel have a conference centre?	**Tem um centro de convenções no hotel?**	Te^n oo^n **se**^{n}-tro je ko^n-ve^n-soy^{n}s noo o-**tew**
Is there a spa/fitness centre?	**Tem um spa/ sala de ginástica?**	Te^n oo^n spa/**sa**-la je zhee-na-stee-ka
Does the hotel have a swimming pool/a private beach?	**O hotel tem piscina/ acesso a praia particular?**	Oo o-**tew** te^n pee-**see**-na/a-**ses**-so a **pra**-ya par-tee-koo-**lar**
I'd like a single room with a shower	**Quero um quarto individual com chuveiro**	Ke-roo oo^n **kwar**-too ee^n-jee-vee-doo-**aw** ko^n shoo-**ver**-oo
I'd like a room with a double bed and a bathroom	**Quero um quarto de casal e banheiro**	Ke-roo oo^n **kwar**-too je ka-**zal** ee ba-**nyer**-oo
I'd like adjoining rooms	**Eu gostaria de quartos conjugados**	Ay-oo gos-ta-ree-a je **kwar**-toos ko^n zhoo-ga-dos
Have you a room with twin beds/a king size bed?	**Há algum quarto duplo/cama king-size disponível?**	Ah al-**goo**^{n} **kwar**-too doo-plo/ ka-ma king-size jee-spo-**nee**-vel
How long will you be staying?	*Por quanto tempo você vai ficar?	Poor kwa^n-too te^n-po vo-seh vy fee-**kar**
Is it for one night only?	*É só por uma noite?	Eh soh poor **oo**-ma no-ee-te
I'd like a room . . .	**Quero um quarto . . .**	Ke-roo oo^n **kwar**-too
for a week	**para uma semana**	pa-ra oo-ma se-ma-na
for two or three days	**para dois ou três dias**	pa-ra do-ees oh trays dee-as
until Friday	**até sexta-feira**	a-teh say-ees-ta-**fay**-ee-ra

What floor is the room on?	Em que andar fica o quarto?	En ke an-**dar** fee-ka oo **kwar**-too
Are there facilities for the disabled?	Há instalações para pessoas com necessidades especiais?	Ah een-sta-la-**soy**ns pa-ra pes-**so**-as kon ne-se-see-da-jes es-pe-sy-**ice**
Have you a room on the first floor?	Tem um quarto no primeiro andar?	Ten oon **kwar**-too noo pree-**may**-ee-roo an-**dar**
May I see the room?	Posso ver o quarto?	**Pos**-so vayr oo **kwar**-too
I'll take this room	Fico com este quarto	**Fee**-koo kon es-te **kwar**-too
I don't like this room	Não gosto deste quarto	Nown **gos**-too **days**-te **kwar**-too
Have you another one?	Tem outro?	Ten o-troo
I'd like a quiet room	Quero um quarto silencioso	**Ke**-roo oon **kwar**-too see-len-syo-so
There's too much noise	Há muito barulho	Ah **mwee**-too ba-**roo**-lyoo
I'd like a room with a balcony	Eu gostaria de um quarto com varanda	**Ay**-oo gos-ta-**ree**-a je oon **kwar**-too kon va-**ran**-da
Have you a room . . .	Tem um quarto . . .	Ten oon **kwar**-too
looking on to the street?	que dê para a rua?	ke day **pa**-ra a **roo**-a
near the swimming pool?	seja perto da piscina?	se-**zha pair**-to da pee-**see**-na
overlooking the sea?	dê para o mar?	day **pa**-ra oo mar

We've only a double/twin-bedded room	*Nós só temos um quarto de casal/duplo	Nohs soh te-mos oo^n kwar-too je ka-zal/doo-plo
This is the only room vacant	*Este é o único quarto vago	Es-te eh oo oo-nee-koo kwar-too va-goo
We shall have another room tomorrow	*Teremos outro quarto amanhã	Te-ray-moos o-troo kwar-too a-ma-nya^n
The room is only available tonight	*O quarto só está vago por esta noite	Oo kwar-too soh es-ta va-goo poor es-ta no-ee-te
Have you nothing cheaper?	Não tem nada mais barato?	Now^n te^n na-da ma-ees ba-ra-too
How much do we pay for the child(ren)?	Quanto pagamos pela(s) criança(s)?	Kwa^n-too pa-ga-moos pe-la(s) kree-a^n-sa(s)
Could you put a cot/an extra bed in the room?	Pode pôr um berço/uma cama extra no quarto, por favor?	Po-je por oo^n ber-so/oo-ma ka-ma es-tra noo kwar-too poor fa-vor
Is the service (and tax)[1] included	O serviço (e taxa) está incluído?	Oo ser-vee-soo (e ta-sha) es-ta ee^n-kloo-ee-doo
Is breakfast included?	O café da manhã está incluído?	O ka-fe da ma-nya es-ta ee^n-kloo-ee-do
How much is the room with full board/without meals?	Quanto é a pensão completa?/ Quanto é o quarto sem refeições?	Kwa^n-too eh a pay^n-sow^n ko^n-ple-la/ kwa^n-too ch oo kwar-too say^n re-fay-soy^{n}s
Do you have a weekly rate?	Tem uma tarifa semanal?	Te^n oo-ma ta-ree-fa se-ma-naw
It's too expensive	É muito caro	Eh mwee-too ka-roo

1. In health resorts only.

How would you like to pay?	*Como você quer pagar?	Ko-moo vo-seh ker pa-gar
Would you fill in the registration form?	*Pode preencher o formulário?	Po-je pre-ayn-shayr oo for-moo-la-ree-oo
Could I see your passport?	*Posso ver seu passaporte?	Pos-soo vayr say-oo pa-sa-por-te
Surname/First name	*Sobrenome/Nome	So-bre-no-me/no-me
Address	*Endereço	En-de-re-so
Date and place of birth	*Local e data de nascimento	Lo-kaw e da-ta je na-see-men-to
Passport number	*Número do passaporte	Noo-me-roo doo pa-sa-por-te
What is your car registration number?	*Qual é o número de registro do seu carro?	Kwal eh oo noo-me-roo je re-zhee-stro doo say-oo ka-hoo

Checking Out

Key Phrases

Can you have my bill ready?	Pode me ver a conta?	Po-je me ver a kon-ta
There is a mistake on the bill	Há um engano na conta	Ah oon ayn-ga-noo na kon-ta
Please store the luggage, we will be back at ...	Por favor guarde nossas malas, nós voltaremos às ...	Poor fa-vor gwar-je nos-sas ma-las, nos vol-ta-re-moos ahs ...

I'd like to leave tomorrow	Eu gostaria de ir embora amanhã	Ay-oo gos-ta-**ree**-a je eer eⁿ-bo-ra a-ma-**nya**
I'll pay by credit card	Eu pagarei com cartão de crédito	Ay-oo pa-ga-**re** koⁿ kar-towⁿ je **kre**-jee-to
I shall be coming back on ... Can I book a room for that date?	Voltarei no dia ... Posso reservar um quarto para essa data?	Vol-ta-**rei** noo jee-a ...**pos**-soo he-zer-**var** ooⁿ kwar-too **pa**-ra es-sa **da**-ta
Could you have my luggage brought down?	Pode trazer a minha bagagem para baixo?	**Po**-je tra-**zayr** a mee-nya ba-ga-zhayⁿ **pa**-ra by-shoo
Please order a taxi for me	Por favor, chame um taxi para mim	Poor fa-**vor** sha-me ooⁿ **tak**-see pa-ra meeⁿ
Thank you for a pleasant stay	Muito obrigado (a) pela agradável estadia	**Mwee**-too o-bree-**ga**-doo (a) pe-la a-gra-**da**-vel es-ta-**jee**-a

Problems and Complaints

The air conditioning/ television doesn't work	O ar condicionado/a televisão não funciona	Oo ahr koⁿ-jee-syo-**na**-do/a te-le vee **zow**ⁿ nowⁿ fooⁿ-**syo**-na
There are no towels in my room	Não há toalhas no meu quarto	Nowⁿ ah too-a-lyas noo **may**-oo kwar-too
There's no soap	Não há sabonete	Nowⁿ ah sa-bo-ne te
There's no (hot) water	Não há água (quente)	Nowⁿ ah a-gwa (kayⁿ-te)
There's no toilet paper in the lavatory	Não há papel higiênico no banheiro	Nowⁿ ah pa-**pel** ee-zhee-e-nee-koo noo ba-nyer-oo
The lavatory won't flush	A privada não dá descarga	A pree-**va**-da nowⁿ da des-**kar**-ga

The toilet is blocked	**A privada está entupida**	A pree-**va**-da- es-**ta** e^n-too-**pee**-da
The shower doesn't work/is flooded	**O chuveiro não funciona/está inundado**	Oo shoo-**ver**-oo now^n foo^n-see-o-na/es-**ta** ee-noo^n-**da**-doo
The light doesn't work	**A luz não acende**	A loosh now^n a-**say**^n-de
The lamp is broken	**A lâmpada está quebrada**	A **la**^n-pa-da es-**ta** ke-**bra**-da
The blind is stuck	**A persiana está emperrada**	A per-**sya**-na es-**ta** e^n-pe-ha-da
The curtains won't close	**As cortinas não fecham**	As koor-**tee**-nas now^n **fay**-sha^n

Camping

Key Phrases

Is there a camping site near here?	**Há uma área de acampamento aqui perto?**	Ah **oo**-ma **a**-ree-a je a-ka^n-pa-**me**^n-to a-**kee** **per**-too
May we camp . . .	**Podemos acampar . . .**	Po-**de**-moos a-ka^n-**par**
on the beach?	**na praia?**	na **pra**-ya
in your field?	**no seu terreno?**	noo **say**-oo te-**hay**-noo
here?	**aqui?**	a-**kee**
Is there drinking water?	**Há água potável?**	Ah **a**-gwa poo-**ta**-vel
electricity?	**eletricidade?**	e-le-tree-see-**da**-je

Can we hire a tent?	Podemos alugar uma barraca?	Po-**de**-moos a-loo-**gar** oo-ma ba-**ha**-ka
Are bathrooms/ showers provided?	Há banheiros/ chuveiros disponíveis?	Ah ba-**nyer**-oos/shoo-ver-oos jee-spo-**nee**-vays
What does it cost per person/day/week?	Quanto custa por pessoa/dia/semana?	Kwa^n-too **koo**-sta poor pes-**so**-a/jee-a/se-**ma**-na
Where are the shops?	Onde ficam as lojas?	O^n-je **fee**-ka^n as **lo**-zhas
Is there . . .	Há/Tem . . .	Ah/Te^n
a launderette?	serviço de lavanderia?	ser-**vee**-so je la-va^n-de-**ree**-a
a playground?	um parquinho?	oo^n par-**kee**-nyo
a restaurant?	um restaurante?	oo^n res-tow-ra^n-te
a swimming pool?	uma piscina?	oo-ma pee-**see**-na
My camping gas has run out	O meu gás acabou	Oo **may**-oo gas a-ka-**bo**
Where can I buy butane gas?	Onde posso comprar gás butano?	O^n-je **pos**-soo ko^n-prar gas boo-**ta**-no
Where do I get rid of rubbish?	Onde posso deixar o lixo?	O^n-je **pos**-soo day- **shar** oo lee-shoo
Should we sort the rubbish (for recycling)?	Devemos separar o lixo (para reciclagem)?	De-**ve**-mos se-pa-**rar** oo lee-shoo (**pa**-ra re-see-kla-zhe^n)
Where can I wash up/wash clothes?	Onde posso lavar a louça/lavar a roupa?	O^n-je **pos**-soo la-var a **lo**-sa/la-var a **ho**-pa
Is there somewhere to dry clothes?	Tem algum lugar para secar a roupa?	Te^n al-**goo**^{n} loo-**gar** pa-ra se-**kar** **ho**-pa

| I'm afraid the campsite is full | *Lamento mas a área de acampamento está lotada | La-**may**ⁿ-too mas a a-ree-a je a-kaⁿ-pa-**me**ⁿ-too es-**ta** lo-ta-da |

Hostels

How long is the walk to the youth hostel?	A que distância está o albergue da juventude?	A ke jees-**ta**ⁿ-see-a es-**ta** oo al-**ber**-ghe da zhoo-vayⁿ-**too**-je
Have you a room/bed for the night?	Tem quarto/cama para esta noite?	Teⁿ **kwar**-too/**ka**-ma pa-ra es-ta no-**ee**-te
How many days can we stay?	Quantos dias podemos ficar?	**Kwa**ⁿ-toos **jee**-as poo-**day**-moos fee-**kar**
Here is my membership card	Aqui está o meu cartão de sócio/membro	A-**kee** es-ta oo **may**-oo kar-**tow**ⁿ je so-see-oo/**may**ⁿ-broo
Do you serve meals?	Servem refeições?	**Ser**-vayⁿ he-fay-ee-**soy**ⁿs
Can I use the kitchen?	Posso usar a cozinha?	**Pos**-soo oo-**zar** a koo-**zee**-nya
Is there somewhere cheap to eat nearby?	Há algum lugar barato onde se possa comer por aqui?	Ah al-**goo**ⁿ loo-**gar** ba-**ra**-too oⁿ-je se **pos**-sa ko-**mayr** poor a-**kee**
Can I rent sheets/a sleeping bag?	Posso alugar lençóis/um saco de dormir?	**Pos**-soo a-loo-**gar** leⁿ-**soys**/ooⁿ sa-koo je door-**meer**
Does the hostel have an internet connection?	O albergue tem acesso à internet?	Oo al-**berg**he teⁿ a-**ses**-so ah internet

Hotels

In your room

chambermaid	a camareira	ka-ma-**ray**-ra
room service	o serviço de quarto	ser-**vee**-soo je **kwar**-too
I'd like breakfast in my room, please	**Quero o café da manhã no meu quarto, por favor**	Ke-roo oo ka-**feh** da ma-nya^n noo **may**-oo **kwar**-too poor **fa-vor**
Can I have more hangers, please?	**Pode me dar mais cabides, por favor?**	Po-je me dar **ma**-ees ka-**bee**-des poor fa-vor
Is there a socket for an electric razor?	**Há tomada para máquina de barbear?**	Ah too-**ma**-da pa-ra ma-**kee**-na je bar-bee-**ar**
Where is the bathroom?	**Onde é o banheiro?**	O^n-je eh oo ba-**nyer**-oo
Is there a shower?	**Há um chuveiro?**	Ah oo^n shoo-**ver**-oo
May I have another blanket/pillow?	**Pode me arrumar uma outra manta/um outro travesseiro?**	Po-je me a-hoo-**mar** oo-ma o-tra ma^n-ta/o-tro tra ves-**sey**-roo
These sheets are dirty	**Estes lençóis estão sujos**	Es-tes le^n soys es-tow^n soo-zhos
I can't open my window; please open it	**Não consigo abrir a janela; pode abri la por favor**	Now^n ko^n-**see**-goo a-breer a zha-ne-la, po-je a-**bree**-la poor fa-vor
It's too hot/cold	**Está quente/frio demais**	Es-ta ke^n-te/free oo je ma-ees
Can the heating be turned up/down?	**Pode aumentar/ diminuir o aquecimento?**	Po-je ow-may^n-**tar**/ jee-mee-noo-**eer** oo a-ke-see-**may**^n-too

Can the heating be turned on/off?	Pode ligar/desligar o aquecimento?	Po-je lee-gar/jes-lee-gar oo a-ke-see-mayn-too
Is the room air-conditioned?	O quarto tem ar condicionado?	Oo kwar-too ten ahr kon-jee-see-oo-na-doo
The air conditioning doesn't work	O ar condicionado não funciona	Oo ahr kon-jee-see-oo-na-doo nown foon-see-o-na
Come in	Entre	Ayn-tre
Put it on the table, please	Ponha em cima da mesa, por favor	Po-nya en see-ma da may-za poor fa-vor
Have you a needle and thread?	Tem uma agulha e linha?	Ten oo-ma a-goo-lya ee leen-nya
Do you have an iron and ironing board?	Você tem um ferro e uma tábua de passar roupa?	Vo-seh ten oon fe-hoo e oo-ma ta-boo-a je pas-sar ho-pa
I'd like these shoes cleaned	Quero estes sapatos limpos	Ke-roo es-tes sa-pa-toos leen-poos
I'd like this dress cleaned	Quero este vestido limpo	Ke-roo es-te ves-tee-do leen-po
I'd like this suit pressed	Quero este terno passado	Ke-roo es-te ter-no pas-sa-doo
When will it be ready?	Quando estará pronto?	Kwan-doo es-ta-ra pron-too
It will be ready tomorrow	*Estará pronto amanhã	Es-ta-ra pron-too a-ma-nyan

Other services

| porter | carregador | ka-he-ga-dor |
| manager | gerente | zhe-rayn-te |

telephonist	telefonista	te-le-fo-**nees**-ta
My key, please	**Minha chave, por favor**	**Mee**-nya **sha**-ve, poor fa-**vor**
A second key, please	**Uma segunda chave, por favor**	**Oo**-ma se-**goo**ⁿ-da **sha**-ve, poor fa-**vor**
I've lost my key	**Perdi a minha chave**	Per-**jee** a **mee**-nya **sha**-ve
Have you a map of the town/an entertainment guide?	**Tem um mapa da cidade/guia de entretenimento?**	Teⁿ ooⁿ **ma**-pa da see-**da**-je/**ghee**-a je eⁿ-tre-te-nee-**me**ⁿ-to
Could you put this in your safe?	**Posso deixar isto no seu cofre?**	**Pos**-soo dey -**shar** ees-too noo **sey**-oo **ko**-fre
Are there any letters for me?	**Há alguma carta para mim?**	Ah al-**goo**-ma **kar**-ta pa-ra meeⁿ
Are there any messages for me?	**Há alguma mensagem para mim?**	Ah al-**goo**-ma mayⁿ-**sa**-zhayⁿ pa-ra meeⁿ
What is the international dialing code?	**Qual é o código internacional para ligação?**	Kwal eh oo **ko**-jee-go eeⁿ-ter-na-syo-nal pa-ra lee-ga-**sow**ⁿ
Could you send a fax for me, please?	**Você pode me mandar um fax, por favor?**	Vo-seh **po**-je me maⁿ-dar ooⁿ fax poor fa-**vor**
Is there a computer for guests to use?	**Há um computador para hóspedes usarem?**	Ah ooⁿ koⁿ-poo-**ta**-dor pa-ra **os**-pe-jes oo-sar-ayⁿ
Is there a charge for this?	**Há uma taxa para isto?**	Ah **oo**-ma **ta**-sha pa-ra ees-lo
Do I need a password?	**Preciso de uma senha?**	Pre-**see**-so je **oo**-ma se-nya

There's a lady/ gentleman to see you	*Há uma senhora/ um senhor perguntando por você	Ah oo-ma se-nyo-ra/oo^n se-nyor per-goo^n-ta^n-doo poor vo-seh
Please ask her/him to come up	Por favor, diga-lhe para subir	Poor fa-vor jee-ga-lye pa-ra soo-beer
I'm coming down immediately	Estou descendo imediatamente	Es-toh de-se^n-doo ee-me-jee-a-ta-may^n-te
Have you any . . .	Você tem . . .	Vo-seh te^n
envelopes?	envelopes?	ay^n-ve-lo-pes
stamps?	selos?	say-loos
Please send the chambermaid/the waiter	A camareira/o garçon, por favor	Ah ka-ma-ray-ra/oo gar-son poor fa-vor
I need a guide/an interpreter	Preciso de um guia/ intérprete	Pre-see-zoo je oo^n ghee-a/ee^n-ter-pre-te
Does the hotel have a babysitting service?	O hotel tem quem cuide de crianças/serviço de babysitter?	Oo o-tew te^n ke^n kwee-je je kree-a^n-sas/ser-vee-soo je babysitter
Where is the dining room?	Onde é a sala de jantar?	O^n-je eh a sa-la je zha^n-tar
What time is breakfast/lunch/ dinner served?	A que horas é o café da manhã/o almoço/o jantar?	A ke o-ras eh oo ka-fe da ma-nya/oo al-mo-so/oo zha^n-tar
Is there a garage?	Tem garagem aqui?	Te^n ga-ra-zhay^n a-kee
Where can I park the car?	Onde posso estacionar o carro?	O^n-je pos-soo es-ta-see-o-nar oo ka-ho

Is the hotel open all night?	**O hotel está aberto toda a noite?**	Oo o-**tew** es-**ta** a-**ber**-too **to**-da a no-**ee**-te
What time does it close?	**A que horas fecha?**	A ke **o**-ras **fay**-ee-sha
Please wake me at . . .	**Por favor me acorde às . . .**	Poor fa-**vor** me a-**kor**-je ahs

APARTMENTS AND HOUSES

Key Phrases

Please could you show us around	**Por favor nos mostre a casa/o apartamento**	Poor fa-**vor** nos **mos**-tre a ka-za/oo a-par-ta-**may**ⁿ-too
How does the heating/hot water work?	**Como é que o aquecimento/a água quente funciona?**	**Ko**-moo eh ke oo a-ke-see-**may**ⁿ-too/a **ah**-gwa **kay**ⁿ-te fooⁿ-see-**o**-na
Please could you show me how this works	**Por favor me mostre como isto funciona**	Poor fa-**vor** me **mos**-tre **ko**-moo **ees**-too fooⁿ-see-**o**-na
Which days does the maid come?	**Quais os dias que a empregada vem?**	**Kwa**-ees os **jee**-as ke a eⁿ-pre-**ga**-da veⁿ
When is the rubbish collected?	**Quando é a coleta de lixo?**	**Kwa**ⁿ-doo eh a ko-**le**-ta je **lee**-shoo
Please could you give me another set of keys	**Por favor você poderia me dar um outro molho de chaves?**	Poor fa-**vor** vo-seh po-de-**ree**-a me dar ooⁿ **o**-troo **mo**-lyoo je **sha**-ves

We have rented an apartment/villa	**Nós alugámos um apartamento/chalet**	Nohs a-loo-**ga**-moos oo^n a-par-ta-**may**^{n}-too/sha-**leh**
Here is our reservation	**Aqui está a nossa reserva**	A-**kee** es-ta a **nos**-sa he-**zer**-va
Is the cost of electricity/of the gas cylinder/of the maid included?	**O preço da eletricidade/do bujão de gás/ da empregada está incluído?**	Oo **pray**-soo da ee-le-tree-see-**da**-je/do boo-**zhow**^{n} je gas/ da e^n-pre-**ga**-da es-ta ee^n-kloo-ee-doo
Where is . . .	**Onde está . . .**	O^n-je es-**ta**
the electricity mains switch?	**o quadro da eletricidade?**	oo kwa-droo da ee-le-tree-see-**da**-je
the fuse box?	**a caixa de fusível?**	a **kay**-sha je foo-**zee**-vel
the light switch?	**o interruptor da luz?**	oo ee^n-te-hoop-**tor** da loosh
the power-point?	**a derivação?**	a de-ree-va-**sow**^{n}
the water mains stopcock?	**a válvula reguladora?**	a **val**-voo-la re-goo-la-**do**-ra
Is there a spare gas cylinder?	**Há um bujão de reserva?**	Ah oo^n boo-**zhow**^{n} je re-**zer**-va
Are gas cylinders delivered?	**Há entrega de bujão?**	Ah e^n-**tre**-ga je boo-**zhow**^{n}
For how long does the maid come?	**A empregada vem por quanto tempo?**	A e^n-pre-**ga**-da ve^n poor kwa^n-too **tay**^{n}-poo
Should we sort the rubbish for recycling?	**Devemos separar o lixo para reciclagem?**	De-**ve**-mos se-pa-**rar** oo lee-shoo pa-ra re-see-**kla**-ge^n
The rubbish hasn't been collected	**O lixo não foi coletado**	Oo **lee**-shoo now^n foy ko-le-**ta**-do

Where can we buy logs for the fire?	**Onde podemos comprar lenha para o fogo?**	O[n]-je po-**de**-moos ko[n]-prar **lay**-nya **pa**-ra oo **fo**-goo
Is there a barbecue?	**Há uma churrasqueira?**	Ah **oo**-ma shoo-has-**key**-ra
Does someone come to service the swimming pool?	**Há alguém que vem fazer serviços na piscina?**	Ah al-**ge**[n] ke ve[n] fa-**zair** ser-vee-**soos** na pee-**see**-na
Is there an inventory?	**Há um inventório?**	Ah oo[n] ee[n]-ve[n]-**toh**-ree-o
This was broken when we arrived	**Isto estava quebrado quando nós chegámos**	**Ees**-too es-**ta**-va ke-**bra**-do **kwa**[n]-doo nohs she-**ga**-mos
We have replaced the broken . . .	**Nós substituímos . . . que estavam quebrados**	Nos soob-stee-too-**ee**-moos . . . ke es-ta-va[n] ke-**bra**-dos
Here is the bill	**Aqui está a conta**	A-**kee** es-**ta** a **ko**[n]-ta
Please return my deposit against damage	**Por favor restitua-me o depósito contra danos**	Poor fa-**vor** hes-tee-**too**-a-me oo de-**po**-zee-too **ko**[n]-tra **da**-noos

Cleaning and Maintenance[1]

bleach	**a água sanitária**	a-gwa sa-nee-**ta**-ree-a
bracket	**o suporte**	soo-**por**-te
broom	**a vassoura**	vas-**so**-ra
brush	**a escova**	es-**ko**-va

---

1. See also Hardware and Outdoors (p. 180).

bucket	o balde	baw-je
butane gas	o gás butano	gas boo-ta-no
charcoal	o carvão	kar-vow^n
clothes line	o varal	va-raw
clothes peg	o prendedor de roupa	pre^n-de-dor je ho- pa
detergent	o detergente	de-ter-zhe^n-te
dustbin	a lixeira	lee-shey-ra
dustpan	a pá de lixo	pah je lee-shoo
fire extinguisher	o extintor	es-tee^n-tor
hammer	o martelo	mar-te-loo
metal	o metal	me-taw
mop	o esfregão	es-fre-gow^n
nails	os pregos	pre-goos
paint	a tinta	tee^n-ta
paint brush	o pincel	pee^n-sew
plastic	o plástico	plas-tee-koo
pliers	o alicate	a-lee-ka- te
rubbish sack	o saco de lixo	sa-koo je lee-shoo
saw	a serra	se-ha
screwdriver	a chave de fenda	sha-ve je fe^n-da
screws	os parafusos	pa-ra-foo-zoos
spanner	a chave inglesa	sha-ve ee^n-glay-za
stainless steel	o aço inoxidável	a-so ee-no-see-da-vew
tile	o azulejo	a-zoo-lay-zhoo

toilet/drain unblocking liquid	o desentupidor líquido para vaso/ralo	des-e^n-too-pee-**dor** lee-kee-do **pa**-ra **va**-zoo/**ha**-loo
vacuum cleaner	o aspirador de pó	as-pee-ra-**dor** je poh
washing powder	o sabão em pó	sa-**bow**^{n} e^n poh
washing-up liquid	o detergente	de-tair-**zhe**^{n}-te
wire	o arame	a-**ra**-me
wood	a madeira	ma-**day**-ra

Furniture and Fittings

armchair	a poltrona	pol-**tro**-na
barbecue	a churrasqueira	shoo-has-**key**-ra
bath	a banheira	ba-**nye**-ra
bed	a cama	**ka**-ma
(woollen) blanket	o cobertor (de lã)	koo-ber-**tor** (je la^n)
bolt (for door)	o parafuso (para porta)	pa-ra-**foo**-zoo (**pa**-ra **por**-ta)
central heating	o aquecimento central	a-ke-see-**me**^{n}-too se^n-**traw**
chair	a cadeira	ka-**day**-ra
clock	o relógio	re-**lo**-zhee-oo
cooker	o fogão	foo-**gow**^{n}
cupboard	o armário	ar-**ma**-ree-oo

curtains	as cortinas	koor-**tee**-nas
cushions	as almofadas	al-moo-**fa**-das
deckchair	a espreguiçadeira	es-pre-ghee-sa-**day**-ra
dishwasher	a máquina de lavar louça	ma-**kee**-na je la-**var** lo-sa
doorbell	a campainha	kaⁿ-pa-**ee**-nya
doorknob	a maçaneta	ma-sa-**ne**-ta
hinge	a dobradiça	doo-bra-**jee**-sa
immersion heater	o aquecedor de imersão	a-ke-se-dor je ee-mer-sowⁿ
iron	o ferro de passar roupa	fe-hoo je pas-sar ho-pa
lamp	a lâmpada	laⁿ-pa-da
lampshade	o abajur	a-ba-**zhoor**
light bulb	a lâmpada	laⁿ-pa-da
lock	a fechadura	fe-sha-**doo**-ra
mattress	o colchao	kol-**show**
mirror	o espelho	es-**pay**-lyoo
oven	o forno	for-noo
padlock	o cadeado	ka-dee-**a**-doo
pillow	o travesseiro	tra-ve-**say**-roo
pipe	o cano	**ka**-noo
plug (*bath/electric*)	o plugue	**ploo**-ghe

radio	o rádio	ha-jee-oo
refrigerator	a geladeira	zhe-la-**day**-ra
sheet	o lençol	le^n-**sow**
shelf	a prateleira	pra-te-**lay**-ra
shower	o chuveiro	shoo-**ve**-roo
sink	a pia	**pee**-a
sofa	o sofá	so-**fa**
stool	o banco	**ba**^{n}-koo
table	a mesa	**may**-za
tap	a torneira	toor-**nay**-ra
television	a televisão	te-le-vee-**zow**^{n}
toilet	o banheiro	ba-**nye**-roo
towel	a toalha	too-**a**-lya
washbasin	a bacía	ba-**see**-a
washing machine	a máquina de lavar roupa	ma-**kee**-na je la-**var** ho-pa
window latch	o trinco da janela	**tree**^{n}-koo da zha-**ne**-la
window sill	o peitoril	pay-ee-to-**reew**

Kitchen Equipment

bottle opener	o abridor de garrafas	a-bri-**dor** je ga-**hah**-fas
bowl	a tigela	tee-**zhe**-la
can opener	o abridor de latas	a-bree-**dor** je **la**-tas

candle	a vela	**ve**-la
chopping board	a tábua de corte	**ta**-boo-a je **kor**-te
coffee pot	a cafeteira	ka-fe-**tay**-ra
colander	o coador	koo-a-**dor**
coolbag	a bolsa térmica	**bol**-sa **tair**-mee-ka
corkscrew	o saca-rolhas	sa-ka-**ho**-lyas
cup	a taça	**tah**-sa
fork	o garfo	**gar**-foo
frying pan	a frigideira	free-zhee-**day**-ra
glass	o copo	**ko**-poo
grill	a grelha	**gre**-lya
ice tray	a fôrma de gêlo	**for**-ma je **zhay**-loo
kettle	a chaleira	sha-**lay**-ra
knife	a faca	**fa**-ka
matches	os fósforos	**fohs**-to-roos
microwave	o micro-ondas	mee-kro-**on**-das
pan (with lid)	a panela (com tampa)	pa-ne-la (koⁿ taⁿ-pa)
plate	o prato	**pra**-too
scissors	a tesoura	te-**zo**-ra
sieve	a peneira	pe-**nay**-ra
spoon	a colher	ko-**lyer**
tea towel	o pano de prato	**pa**-noo je **pra**-too
torch	a lanterna	laⁿ-**ter**-na

Parts of a House and Grounds

balcony	a varanda	va-**ra**^{n}-da
bathroom	o banheiro	ba-**nye**-roo
bedroom	o quarto	**kwar**-too
ceiling	o teto	**teh**-too
chimney	a chaminé	sha-mee-**neh**
corridor	o corredor	koo-he-**dor**
door	a porta	**por**-ta
fence	a cerca	**ser**-ka
fireplace	a lareira	la-**rey**-ra
floor	o chão	show^n
garage	a garagem	ga-**ra**-zhay^n
garden	o jardim	zhar-**jee**^{n}
gate	o portão	poor-**tow**^{n}
hall	a entrada	ay^n-**tra**-da
kitchen	a cozinha	koo-**zee**-nya
living room	a sala de estar	**sa**-la je es-**tar**
patio	o pátio	**pa**-tee-oo
roof	o telhado	te-**lya**-doo
shutters	as persianas	per-see-a-nas
stairs	as escadas	es-**ka**-das
swimming pool	a piscina	pee-**see**-na
terrace	o terraço	te-**ha**-soo

| wall | a parede | pa-re-je |
| window | a janela | zha-ne-la |

Problems

The drain is blocked	O ralo está entupido	Oo ha-lo es-ta en-too-pee-doo
The pipe/sink is blocked	O cano/a pia está entupido(a)	Oo ka-noo/a pee-a es-ta en-too-pee-doo(a)
The toilet doesn't flush	A privada não dá descarga	Ah pree-va-da nown dah jes-kar-ga
There's no water	Não há água	Nown ah a-gwa
We can't turn the water off	Não conseguimos fechar a torneira	Nown kon-se-ghee-moos fe-shar a tor-ney-ra
We can't turn the shower on	Não conseguimos ligar o chuveiro	Nown kon-se-ghee-moos lee-gar oo shoo-ve-roo
There is a leak (water, gas)	Há um vazamento (de água, gás)	Ah oon va-za-men-to (je a-gwa, gas)
There is a broken window	Há uma janela quebrada	Ah oo-ma zha-ne-la ke-bra-da
The shutters won't close	As persianas não fecham	As per-see-a-nas nown fay-shown
The window won't open/shut	A janela nao abre/fecha	A zha-ne-la nown a-bre/fay-sha
The electricity has gone off	Acabou a luz	A loo-be a loosh

The heating/cooker/ refrigerator/boiler doesn't work	O aquecimento/o fogão/a geladeira/a caldeira não funciona	Oo a-ke-see-**may**n-too/ oo foo-**gow**n/a zhe-la-**dey**-ra/a kal-**dey**-ra nown foon-see-**o**-na
The lock is stuck	A fechadura está encravada	A fe-sha-**doo**-ra es-**ta** en-kra-**va**-da
This is broken	Isto está quebrado	**Ees**-too es-**ta** ke-**bra**-do
This needs repairing	Isto precisa de conserto	**Ees**-too pre-**see**-za je kon-**sayr**-too
The apartment/ house has been burgled	O apartamento/a casa foi roubado(a)/ arrombado(a)	Oo a-par-ta-**may**n-too/a ka-za **fo**-ee ho-**ba**-doo (a)/ a-hon-**ba**-doo(a)

COMMUNICATIONS

Key Phrases

Is there an internet café near here?	Há algum café com acesso à internet aqui perto?	Ah al-goo^n ka-**feh** ko^n a-**ses**-soo ah internet a-**kee** per-too
Do I need a password?	Preciso de uma senha?	Pre-**sec** zoo je oo-ma se-nya
Can I print this?	Posso imprimir isto?	Pos-so eem-pree-**meer** ees-too
What is your email address?	Qual é seu email?	Kwal eh **say**-oo email
I want to get a local sim card for this phone	Eu quero um sim card/chip local para este celular	**Ay**-oo ke-roo oo^n sim card/chip lo-**kaw** pa-ra **es**-te se-loo-lar
Where's the nearest post office?	Onde fica a agência de correio mais próxima?	O^n-je fee ka a a-rje^n-sya je koo-**hay**-oo ma-ees pro-see-ma

Email and Internet

Can I access the Internet?	Posso acessar à internet?	Pos-so a-ses-**sar** ah internet
Can I check my emails?	Posso checar meus emails?	Pos-so she-**kar** me-oos emails

Can I use any computer?	Posso usar qualquer computador?	Pos-so oo-zar kwal-ker ko^n-poo-ta-dor
How much does it cost for an hour/half an hour?	Quanto custa por uma hora/ meia hora?	Kwa^n-too koo-sta poor oo-ma o-ra/me-ya o-ra
How do I turn on the computer?	Como eu ligo o computador?	Ko-moo ay-oo lee-goo oo ko^n-poo-ta-dor
How do I log on/off?	Como eu faço log in/off?	Ko-moo ay-oo fa-so login/off
The computer doesn't respond	O computador não está respondendo	Oo ko^n-poo-ta-dor now^n es-ta he-spo^n-de^n-doo
The computer has frozen	O computador travou	Oo ko^n-poo-ta-dor tra-vow
Can you change this to an English keyboard?	Você pode mudar isto para um teclado inglês?	Vo-seh po-je moo-dar ees-too pa-ra oo^n te-kla-doo een-glays
Where is the @/ at sign on the keyboard?	Onde fica o sinal de arroba no teclado?	O^n-je fee-ka oo see-naw je a-ho-ba no te-kla-do
Does this café have wi-fi?	Este café tem wi-fi?	Es-te ka-feh te^n wi-fi
Is there a connection fee?	Tem alguma taxa para conexão?	Te^n al-goo-ma ta-sha pa-ra ko-nek-sow^n
My email address is...	O meu endereço de email é...	Oo me-oo ee^n-de-re-soo je email eh
Did you get my email?	Você recebeu meu email?	Vo-seh he-se-be-oo me-oo email

Email me, please	**Por favor, me mande um email**	Poor fa-**vor** me **ma**ⁿ-je ooⁿ email
Do you have a website?	**Você tem um website?**	**Vo**-seh teⁿ ooⁿ website
Please find attached …	**Segue em anexo(a) …**	**Se**-ghe eⁿ a-**nek**-so(a)

Faxing and Copying

Can I send a fax?	**Posso mandar um fax?**	**Pos**-so maⁿ-**dar** ooⁿ fax
Can I receive a fax here?	**Posso receber fax aqui?**	**Pos**-so he-se-**ber** fax a-**kee**
How much does it cost per page?	**Quanto custa por página?**	**Kwa**ⁿ-too **koos**-ta poor pa-zhee-na
Do you have a fax machine?	**Você tem uma máquina de fax?**	**Vo**-seh teⁿ oo-ma ma-kee-na je fax
What is your fax number?	**Qual é o seu número de fax?**	**Kwal** eh oo say-oo **noo**-me roo je fax
Please resend your fax	**Você pode me reenviar seu fax**	**Vo**-seh **po**-je me he-en-vee-ar **say**-oo fax
Can I make photocopies here?	**Posso tirar xerox aqui?**	Pos soo tee-rar sherox a-**kee**
Can you scan this for me?	**Você pode escanear isto para mim?**	**Vo**-seh **po**-je es-ka-ne-ar **ees**-to **pa**-ra meeⁿ

Post

Where's the main post office?	**Onde é a agência principal dos correios?**	On-je eh a a-**zhe**n-sya preen-see-**pal** doos koo-**hay**-oos
Where's the nearest post office?	**Onde é a agência de correios mais próxima?**	On-je eh a a-**zhe**n-sya je koo-**hay**-oos ma-ees pro-see-ma
What time does the post office open/close?	**A que horas abrem/fecham os correios?**	A ke **o**-ras a-brayn/**fay**-shan oos koo-**hay**-oos
Where's the post box?	**Onde há uma caixa de correio?**	On-je ah **oo**-ma **ky**-sha je koo-**hay**-oo
Which counter do I go to for stamps?	**Qual é o balcão para selos?**	Kwal eh oo bal-**kow**n pa-ra se-loos
How much is a postcard to . . . ?	**Que franquia levam os postais para . . . ?**	Ke fran-**kee**-a le-van oos pos-ta-ees **pa**-ra
How much is airmail to . . . ?	**Quanto custa um correio aéreo para . . . ?**	**Kwa**n-too **koo**-sta oon koo-**hay**-oo **aeh**-ree-oo **pa**-ra
It's inland	**É dentro do território nacional**	Eh **de**n-troo doo te-hee-to-ree-oo na-see-o-**naw**
Give me three stamps for . . . , please	**Por favor me dê três selos para . . .**	Poor fa-**vor** me de tres se-loos **pa**-ra
I'd like to send this letter express	**Quero mandar esta carta expresso**	Ke-roo man-**dar** es-ta **kar**-ta es-**pre**-soo
I'd like to register this letter	**Quero registrar esta carta**	**Ke**-roo he-zhees-**trar** es-ta **kar**-ta
I want to send a parcel	**Quero mandar um pacote**	**Ke**-roo man-**dar** oon pa-**ko**-te

Are there any letters for me?	Há alguma carta para mim?	Ah al-goo-ma kar-ta pa-ra mee^n
What is your name?	*Qual é o seu nome?	Kwal eh oo say-oo no-me
Have you any means of identification?	*Tem algum documento de identificação?	Te^n al-goo^n do-koo-may^n-too je ee-day^n-tee-fee-ka-sow^n

Telephone, Mobiles and SMS

Do you have a mobile/cell phone?	Você tem um celular?	Vo seh te^n oo^n se-loo-lar
What is your mobile/cell number?	Qual é o número do seu celular?	Kwal eh oo noo-me-roo do say-oo se-loo-lar
My mobile/cell phone doesn't work here	Meu celular não funciona aqui	Mee-oo se-loo-lar now^n foo^n-see-o-na a-kee
I'd like to get a local SIM card for this phone	Eu gostaria de ter o SIM card/ chip local para esse telefone	Ay-oo gos-ta-ree a je ter oo SIMcard/chip lo-kaw pa ra es-se te-le-fo-ne
Can you give me his mobile/cell number?	Você pode me dar o número do celular dele?	Vo seh po-je me dar oo noo-me-roo doo se-loo-lar de le
I'll send you a text/SMS	Vou te mandar um texto/sms	Vo te ma^n-dar oo^n tex-to/sms
Where's the nearest phone box?	Onde é a cabine telefônica mais próxima?	O^n je eh a ka-bee-ne te-le-fo-nee-ka ma ees pro-see-ma
I want to make a phone call	Eu quero fazer uma ligação/chamada	Ay-oo ke-roo fa-zair oo-ma lee-ga-sow^n/ sha-ma-da

May I use your phone?	Posso usar o seu telefone?	Pos-soo oo-zar oo say-oo te-le-fo-ne
Do you have a telephone directory for ... ?	Tem uma lista telefônica de ... ?	Te^n oo-ma lees-ta te-le-fo-nee-ka je
What is the country/area code for ... ?	Qual é o código internacional/código de área para ..?	Kwal eh oo ko-jee-goo een-ter-na-see-o-naw/ ko-jee-goo je ah-ree-a-pa-ra
Can I dial international direct?	Posso fazer uma chamada internacional diretamente?	Pos-soo fa-zair oo-ma sha-ma-da een-ter-na-see-o-naw jee-re-ta-me^n-te
Please get me ...	Por favor me dê kadal ...	Poor fa-vor me de
I'd like to telephone England	Quero telefonar para Inglaterra	Ke-roo te-le-fo-nar pa-ra ee^n-gla-te-ha
I was cut off; can you reconnect me?	A ligação caiu; pode me conectar de novo?	Ah lee-ga-sow^n kah-ee-oo po-je me ko-nek-tar je no-vo
The line is engaged	*A linha está ocupada	Ah lee-nya es-ta o-koo-pa-da
There's no reply	*Não respondem	Now^n res-po^n-day^n
You have the wrong number	É engano	Eh e^n-ga-noo

On the phone

Hello	Alô	A-lo
I want extension ...	Quero a extensão ...	Ke-roo a es-tay^n-sow^n
May I speak to ...	Posso falar com o/a ...	Pos-soo fa-lar ko^n oo/a

(Name) speaking	**Aqui quem fala é o/a**	A-**kee** ken fa-la eh oo/a
Who's speaking?	**Quem fala?**	Kayn fa-la
Hold the line	***Não desligue**	Nown dezh-lee-ghe
He's not here	***Ele não está aqui**	E-le nown es-ta a-kee
When will he be back?	**Quando ele volta?**	Kwan-doo e-le **vol**-ta
Will you take a message?	**Você pode dar um recado ... ?**	Vo-seh **po**-je dar oom he-ka doo
Tell him that ... phoned	**Diga para ele que ... telefonou**	**Jee**-ga pa-ra e-le ke ... te-le fo no
I'll ring again later	**Telefonarei mais tarde**	Te le-fo-na-**ray** ma-ees **tar**-je
Please ask him to phone me	**Por favor diga para ele me telefonar**	Poor fa-**vor** jee-ga pa-ra e-le me te le-fo-**nar**
Please repeat that	**Por favor repita isso**	Poor fa-**vor** he-**pee**-ta ees-soo
Please speak slowly	**Por favor fale devagar**	Poor fa-**vor** fa-le je-va-gar
What's your number?	***Qual é o seu número?**	Kwal eh oo **say**-oo noo-me-roo
My number is ...	**O meu número é ...**	Oo may-oo noo-me-roo eh
I can't hear/don't understand you	**Eu não consigo te ouvir/entender**	Ay-oo nown kon-see goo le o-veer/en-ten-der

DISABLED TRAVELLERS

Key Phrases

Is there a disabled parking area?	Há vagas de estacionamento para deficientes físicos?	Ah **va**-gas je es-ta-see-o-na-**me**ⁿ-too **pa**-ra de-fee-see-**e**ⁿ-tes **fee**-zee-kos
Are there facilities for the disabled?	Há instalações para deficientes físicos?	Ah eeⁿ-sta-la-**soy**ⁿs **pa**-ra de-fee-see-**e**ⁿ-tes **fee**-zee-kos
I want to book a wheelchair (from the check-in desk to the plane)	Gostaria de reservar uma cadeira de rodas (do balcão de check-in ao avião)	Gos-ta-**ree**-a je he-zer-var **oo**-ma ka-**dey**-ra je **ho**-das (doo bal-**kow**ⁿ je check-in aw a-vee-**ow**ⁿ)
I need a bedroom on the ground floor/ near the lift	Preciso de um quarto no térreo/ perto do elevador	Pre-**see**-zoo je ooⁿ **kwar**-too noo **te**-heo/**per**-too doo e-le-va-**dor**
Does the bus take wheelchairs?	O ônibus é adaptado para cadeirantes?	Oo **oh**-nee-boos eh ad-ap-**ta**-doo **pa**-ra ka-dey-**ra**ⁿ-tes

Access

Can we borrow/hire a wheelchair?	Podemos emprestar/ alugar uma cadeira de rodas?	Po-**de**-mos eⁿ-pres-**tar**/ a-loo-**gar** **oo**-ma ka-**dey**-ra je **ho**-das

I'd like to reserve a wheelchair, please	**Gostaria de reservar uma cadeira de rodas, por favor**	Gos-ta-**ree**-a je re-zer-**var** **oo**-ma ka-**dey**-ra je **ho**-das poor fa-**vor**
Is it possible to visit the old town/the site in a wheelchair?	**É possível visitar o centro velho da cidade/ o local em uma cadeira de rodas?**	Eh pos-**see**-vel vee-zee-tar oo se^n-troo **veh**-lyoo da see-**da**-je /oo lo-**kaw** e^n **oo**-ma ka-**dey**-ra je **ho**-das
Is there wheelchair access to the gallery/ stadium/theatre?	**Há acessibilidade para cadeirantes no museu/estádio/ teatro?**	Ah a-ses-see-bee-lee-**da**-je **pa**-ra ka-dey-ra^n-tes noo **moo**-se-oo/es-**ta**-jee-oo/te-**ah**-troo
Are the paths in the garden/park suitable for wheelchairs?	**Há trilhas no jardim/parque com acessibilidade para cadeirantes?**	Ah **tree**-lyas noo zhar jee^n /par-ke ko^n a-ses-see-bee-lee-**da**-je **pa**-ra ka-dey-ra^n tes
Is there a wheelchair ramp?	**Há rampas de acesso para cadeirantes?**	Ah ha^n-pas je a-ses-soo **pa**-ra ka-dey-ra^n-tes
Are there seats reserved for the disabled?	**Há assentos reservados para deficientes físicos?**	Ah as-se^n-toos he-ser-**va**-doos **pa**-ra de-fee-see-e^n-tes fee-zee-kos
Is there a table with place for a wheelchair?	**Há mesa adaptada para cadeirantes?**	Ah **may**-za a-dap-**ta**-da **pa**-ra ka-dey-ra^n-tes
Are mobility scooters allowed inside?	**É permitido o uso de cadeiras de rodas motorizadas dentro do local?**	Eh per-mee-**tee**-doo oo oo-zoo je ka-**dey**-ras je **ho**-das mo-to-ree-za-das de^n-troo doo lo-**kaw**
Where is the lift?	**Onde fica o elevador?**	O^n-je **fee**-ka oo e-le-**va** dor

Are there disabled toilets?	Há banheiros com acessibilidade para deficientes físicos?	Ah ba-**nye**-roos ko^n a-ses-see-bee-lee-**da**-je **pa**-ra de-fee-see-e^n-tes **fee**-zee-kos
Is there a reduction for the disabled?	Há descontos para deficientes físicos?	Ah des-**ko**^{n}-tos **pa**-ra de-fee-see-e^n-tes **fee**-zee-kos
Are guide dogs allowed?	Cães-guia são permitidos?	Ka^n-es-**ghee**-a sow^n per-mee-**tee**-dos
I can't walk far	Eu não posso andar longas distâncias	**Ay**-oo now^n **pos**-soo a^n-**dar** lo^n-gas jees-**ta**^{n}-see-as
I can't climb stairs	Eu não posso subir escadas	**Ay**-oo now^n **pos**-soo soo-**beer** es-**ka**-das
Is the bathroom equipped for the disabled?	O banheiro é adaptado para deficientes físicos?	Oo ba-**nye**-roo eh a-dap-**ta**-doo **pa**-ra de-fee-see-e^n-tes **fee**-zee-kos

Assistance

Please could you hold the door open?	Por favor, pode segurar a porta para mim?	Poor fa-**vor** **po**-je se-goo rar a **por**-ta **pa**-ra mee^n
Can you help me?	Pode me ajudar?	**Po**-je me a-zhoo-**dar**
I am deaf; please speak louder	Sou surdo; por favor, fale mais alto	So **soor**-doo poor fa-**vor** **fa**-le **ma**-ees **al**-too
Could you help me cross the road, please?	Pode me ajudar a atravessar a rua, por favor?	**Po**-je me a-joo-**dar** a at-ra-ves-**sar** a **hoo**-a poor fa-**vor**

Travel

Does the bus take wheelchairs?	**O ônibus é adaptado para cadeirantes?**	Oo **oh**-nee-boos eh ad-ap -ta-doo **pa**-ra ka-dey-ra^n -tes
Can I get onto the train/plane with a motorised wheelchair?	**Posso entrar no trem/avião com uma cadeira de rodas motorizada?**	**Pos**-soo e^n-**trar** no tre^n /a-vee-**ow**^{n} ko^n **oo**-ma ka-**dey**-ra je **ho**-das mo-to-ree-**za**-da
Could you order a taxi that will take a wheelchair?	**Você pode pedir um taxi adaptado para cadeirantes?**	**Vo**-seh po-je pe-**jeer** oo^n tak-see ad-ap-**ta**-do pa-ra ka-dey-ra^n-tes

EATING OUT

Key Phrases

Can you suggest a good/cheap/ vegetarian restaurant?	**Pode recomendar um bom restaurante?/ um restaurante barato?/ um restaurante vegetariano?**	Po-je re-koo-may^n-**dar** oo^n bo^n res-tow-**ra**^{n}-te/ oo^n res-tow-**ra**^{n}-te ba-**ra**-too/ oo^n res-tow-**ra**^{n}-te ve-zhe-ta-ree-**a**-noo
I've reserved a table; my name is . . .	**Tenho uma mesa reservada; o meu nome é . . .**	Te-nyoo **oo**-ma **may**-za re-zer-**va**-da; oo **may**-oo **no**-me eh
May I see the menu/ the wine list, please?	**Posso ver o cardápio/ a carta de vinhos, por favor?**	**Pos**-soo ver oh kar-**dah**-pyo/a **kar**-ta je **vee**-nyos poor fa-**vor**
What is your dish of the day?	**Qual é o prato do dia?**	Kwal eh oo **pra**-too doo **jee**-a
The bill, please	**A conta, por favor**	A **ko**^{n}-ta poor fa-**vor**
Does it include service?	**Inclui o serviço?**	Ee^n-**klwy** oo ser-**vee**-soo
It was very good	**Estava muito bom**	Es-**ta**-va **mwee**-too bo^n

I'd like to book a table for four at one o'clock	**Queria reservar uma mesa para quatro, para a uma hora**	Ke-**ree**-a he-zer-**var** **oo**-ma **may**-za pa-ra **kwa**-troo **pa**-ra a **oo**-ma **o**-ra
We did not make a reservation	**Não fizemos reserva**	Now^n fee-**ze**-moos he-**zer**-va

Have you got a table for three?	**Tem uma mesa para três?**	Te^n **oo**-ma **may**-za pa-ra tres
We'd like a table where there is room for a wheelchair	**Nós gostaríamos de uma mesa com espaço para cadeira de rodas**	Nohs gos-tar-**ee**-a-moos je **oo**-ma **may**-za ko^n es-pa-soo pa-ra ka-**dey**-ra je **ho**-das
Do you have a high chair?	**Tem uma cadeirinha alta?**	Te^n **oo**-ma ka-dey-**ree**-nya **al**-ta
Is there a table . . .	**Tem uma mesa . . .**	Te^n **oo**-ma **may**-za
by the window?	**perto da janela?**	**per**-too da zha-ne-la
in the corner?	**no canto?**	noo ka^n-**too**
on the terrace?	**no terraço?**	noo te-**ha**-soo
This way, please	*Por aqui, por favor	Poor a-**kee** poor fa-**vor**
We shall have a table free in half an hour	*Teremos uma mesa livre dentro de meia hora	Te-re-moos oo-ma **may**-za **lee**-vre day^n-troo je me-ee-a o-ra
We don't serve lunch until half past twelve	**Não servimos almoço até ao meio dia e meia**	Now^n ser-**vee**-moos al-mo-soo a-**teh** aoo me-yoo **jee**-a e me-ya
We don't serve dinner until eight o'clock	*Não servimos jantar até às oito horas	Now^n ser-**vee**-moos zha^n-tar a **teh** ahs oy-too o-ras
Sorry, the kitchen is closed	*Desculpe, mas a cozinha está fechada	Des-**kool**-pe mas a koo-zee-nya es ta fe-**sha**-da
Where are the toilets?	**Onde ficam os banheiros?**	O^n-je fee-ka^n oos ba-nye-roos
The toilets are downstairs	*Os banheiros ficam lá em baixo	Ous ba-**nye**-roos fee-ka^n lah e^n **by**-shoo

We are in a hurry	**Estamos com pressa**	Es-**ta**-moos ko[n] **pres**-sa
Do you serve snacks?	**Servem lanches?**	**Ser**-vay[n] la[n]-shes
I am a vegetarian	**Sou vegetariano(a)**	So ve-zhe-ta-ree-**a**-noo(a)
I am allergic to wheat/nuts	**Sou alérgico(a) a trigo/a nozes**	So al-**er**-zhee-koo(a) a **tree**-goo/a **no**-zes
I am allergic to dairy products	**Tenho intolerância à lactose**	**Te**-nyoo ee[n]-to-le-**ra**[n]-sya ah lak-**to**-ze

Ordering

cover charge	***couvert**	koo-**vert**
service and VAT included	***serviço e IVA incluídos**	ser-**vee**-soo e **ee**-va ee[n]-**klwee**-doos
service and VAT not included	***serviço e IVA não incluídos**	ser-**vee**-soo eh ee-va now[n] een-**klwee**-doos
service charge	***a taxa de serviço**	**ta**-sha je ser-**vee**-soo
waiter/waitress (*addressing*)	**garçon/garçonete**	**gar**-so[n]/gar-so-**neh**-te
May I see the menu?	**Posso ver o cardápio?**	**Pos**-soo ver oo kar-**da**-pyo
Is there a set menu?	**Há menu do dia/ menu turístico?**	Ah me-**noo** doo **jee**-a/ me-**noo** too-**rees**-tee-koo
first course/main course/side dish	**entrada/prato principal/ acompanhamento**	e[n]-**tra**-da/**pra**-too pree[n]-see-**pal**/a-ko[n]-pa-nya-me[n]-too
I'd like something light	**Gostaria de uma comida leve**	Gos-ta-**ree**-a je **oo**-ma ko-**mee**-da **le**-ve

Do you have a children's menu?	**Tem menu infantil?**	Te^n me-**noo** ee^n-fa^n-**teel**
What is your dish of the day?	**Qual é o prato do dia?**	Kwal eh oo **pra**-too doo **jee**-a
What do you recommend?	**O que recomenda?**	Oo ke re-ko-**me**^{n}-da
Can you tell me what this is?	**Pode me dizer o que é isto?**	**Po**-je me dee-**zayr** oo ke eh **ees**-too
What is the speciality of the restaurant/of the region?	**Qual é a especialidade do restaurante/da região?**	Kwal eh a es-pe-see-a-lee-**da**-je doo res-tow-ra^n-te/da re-**zhyow**^{n}
Do you have any vegetarian dishes?	**Tem pratos vegetarianos?**	Te^n **pra**-toos ve-zhe-ta-ree-a-noos
Would you like to try...?	*Gostaria de provar...?	Gos-ta-**ree**-a je pro-var
There's no more...	*Já não há...	Zhah now^n ah
I'd like...	Quero...	**Ke**-roo
May I have peas instead of beans?	**Pode me dar ervilhas em vez de feijão?**	**Po**-je me dar er-**vee**-lyas ay^n vays je fay-ee-**zhow**^{n}
Is it hot or cold?	**Este prato é quente ou frio?**	**Es**-te pra-too eh kay^n-te o free-oo
Without sauce/oil, please	Sem molho/azeite, por favor	So^n mo-lyoo/a-zay-te poor fa-vor
Some more bread, please	**Mais pão, por favor**	**Ma**-ees pow^n poor fa-**vor**
A little more...	Um pouco mais...	Oo^n po-koo **ma**-ees

Salt and pepper/ napkins, please	Sal e pimenta/ guardanapos, por favor	Sahl e pee-**me**^{n}-ta/gwar-da-**na**-poos poor fa-**vor**
How would you like it cooked?	*Que ponto de cozimento?	Ke **po**^{n}-to je ko-zee-**me**^{n}-too
rare/medium/well done	mal passado/ao ponto/ bem passado	mal pas-**sa**-doo/ow **po**^{n}-too/be^n pas-**sa**-doo
Would you like a dessert?	Quer sobremesa?	Ker so-bre-**me**-za
Something to drink?	*Algo para beber?	**Al**-goo **pa**-ra be-**ber**
The wine list, please	A carta de vinhos, por favor	A **kar**-ta je **vee**-nyos poor fa-**vor**
Do you have a local beer?	Tem uma cerveja local?	Te^n **oo**-ma ser-**ve**-zha lo-**kaw**

Paying

The bill, please	A conta, por favor	A **ko**^{n}-ta poor fa-**vor**
Does it include service?	O serviço está incluído?	Oo ser-**vee**-soo es-**ta** een-**klwee**-doo
Please check the bill; I don't think it's correct	Reveja a conta, por favor; penso que não está certa	Re-**vay**-zha a **ko**^{n}-ta poor fa-**vor**; **pe**^{n}-soo ke now^n es-**ta ser**-ta
What is this amount for?	Para que é esta quantia?	**Pa**-ra ke eh **es**-ta kwa^n-**tee**-a
I didn't have soup	Não comi sopa	Now^n koo-**mee so**-pa

May we have separate bills?	**Pode nos dar contas separadas?**	Po-je noos dar ko^n-tas se-pa-ra-das
Do you take credit cards?	**Aceita cartão de crédito?**	A-**say**-ee-ta kar-**tow**^{n} je **kreh**-jee-too
Keep the change	**Pode ficar com o troco**	Po-je fee-**kar** ko^n oo **tro**-koo

Compliments

It was very good	**Estava muito bom**	Es-ta-va **mwee** -too bo^n
We enjoyed it, thank you	**Gostei muito, obrigado (a)**	Goos **tay**-ee **mwee**-too o-bree-**ga**-doo (a)
The food was delicious	**A comida estava deliciosa**	A ko-**mee**-da es ta-va de-lee-see-**o**-sa
Especially...	**Especialmente...**	E-spe-see-al-**me**^{ii}-te

Complaints

We've been waiting a long time for our drinks	**Nós estamos esperando nossas bebidas já faz tempo**	Nohs es-**ta**-mos es-pe-ra^n-doo **nós**-sas be-**bee** das zha faz te^n-poo
Why is the food taking so long?	**Por que é que a comida está demorando tanto?**	Poor-ke eh ke a koo-**mee**-da es ta de-mo-ra^n-doo ta^n-too
This isn't what I ordered; I'd like...	**Isto não foi o que pedi, eu quero...**	Ees-too now^n foy oo ke pe-**dee ay**-oo ke-roo
This is bad	**Isto não está bom**	**Ees**-too now^n es-**ta** bo^n

This is uncooked/overcooked	Está pouco cozido/passou do ponto	Es-**ta po**-koo koo-**zee**-doo/pas-**so** doo **po**ⁿ-too
This is stale	Isto não está fresco	Ees-too nowⁿ es-**ta** fres-koo
This is cold/too salty	Está frio/muito salgado	Es-**ta free**-oo/**mwee**-too sal-**ga**-doo
This plate/knife/spoon/glass is not clean	Este prato/faca/colher/copo não está limpo	Es-te **pra**-too/**fa**-ka/koo-lyer/**ko**-poo nowⁿ es-**ta** leeⁿ-poo
I'm sorry; I will bring you another	*Desculpe, vou trazer outro	Des-**kool**-pe vo tra-**zer** o-troo

Breakfast

breakfast	café da manhã	ka-**feh** da **ma**-nya
Help yourselves at the buffet	*Sirva-se na mesa do buffet	**Seer**-va-se na **may**-za doo boo-**fay**
A large white coffee/a black coffee, please	Um café com leite duplo/um café, por favor	Ooⁿ ka-**feh** koⁿ **lay**-te **doo**-ploo/ooⁿ ka-**feh** poor fa-**vor**
I'd like a decaffeinated coffee/hot chocolate	Quero um café descafeinado/um chocolate quente	Ke-roo ooⁿ ka-**feh** des-ka-fey-**na**-doo / ooⁿ shoo-koo-la-te **kay**ⁿ-te
I would like . . .	Quero . . .	**Ke**-roo
tea with milk/lemon	chá com leite/limão	shah koⁿ **lay**-te/lee-**mow**ⁿ
China tea	chá da China	shah da **shee**-na
Indian tea	chá da Índia	shah da **ee**ⁿ-jy-a

green tea	chá verde	shah **ver**-de
camomile tea	chá de camomila	shah je ka-mo-**mee**-la
herbal tea	chá de ervas	shah je **er**-vas
mint tea	chá de hortelã	shah je or-te-**la**^{n}
Do you have sweetener?	**Tem adoçante?**	Te^n a-do-**sa**^{n}-te
May we have some sugar, please?	**Pode nos dar açúcar, por favor?**	Po-je noos dar a-**soo**-kar poor fa-**vor**
a roll and butter	um pão e manteiga	oo^n paw^n e ma^n-**tay**-ga
toast	torradas	too-ha-das
More butter, please	**Mais manteiga, por favor**	Ma-ees ma^n-**tay**-ga poor fa **vor**
Have you some jam/honey?	**Tem geleia/mel?**	Tay^n zhe-**ley**-a/mel
I would like . . .	**Eu gostaria de . . .**	Ay-oo gos-ta-**ree**-a je
a soft boiled egg	um ovo cozido mole	oo^n o-voo koo-**zee**-doo **mo** le
a hard-boiled egg	um ovo cozido duro	oo^n **o**-voo koo-zee-doo doo-roo
a fried egg	um ovo frito	oo^n o-voo **free**-loo
a poached egg	um ovo escalfado	oo^n o-voo es-kal-fa-doo
scrambled eggs	ovos mexidos	o-voos me-shee-doos
What fruit juices do you have?	**Que sucos de fruta tem?**	Ke **soo**-koos je **froo**-ta te^n
Orange/grapefruit/tomato juice	**suco de laranja/toranja/tomate**	soo-koo je la-**ra**^{n}-zha/to-**ra**^{n}-zha/to-ma-te

cereal	o cereal	se-re-**aw**
fresh fruit	a fruta fresca	**froo**-ta **frays**-ka
ham	o presunto	pre-**soo**ⁿ-too
cheese	o queijo	**key**-zhoo
yoghurt	o yogurte	yo-**goor**-te

Drinks[1]

bar	bar	bar
What will you have to drink?	*O que deseja desejam beber?	Oo ke de-**zay**-zhaⁿ be-**ber**
A (half) bottle of the local wine, please	Uma (meia) garrafa de vinho local	**Oo**-ma (**may**-a) ga-**ha**-fa je **vee**-nyoo lo-**kal**
I'd like to see the wine list	Gostaria de ver a carta de vinho	Gos-ta-**ree**-a je ver ah **kar**-ta je **vee**-nhoo
Do you serve wine by the glass?	Servem vinho ao copo?	**Ser**-vayⁿ **vee**-nyoo aoo **ko**-poo
carafe/glass	jarra/taça	**zha**-ha/**tas**-sa
bottle/half bottle	garrafa/meia garrafa	ga-**ha**-fa/**may**-a ga-**ha**-fa
Do you have draught beer?	Tem chope?	Teⁿ **sho**-pe
light/dark beer	cerveja clara/escura	ser-**ve**-zha **kla**-ra/es-**koo**-ra

1. For the names of beverages, see pp. 96, 115.

Two more beers	Mais duas cervejas	Ma-ees doo-as ser-vay-zhas
neat/on the rocks	simples/com gêlo	seen-ples/kon zhay-loo
with water/soda water	com água/soda	kon a-gwa/so-da
mineral water (with/without gas)	água mineral (com/sem gás)	a-gwa mee-ne-ral (kon/sen gas)
ice cubes	cubos de gelo	koo-boos je zhe-loo
Cheers!	Saúde!	Sa-oo-je
apple juice	suco de maçã	soo koo je ma-san
orange juice	suco de laranja	soo-koo je la-ran-zha
fruit juice	suco de frutas	soo-koo je froo-tas
What smoothies do you have?	Que sabor de vitaminas você tem?	Ke sa-bor je vee-ta-mee-nas vo-seh ten
I'd like a glass of water, please	Um copo de água, por favor	Oon ko-poo je a-gwa poor fa-vor
The same again, please	O mesmo novamente, por favor	Oo mes-moo no-va-mayn-te poor fa vor
Three black coffees and one with cream	Três cafés e um café com natas	Trays ka-fehs ee oon ka-feh kon na-tas
decaffeinated coffee	café descateinado	ka-feh jes ka foy na-doo
tea with milk/lemon	chá com leite/limão	shah kon lay-te/lee-mown
iced coffee	café gelado	ka-feh zhe-la-doo
iced tea	chá gelado	shah zhe-la-doo

Quick Meals

café	café	ka-**feh**
snack bar	lanchonete	la^n-sho-**neh**-te
What is there to eat?	O que tem para comer?	Oh ke te^n **pa**-ra ko-**mer**
We are in a hurry; can you suggest something that won't take long?	Nós estamos com pressa; o que você sugere que não levará muito tempo?	Nohs es-**ta**-moos ko^n **pres**-sa; oo ke **voh**-se soo-**zhe**-re ke now^n le-va-**ra** mwee-too te^n-poo
I only want a snack	Só quero um lanche	So **ke**-roo oo^n **la**^n-she
Is it to eat here or to take away?	*É para comer agora ou para levar?	Eh **pa**-ra ko-**mer** a-**go**-ra o **pa**-ra le-**var**
It's to take away	É para levar	Eh **pa**-ra le-**var**
What sandwiches do you have?	Que sanduíches tem?	Ke sa^n-d-**wee**-shes te^n
cheese	queijo	**key**-zhoo
cooked ham	presunto cozido	pre-**zoo**^n-too ko-**zee**-doo
cured ham	presunto defumado	pre-**zoo**^n-too de-foo-**ma**-doo
salami	salame	sa-**la**-me
toasted ham and cheese	misto quente	**mees**-too **ke**^n-te
I'd like a ...sandwich with/without butter	Quero um sanduíche de ... com/sem manteiga	**Ke**-roo oo^n sa^n-d-**wee**-she je ... ko^n/se^n ma^n-**tey**-ga

roll baked with cheese inside	**pão de queijo**	pow[n] je **ke**-zhoo
roll with roast beef, mozzarella, tomato and pickled cucumber	**bauru**	**bow**-roo
small cakes of chicken and catupiry (cream cheese)	**coxinhas**	ko-**shee**-nyas
black-eyed pea croquettes	**acarajé**	a-ka-ra-**zheh**
cheese/salt cod pasties	**pastéis de queijo/ bacalhau**	pas-te-ees je **key**-zhoo/ ba-ka-**lyow**
chicken/prawn pies	**tortas de frango/ camarão**	**tor**-tas je **fran**-goo/ka-ma-**row**[n]
What are those things over there?	**O que são aquelas coisas?**	Oo ke sow[n] a-ke-las ko-ee-zas
What are they made of?	**De que são feitas?**	De ke sow[n] **fay tas**
What is in them?	**O que têm dentro?**	Oo ke te[n] day[n] troo
I'll have one of these, please	**Quero um destes, por favor**	Ke-roo oo[n] **days**-tes poor fa-**vor**
I'm sorry, we've run out	†**Desculpe, não temos mais**	Des-**kool**-pe now[n] te-moos may-ees
a cheese omelette	**um omelete de queijo**	oo[n] ome-**le**-te je **ke**-zhoo
a plain omelette	**um omelete simples**	oo[n] ome-**le**-te **seen**-ples
biscuits	**os biscoitos/as bolachas**	bees-**koy**-toos/boo-la-shas

bread	**o pão**	pow^n
butter	**a manteiga**	ma^n-**tay**-ga
cheese	**o queijo**	**key**-zhoo
chips	**as batatas fritas**	ba-**ta**-tas **free**-tas
chocolate bar	**a barra de chocolate**	**ba**-ha je sho-ko-**la**-te
cold cuts	**as carnes frias**	**kar**-nes **free**-as
eggs	**os ovos**	**o**-voos
ham	**o presunto**	pre-**soo**^{n}-too
ice cream	**o sorvete**	sor-**ve**-te
pancake	**a panqueca**	pa^n-**ke**-ka
pastries (*savoury*)	**os folhados**	fo-**lya**-doos
pickles	**os picles**	**pee**-kles
roll	**o pão**	pow^n
salad	**a salada**	sa-**la**-da
sausage	**a salsicha**	sal-**see**-sha
snack	**lanche/petisco**	la^n-she/pe-**tees**-koo
soup	**a sopa**	**so**-pa
tomato	**o tomate**	to-**ma**-te

Restaurant Vocabulary

bill	a conta	ko^n-ta
bowl	a tigela	tee-**zhe**-la
bread	o pão	pow^n
butter	a manteiga	ma^n-**tay**-ga
course (dish)	o prato	**pra**-too
cream	o creme	**kre**-me
cup	a xícara	**shee**-ka-ra
dessert	a sobremesa	so-bre-**me**-za
dressing	o molho	mo-lyoo
dish of the day	o prato do dia	**pra**-too do **jee**-a
first course/starter	a entrada	e^n-**tra**-da
fork	o garfo	**gar**-foo
glass	o copo	**ko**-poo
glass (*wine*)	a tassa	**tas**-sa
headwaiter	o maitre	**me**-tre
hungry (to be)	ter fome	ter **fo**-me
knife	a faca	**fa**-ka
menu	o menu/o cardápio	me-noo/kar-**da**-pio
mustard	a mostarda	moos-**tar**-da
napkin	o guardanapo	guar-da-**na**-poo
oil	o óleo	**o**-lyo
olive oil	o azeite	a-**zay**-te

pepper	a pimenta	pee-**me**ⁿ-ta
pickles	os picles	**pee**-kles
plate	o prato	**pra**-too
salt	o sal	sow
sauce	o molho	**mo**-lyoo
saucer	o pires	**pee**-res
service	o serviço	ser-**vee**-soo
spoon	a colher	koo-**lyer**
straw	o canudo	ka-**noo**-doo
sugar	a açúcar	a-**soo**-kar
sweetener	o adoçante	a-do-**sa**ⁿ-te
table	a mesa	**may**-za
tablecloth	a toalha de mesa	too-a-lya je **may**-za
thirsty (to be)	ter sede	ter **say**-de
tip	a taxa de serviço/ gorjeta	**ta**-sha je ser-**vee**-soo/ gor-**zhe**-ta
toilets	os banheiros	ba-**nyer**-oos
toothpick	o palito	pa-**lee**-too
tomato sauce	o molho de tomate	**mo**-lyo je to-**ma**-te
vegetarian	o vegetariano	ve-zhe-ta-ree-**a**-noo
vinegar	o vinagre	vee-**na**-gre
waiter	o garçon de mesa	**gar**-soʰ je **may**-za
waitress	a garçonete de mesa	gar-so-**neh**-te de **may**-za
water	a água	**a**-gwa
wine list	a carta de vinhos	**kar**-ta je **vee**-nyoos

THE MENU

Dishes that are specific to one country are marked *B* for Brazil and *P* for Portugal

Starters

acarajé *B*	black-eyed pea croquettes
ameijoas à Bulhão Pato *P*	clams with garlic and coriander
anchovas	anchovies
azeitonas	olives
biqueirões	fresh anchovies
bolinhos de bacalhau	salt cod pasties
coxinhas de galinha *B*	small cakes of chicken and catupiry (cream cheese)
empadas de camarão *B*	prawn pasties
empadas de galinha	chicken pasties
linguiça grelhada	grilled spicy sausage
ostras	oysters
presunto (fumado) *P*	(smoked) ham
salada de palmito *B*	palm heart salad
salada de quiabo *B*	okra salad
sardinhas	sardines

Sopas / Soups

açorda *P*	bread and garlic soup
açorda de bacalhau *P*	bread and garlic soup with salt cod
caldo	consommé
caldo verde	spring cabbage or kale and chouriço
canja de galinha	chicken soup
creme de palmito *B*	palm heart soup
sopa de feijão	bean soup
sopa de legumes *P*	vegetable soup
sopa de marisco	shellfish soup
sopa de milho *B*	corn soup
sopa da pedra *P*	stone soup (dried beans, vegetables and sausage)
sopa de peixe	fish soup
sopa de siri *B*	crab soup

Peixe / Fish

ameijoas	clams
atum	tuna
bacalhau	salt cod
bacalhau à Gomes de Sá P	salt cod with potatoes, onions and garlic
besugo	sea bream
bolinhos de bacalhau	salt cod pasties

calamares/lulas com tinta	squid cooked in their own ink
caldeirada de peixe *P*	fish stew
caldeirada rica *P*	rich stew with a variety of fish
caranguejo (de mar)	crab
caranguejo (de rio)	crayfish
cherne	bass
choco	cuttlefish
enguias	eels
goraz	bream
lagosta	lobster
linguado	sole
mariscada *B*	fish and seafood stew
mexilhão	mussels
moqueca de camarão/peixe *B*	shrimp/fish stew
peixe espada	swordfish
peixe frito	fried fish
peixe vermelho	snapper
pescada	hake
polvo	octopus
raia	skate
robalo	turbot
salmão	salmon
salmonete	red mullet

sardinhas	sardines
vatapá *B*	seafood stew in coconut and peanut sauce

Carne / Meat

almôndegas	meatballs/rissoles in a spicy sauce
bife	steak
cabrito	kid goat
carne assada (de vaca)	roast beef
carne de porco à Alentejana *P*	pork with clams
carne guisada	beef stew
borrego/carneiro (assado)	(roast) lamb
chouriço	sausage made from spiced, cured pork
churrascos *B*	grilled meats with garnishes
cozido *P*	meat and vegetable stew
enchidos	spiced sausages
escalope	escalope
feijoada	rich bean stew with pork and sausages
filé de carne	fillet of beef
guisado de vitela	braised veal
iscas	liver steaks
leitão	suckling pig
língua	tongue

linguiça	spicy sausage
lombo	loin
morcela	black pudding
pé de porco	pig's trotters
picadinho B	chopped meat
presunto	cured ham
quiabada B	beef and okra stew
rabada B	oxtail stew
rabo de vaca (boi)	oxtail
salpicão	smoked, spicy pork sausage
salsicha	sausage
toucinho	bacon
tutu à Mineira B	creamed beans and grilled pork
vitela	veal

Aves e Caça / Game and Poultry

coelho	rabbit
coelho à caçadora P	hunter's rabbit (Rabbit stew with red wine)
faisão	pheasant
frango	chicken
frango de piri-piri P	chicken with a chilli and olive oil dressing

galinha	chicken
galo	cock
ganso	goose
javali	wild boar
lebre	hare
pato	duck
pato bravo	wild duck
perdiz	partridge
peru	turkey
pombo	pigeon
xinxim de galinha *B*	chicken and shrimps with peanuts and cashews

Pratos com amidos e grãos/ Dishes based on starches and grains

arroz de bacalhau	rice with salt cod
arroz de caril *P*	curry and rice
arroz de galinha	rice with chicken
arroz de pato *P*	rice with duck
arroz de peixe *P*	rice with fish
arroz de polvo *P*	octopus with race
cuzcuz de milho *B*	corn couscous

cuzcuz paulista *B*	couscous with prawns
farofa *B*	cassava meal prepared in a variety of ways to accompany main dishes
tapioca *B*	roasted cassava meal served as starchy mash

Legumes e Verduras/ Vegetables and Salads

abóbora	pumpkin
agrião	watercress
aipim/mandioca	cassava
aipo	celery
alcachofra	artichoke
alface	lettuce
alho	garlic
alho porro/alho francês	leek
azeitonas	olives
batatas	potatoes
beringela	aubergine/eggplant
beterraba	beetroot
cebola	onion
cenoura	carrot
coentros	coriander

cogumelos	mushrooms
couve	cabbage/greens
couve-flor	cauliflower
ervilhas	peas
espargo	asparagus
espinafre	spinach
favas	broad beans
feijão	beans
grão de bico	chickpeas
mandioca frita *B*	fried yucca strips
milho	corn
nabo	turnip
palmito	palm heart
pepino	cucumber
pimento	pepper
quiabo	okra
rabanete	radish
salada	salad
salsa	parsley
tomate	tomato
xuxu	chayote

Sobremesa/Dessert

abacaxi com vinho *B*	pineapple with red wine
arroz doce	rice pudding
beijinho *B*	coconut truffle
bolinho frito	fritter
bolo	cake
brigadeiro *B*	chocolate truffle
cocada *B*	coconut dessert
compota	fruit compote
creme de abacate *B*	avocado mousse
doce de abóbora	pumpkin dessert
doce de ovos *P*	candied egg yolk dessert
pastéis de nata *P*	custard tarts
pudim flan *P*	crème caramel
queijadas *P*	cheese tartlets
quindim *B*	dessert of egg yolks, sugar and coconut
sorvete	sorbet
suspiro	meringue
torta de fruta	fruit tart
torrão	nougat
toucinho do céu *P*	rich egg and almond dessert

Frutas Frescas e Secas/
Fruit and Nuts

abacate	avocado
abacaxi	pineapple
açaí	rainforest berry
alperce	apricot
ameixa	plum
amêndoa	almond
amendoim	peanut
avelã	hazelnut
banana	banana
caju	cashew
castanha	chestnut
castanha do pará	Brazil nut
cereja	cherry
cupuaçu	rain forest fruit
figo	fig
goiaba	guava
jaboticaba	rain forest fruit
jaca	jackfruit
laranja	orange
limão	lemon

maçã	apple
maracujá	passion fruit
melancia	watermelon
melão	melon
morango	strawberry
noz	walnut
papaia	papaya
passa	raisin
pêra	pear
pêssego	peach
romã	pomegranate
sapoti	sapodilla
tâmara	date
tangerina	tangerine
toranja	grapefruit
uva	grape

Some Cooking Methods

assado	roast
com manteiga/óleo	with butter/oil
churrasco	barbecued (on a spit)
cozido	boiled

cozido a vapor	steamed
cozido em fogo baixo	stewed
cozido no forno	baked
defumado/fumado	smoked
em puré/creme	pureed/creamed
cru	raw
escaldado/escalfado	poached
frito	fried
grelhado	grilled
grelhado na braza	barbecued
guizado	braised
marinado	marinated
carne	meat
mal passada	rare
ao ponto	medium
bem passada	well done
recheado	stuffed
quente/frio	hot/cold

Bebidas/ Drinks

água	water
água com gás	sparkling water

água de coco	coconut water
água mineral	mineral water
água sem gás	still water
bebidas alcoólicas	alcoholic drinks
brande	brandy
café	coffee (black)
café com leite	white coffee
caipirinha	cachaça (rum) cocktail
cerveja	beer
chope	draught
clara	light
em lata	in a can
engarrafada	bottled
escura	dark
chá	tea
de camomila	camomile
da China	China
de ervas	herb
de hortelã	mint
da Índia	Indian
de limão	lemon
gelado com limão	iced tea with lemon
champanhe	champagne

chimarrão	drink infused from yerba maté
chocolate em pó/cacau	cocoa
chocolate quente	hot chocolate
cidra	cider
conhaque	cognac
guaraná	soft drink
laranjada	orangeade
leite (quente)	(hot) milk
licor	liqueur
limonada	lemonade, lemon squash
milkshake/batido	milkshake
sucos/sumos	juices
suco de laranja	orange juice
suco de maçã	apple juice
suco de tomate	tomato juice
suco de toranja	grapefruit juice
suco de uva	grape juice
vinho	wine
branco	white
da Madeira	Madeira
doce	sweet
do Porto	Port

espumante	sparkling
rosé	rosé
seco	dry
tinto	red
verde	light wine, made from not fully matured grapes

EMERGENCIES[1]

Key Phrases

Fire brigade	**Corpo de bombeiros**	**Kor**-poo je boⁿ-**bey**-roos
Police	**Polícia**	Po-**lee**-sya
Emergency medical service	**Assistência médica de emergência**	As-sees-**te**ⁿ-sya **me**-dee-ka je e-mer-**zhe**ⁿ-sya
Ambulance service	**Serviço de ambulância**	Ser-**vee**-soo je aⁿ-boo-laⁿ-sya
Help!	**Socorro!**	So-**ko**-ho
Danger!	**Perigo!**	Pe-ree-goo
Call the police	**Chame a polícia**	**Sha**-me a po-**lee**-sya
Call a doctor	**Chame um médico**	**Sha**-me ooⁿ **me**-jee-koo
Call an ambulance	**Chame uma ambulância**	**Sha**-me **oo**-ma aⁿ-boo-laⁿ-sya
A&E hospital	**Pronto-socorro**	**Pro**ⁿ-too-so-**ko**-hoo
My son/daughter is lost	**O meu filho/a minha filha se perdeu**	**Oo** may-oo **fee**-lyo/a **mee**-nya **fee**-lya se per-**de**-oo

1. For car breakdown, see 'by car', p. 30. For problems with a house rental, see 'apartments and houses', p. 66.

Emergency numbers:	Portugal	Brazil
	110 police	190 police
	112 ambulance (service)	192 ambulance (service)
	112 fire brigade	193 fire brigade

Where's the police station?	Onde fica a delegacia de polícia?	On-je fee-ka a de-le-ga-sya je poo-lee-sya
Where is the British consulate?	Onde é o consulado britânico?	On-je eh oo kon-soo-la-doo bree-ta-nee koo
Please let the consulate know	Por favor, comunique ao consulado	Poor fa-vor koo-moo-nee-ken ow kon-soo-la-doo
I want to speak to someone from the embassy	Eu quero falar com alguém da embaixada	Ay-oo ke-ro fa-lar kon al-gen da en-bay-sha-da
I want a lawyer who speaks English	Preciso de um advogado que fale inglês	Pre-see-zoo je oon ad-vo-ga-doo ke fa-le een-gles
It's urgent	É urgente	Eh oor-zhayn-te
Can you help me?	Pode me ajudar?	Po-je me a-zhoo-dar

Accidents[1]

Call a doctor	Chame um médico	Sha-me oon me-jee koo
Call an ambulance	Chame uma ambulância	Sha-me oo-ma an-boo-lan-sya

1. See also doctor (p. 132).

Where is the nearest A&E hospital?	**Onde fica o pronto-socorro mais próximo?**	O^n-je **fee**-ka oo **pro**^{n}-too so-**ko**-hoo **ma**-ees **pro**-see-moo
paramedic	**paramédico**	pa-ra-**me**-jee-koo
lifeguard	**salva-vidas**	**sal**-va-**vee**-das
There has been an accident	**Houve um acidente**	**O**-ve oo^n a-see-**day**^{n}-te
Is anyone hurt?	**Alguém se machucou?**	Al-**ge**^{n} se ma-**shoo**-ko
Do you need help?	**Precisa de ajuda?**	Pre-**see**-za je a-**zhoo**-da
emergency exit	**Saída de emergência**	Sa-**ee**-da je e-mer-**zhe**^{n}-sya
fire extinguisher	**Extintor de incêndio**	Es-**tee**^{n}-**tor** je ee^n-**se**^{n}-jee-o
He's badly hurt	**Está bastante ferido**	Es-**ta** bas-**ta**^{n}-te fe-**ree**-doo
He has fainted	**Ele desmaiou**	**E**-le dezh-**may**-o
He's losing blood	**Ele está perdendo sangue**	**E**-le es-**ta** per-**de**^{n}-doo **sa**^{n}-ghe
Please get . . .	**Por favor traga . . .**	Poor fa-**vor** **tra**-ga
a blanket	**uma manta**	**oo**-ma **ma**^{n}-ta
some bandages	**ataduras**	a-ta-**doo**-ras
some water	**água**	**a**-gwa
I've broken my glasses	**Quebrei meus óculos**	Ke-**bray** **me**-oos **o**-koo-loos
I can't see	**Não consigo ver**	Now^n ko^n-**see**-goo ver
A child has fallen in the water	**Uma criança caiu na água**	**Oo**-ma kree-**a**^{n}-sa ka-**yoo** na **a**-gwa

A woman is drowning	Uma mulher está se afogando	Oo-ma moo-lyer es-ta se a-foo-ga^n-doo
She can't swim	Ela não sabe nadar	E-la now^n sa-be na-dar
There's a fire	Há um incêndio	Ah oo^n ee^nse^n-jee-o
I had an accident	Eu sofri um acidente	Ay-oo so-free oo^n a-see-de^n-te
The other driver hit my car	O outro motorista bateu no meu carro	Oo o-troo mo-to-rees-ta ba-te-oo noo me-oo ka-ho
It was my/his fault	Foi minha culpa/ culpa dele	Foy mee-nya kool-pa/kool-pa de-le
I didn't understand the sign	Não compreendi o sinal	Now^n ko^n-pre-ay^n-jee oo see-naw
May I see your . . .	*Posso ver	Pos-soo vay
driving licence?	a sua carta/ carteira de motorista?	a soo-a kar-ta /kar-tey-ra je mo-to-rees-ta
insurance certificate?	o seu certificado de seguro?	oo say-oo ser-tee-fee-ka-doo je se-goo-roo
vehicle registration papers?	certificado de registro de veículo?	ser-tee-fee-ka-doo je re-zhees-tro je ve-ee-koo-loo
Apply to the insurance company	*Dirija-se à companhia de seguros	Jee-ree-zha-se ah ko^n-pa-nyee-a je se-goo-roos
What is the name and address of the owner?	*Como se chama e qual é o endereço do proprietário?	Ko-moo se sha-ma e kwal eh oo e^n-de-re-soo doo pro-pree-ay-ta-ree-oo
Are you willing to act as a witness?	Está disposto a servir de testemunha?	Es-ta jees-pos-too a ser-veer je tes-te-moo-nya

Can I have your name and address, please?	**Pode me dar o seu nome e endereço?**	**Po**-je me dar oo **say**-oo **no**-me e e^n-de-**re**-soo
You must make a statement	***Você tem que fazer uma declaração**	**Vo**-seh te^n ke fa-**zayr** oo-ma de-kla-ra-**sow**^{n}
I want a copy of the police report	**Eu quero uma cópia do relatório policial**	**Ay**-oo **ke**-roo oo-ma **ko**-pee-a doo re-la-**to**-ree-oo po-lee-see-**aw**
You were speeding	***Você estava em alta velocidade**	**Vo**-seh es-**ta**-va e^n **al**-ta ve-lo-see-**da**-je
How much is the fine?	**Quanto é a multa?**	**Kwa**^{n}-too eh a **mool**-ta

Lost Property

My luggage is missing	**A minha bagagem desapareceu**	A **mee**-nya ba-ga-**zhe**^{n} de-za-**pa**-re-se-oo
Has my luggage been found yet?	**Já encontraram a minha bagagem?**	Zhah e^n-ko^n-tra-**ra**^{n} a **mee**-nya ba-ga-**zhe**^{n}
My luggage has been damaged	**A minha bagagem foi danificada**	A **mee**-nya ba-ga-**zhe**^{n} foy da-nee-fee-**ka**-da
I have lost . . .	**Perdi . . .**	Per-**jee**
my camcorder	**a minha filmadora**	a **mee**-nya feel-ma-**do**-ra
my credit card	**o meu cartão de crédito**	o **may**-oo kar-**tow**^{n} je **kreh**-jee-too
my luggage	**a minha bagagem**	a **mee**-nya ba-**ga**-zhe^n
my keys	**as minhas chaves**	as **mee**-nyas **sha**-ves

my mobile phone	o meu celular	oo **may**-oo se-loo-**lar**
my passport	o meu passaporte	oo **may**-oo pa-sa-**por**-te
I've locked myself out	**Eu me tranquei do lado de fora**	**Ay**-oo me **tra**ⁿ-kay doo la-doo je **fo**-ra
Where is the lost property office?	**Onde fica a seção de achados e perdidos?**	**O**ⁿ-je **fee**-ka a se-**sow**ⁿ je a-**sha**-dos e per-**jee**-dos
I found this in the street	**Encontrei isto na rua**	**Ay**ⁿ-koⁿ-**tray** ees-too na **hoo**-a

Missing Persons

My son/daughter is lost	**O meu filho/a minha filha se perdeu**	Oo **may**-oo fee-lyoo/**fee**-lya se per-**day**-oo
He is ... years old, and wearing a blue shirt and shorts	**Ele tem ... anos, e está vestindo uma blusa azul e shorts**	**E**-le teⁿ ... **a**-nos e es-ta ves-**tee**ⁿ-doo oo-ma **bloo**-za a-**zool** e shorts
This is his photo	**Esta é a foto dele**	**Es**-ta eh a **foh**-to de-le
Could you help me find him?	**Pode me ajudar a achá lo?**	**Po**-je me a-joo-**dar** a a-**sha**-lo
Have you seen a small girl with brown curly hair?	**Você viu uma garotinha de cabelo castanho cacheado?**	Vo-**seh vee**-oo oo-ma ga-ro-**tee**-nya je ka-be-loo kas ta nyo ka-she-a-doo
I've lost my wife	**Eu me perdi da minha mulher**	**Ay**-oo me per-jee da mee-nya moo-**lyer**
Could you ask for ... over the loudspeaker?	**Você pode anunciar ... no alto-falante?**	Vo-seh **po**-je a-nooⁿ-see-ar noo al-too-fa-**la**ⁿ-te

Theft

I've been robbed/ mugged	**Eu fui roubado/ assaltado**	**Ay**-oo **foo**-ee ro-**ba**-doo/ as-sal-**ta**-doo
Did you have any jewellery/valuables on you?	**Você tinha alguma jóia/coisas de valor com você?**	**Vo**-seh **tee**-nya al-**goo**-ma **zho**-ya/ko-**ee**-sas je va-**lor** kon **vo**-seh
Were there any witnesses?	**Havia testemunhas?**	Ah-**vee**-a tes-te-**moo**-nyas
My bag/wallet has been stolen	**Roubaram a minha bolsa/ carteira**	Ro-**ba**-ran ah **mee**-nya **bol**-sa/kar-**tey**-ra
Some things have been stolen from our car	**Algumas coisas foram roubadas do nosso carro**	Al-**goo**-mas **ko**-ee-sas fo-ran ro-**ba**-das do **nos**-soo **ka**-ho
It was stolen from our room	**Foi roubado do nosso quarto**	Foy ro-**ba**-doo do **nos**-soo **kwar**-too

ENTERTAINMENT[1]

Key Phrases		
Is there an entertainment guide?	**Há um guia de entretenimento?**	Ah oo^n **ghee**-a je e^n-tre-te-nee-**me**^{n}-too
What is there for children?	**O que tem para crianças?**	Oh ke te^n **pa**-ra kree-a^n-sas
Do you have a programme for the festival?	**Você tem a programação do festival?**	**Vo**-seh te^n a pro-gra-ma-sow^n doo fes-tee-**vaw**
The cheapest seats, please	**Os ingressos mais baratos, por favor**	Oos ee^n-**gres**-sos ma-ees ba-ra-toos, poor fa-**vor**

What is there to do/ see here?	**O que tem para fazer/ ver aqui?**	Oo ke te^n pa-ra fa-**zair**/ver a **kee**
Is there a playground nearby?	**Há algum parquinho aqui perto?**	Ah al-**goo**^{n} par-kee-nyo a-**kee** per-too
Is the circus on?	**Tem algum circo se apresentando?**	Te^n al-**goo**^{n} seer-koo se a-pre-se^n-**ta**^{n}-do
What time is the fireworks display?	**A que horas começa a queima de fogos?**	A ke o-ras ko-me-sa a kay-ma je fo-goos
How far is it to the amusement park?	**Qual é a distancia do parque de diversões?**	Kwal eh a jees-**ta**^{n}-see-a do **par**-ke je jee-ver-soy^{n}s
Is there a casino?	**Há um cassino?**	Ah oo^n kas-**see**-noo

1. See also GOING OUT (p. 150).

What do the local festivities celebrate?	**O que celebram as festas/ festivais locais?**	Oo ke se-le-**bra**^{n} as **fes**-tas/fes-tee-**va**-ees lo-**ka**-ees
cabaret	**o cabaré**	ka-ba-**reh**
casino	**o cassino**	kas-**see**-noo
concert	**o concerto**	ko^n-**sair**-too
disco	**a discoteca**	jees-ko-**te**-ka
waterpark	**o parque aquático**	**par**-ke a-**kwa**-tee-koo
zoo	**o jardim zoológico**	zhar-**jee**^{n} zoo-o-**lo**-zhee-koo

Booking Tickets

I'd like two seats for tonight	**Quero dois lugares para esta noite**	Ke-roo **do**-ees loo-**ga**-res **pa**-ra **es**-ta **no**-ee-te
I'd like to book seats for Thursday	**Quero reservar lugares para quinta-feira**	Ke-roo he-zer-**var** loo-**ga**-res **pa**-ra **kee**^{n}-ta-**fay**-ra
Is the matinée sold out?	**A matiné está esgotada?**	A ma-tee-**neh** es-ta ezh-go-**ta**-da
Where do you want to sit?	**Onde se quer sentar?**	O^n-je se ker se^n-**tar**
I'd like seats . . .	**Queria lugares . . .**	Ke-**ree**-a loo-**ga**-res
by the aisle	**no corredor**	noo ko-he-**dor**
in the circle	**no balcão**	noo bal-**kow**^{n}
in the gallery	**na galeria/geral**	na ga-le-**ree**-a/zhe-**raw**
in the stalls	**na plateia**	na pla-**tay**-a

I'd like a seat at the front	**Queria um lugar na frente do palco**	ke ree-a ooⁿ loo-gar na freⁿ-te doo pal-koo
The cheapest seats	**Os ingressos mais baratos**	Oos eeⁿ-gres-sos ma-ees ba-ra-toos
Are there any concessions?	**Há meia-entrada?**	Ah me-ya eⁿ-tra-da
Are they good seats?	**São bons lugares?**	Sowⁿ boⁿs loo-ga-res
Where are these seats?	**Onde ficam estes lugares?**	Oⁿ-je fee-kaⁿ es-tes loo-ga-res
This is your seat	***Este é o seu lugar**	Es-te eh oo say-oo loo-gar
That performance is sold out	***Aquela apresentação está esgotada**	A-ke-la a-pre-sen-ta-sowⁿ es-ta es-go-ta-da
Everything is sold out	***Está tudo esgotado**	Es-ta too-doo es-go-ta-doo
Standing room only	***Somente lugares em pé**	So-meⁿ-te loo-ga-res eⁿ peh
Pick the tickets up before the performance	***Retire os ingressos antes da apresentação**	He-tee-re oos eeⁿ-gres-sos aⁿ-tes da a-pre-seⁿ-ta-sowⁿ

Cinema, Theatre and Live Music

chamber music	**a música de câmara**	moo-see-ka je ka-ma-ra
film	**o filme**	feel-me
modern dance	**a dança moderna**	daⁿ-sa mo-der-na

opera	a ópera	o-pe-ra
play	a peça	pes-sa
recital	o recital	he-see-taw
What's on at the cinema/theatre?	O que está passando no cinema/teatro?	Oo ke es-ta pas-sa^n-doo noo see-nay-ma /tee-a-troo
Is it the original version?	É a versão original?	Eh a ver-sow^n o-ree-zhee-naw
Are there subtitles?	Tem legendas?	Te^n le-zhe^n-das
Is it dubbed?	É dublado?	Eh doo-bla-doo
Is there a concert on?	Há algum concerto?	Ah al-goo^n kon-sayr-too
Is there a support band?	Tem alguma banda de abertura?	Te^n al-goo-ma ba^n-da je a-ber-too-ra
What time does the main band start?	Que horas começa a banda principal?	Ke o-ras ko-me-sa a ba^n-da pree^n-see-paw
Who is . . .	Quem está . . .	Kay^n es-ta . . .
acting?	atuando?	a-too-a^n-doo
conducting?	regendo?	re-zhe^n-doo
directing?	dirigindo?	jee-ree-zhe^n-doo
singing?	cantando?	ka^n-ta^n-doo
When does the ballet start?	A que horas começa o ballet?	A ke o-ras ko-me-sa oo ballet
What time does the performance end?	A que horas termina a apresentação?	A ke o-ras ter-mee-na a a-pre-se^n-ta-sow^n

A programme, please	Um programa, por favor	Oo^n proo-**gra**-ma poor fa-**vor**
Where is the cloakroom?	Onde fica a chapelaria?	O^n-Je **fee**-ka a sha-pe la-**ree**-a

Clubs and Discos

Can you recommend a good show/a disco?	Você pode sugerir um bom show/uma boate?	Vo-seh **po**-je soo-zhe-**reer** oo^n bo^n show/**oo**-ma **bwa**-te
Which is the best nightclub?	Qual é a melhor boate?	Kwal eh a me-**lyor bwa**-te
Is there a jazz club here?	Há aqui algum clube de jazz?	Ah a-**kee** al-**goo**^{n} **kloo**-be je zhaz
Where can we go dancing?	Onde podemos ir dançar?	O^n-Je po-de-moos eer da^n-**sar**
Would you like to dance?	Quer dançar?	Ker da^n-**sar**

HEALTH

Dentist

Key Phrases		
I need to see a dentist	**Tenho de ir ao dentista**	Te-nyoo je eer ow day^n-**tees**-ta
Can you recommend one?	**Pode me recomendar um?**	**Po**-je me he-ko-me^n-**dar** oo^n
I've lost a filling	**Perdi uma obturação**	Per-**jee oo**-ma ob-too-ra-**sow**^{n}
Can you do it now?	**Pode fazer uma obturação agora?**	**Po**-je fa-**zair oo**-ma ob-too-ra-**sow**^{n} a-**go**-ra
Can you fix it (temporarily)?	**Pode consertá-la (temporariamente)?**	**Po**-je ko^n-ser-**ta**-la (tay^n-po-**ra**-ree-a-may^n-te)

Can I make an appointment?	**Posso agendar uma consulta?**	**Pos**-soo a-zhe^n-**dar oo**-ma ko^n-**sool**-ta
As soon as possible	**O mais rápido possível**	Oo **ma**-ees **ha**-pee-doo po-**see**-vel
I have toothache	**Estou com dor de dentes**	**Es**-toh ko^n dor je **day**^{n}-tes
This tooth hurts	**Este dente está doendo**	**Es**-te **day**^{n}-te es-**ta** do-e^n-doo

Can you fill the tooth?	**Pode obturar o dente?**	Po-je ob-too-**rar** oo dayⁿ-te
I do not want the tooth taken out	**Não quero arrancar o dente**	Nowⁿ ke-roo a-haⁿ-**kar** oo dayⁿ-te
Please give me an injection first	**Por favor, me dê primeiro uma injeção**	Poor fa-**vor** me day pree-**may**-ee-roo **oo**-ma eeⁿ-zhe-**sow**ⁿ
My gum is swollen	**Minha gengiva está inflamada**	**Mee**-nya zhayⁿ-**zhee**-va es-ta eeⁿ-fla-**ma**-da
My gum keeps bleeding	**Minha gengiva está sangrando**	**Mee**-nya zhayⁿ-**zhee**-va es-ta saⁿ-**gra**ⁿ doo
I have broken my dentures	**Eu quebrei minha dentadura**	**Ay**-oo ke-**brey** mee-nya deⁿ-ta-**doo**-ra
You're hurting me	**Você está me machucando**	Vo-seh es-**ta** me ma-shoo **ka**ⁿ-doo
Please rinse your mouth	***Enxague a boca, por favor**	Eⁿ sha-gue a bo-ka poor fa-**vor**
I need to X-ray your teeth	***Tenho que tirar uma radiografia dos seus dentes**	**Te**-nyoo ke tee-**rar** oo-ma ha-jee-oo-gra-**fee-a** doos say-oos dayⁿ-tes
You have an abscess	***Tem um abcesso**	Teⁿ ooⁿ ab-**se**-soo
The nerve is exposed	***O nervo está exposto**	Oo **nayr**-voo es-ta es-**pos**-too
This tooth can't be saved	***Este dente não se pode salvar**	Es-te dayⁿ-te nowⁿ se **po**-je sal-var
How much do I owe you?	**Quanto lhe devo?**	Kwaⁿ-too lye day voo
When should I come again?	**Quando devo voltar?**	Kwaⁿ-doo de-voo vol-**tar**

Doctor

Key Phrases

I must see a doctor. Can you recommend one?	**Preciso de um médico; pode me recomendar um?**	Pre-**see**-zoo je ooⁿ **me**-jee-ko; **po**-je me he-ko-meⁿ-**dar** ooⁿ
Please call a doctor	**Chame um médico, por favor**	**Sha**-me ooⁿ **me**-jee-koo poor fa-**vor**
I suffer from ... Here is a list of my medication	**Sofro de ... Aqui está uma lista com os meus medicamentos**	**So**-fro je ... A-**kee** es-**ta** oo-ma **lees**-ta koⁿ oos me-oos me-jee-ka-**me**ⁿ-toos
I have a heart condition	**Tenho um problema cardíaco**	**Te**-nyoo ooⁿ pro-**ble**-ma kar-**jee**-a-koo
I am diabetic	**Sou diabético**	So jee-a-**be**-tee-koo
I suffer from asthma	**Tenho asma**	**Te**-nyoo **as**-ma
I have had a high temperature since yesterday	**Estou com febre alta desde ontem**	**Es**-toh koⁿ **fe**-bre **al**-ta **des**-je oⁿ-te^m
My stomach is upset	**Estou mal do estômago**	**Es**-toh mal doo es-**to**-ma-goo

Is there a doctor's surgery nearby?	**Há um consultório médico aqui perto?**	Ah ooⁿ koⁿ-sool-**to**-ree-oo **me**-jee-koo a-**kee** **per**-too
When can the doctor come?	**Quando poderá vir o médico?**	**Kwa**ⁿ-doo po-de-**ra** veer oo **me**-jee-koo

Does the doctor speak English?	O médico fala inglês?	Oo me-jee-koo fa-la eeⁿ-glays
Can I make an appointment for as soon as possible?	Posso marcar uma consulta o mais cedo possível?	Pos-soo mar-kar oo-ma koⁿ-sool-ta oo ma-ees say-doo poo-see-vew
I'd like to find a pediatrician	Gostaria de encontrar um pediatra	Gos-ta-ree-a je eⁿ-koⁿ-trar ooⁿ pe-dee-a-tra

Medication

I take daily medication for . . .	Tomo remédio diariamente para . . .	To-moo he-mé-dee-oo jee-a-ree-a-meⁿ-le pa-ra
I suffer from . . . Here is a list of my medication	Sofro de . . . Aqui está a lista dos meus medicamentos	So-fro je . . . A-kee es-ta a lees-ta doos me-oos me-jee-ka-meⁿ-toos
This is a copy of my UK prescription. Could you please prescribe . . . for me?	Esta é uma cópia da minha prescrição médica feita no Reino Unido. Por favor, pode me dar uma prescrição para . . .	Es-ta eh oo-ma ko-pee-a da mee-nya pre-skree-sowⁿ me-jee-ka fay-ta noo he-ee-noo oo-nee-doo. Poor fa-vor po-je me dar oo-ma pre-skree-sowⁿ pa-ra

Symptoms and conditions

I am ill	Estou doente	Es-toh doo-ayⁿ-te
I have high/low blood pressure	Tenho pressão baixa/alta	Te-nyoo pres-sowⁿ ba-ee-sha/al-ta
I have a heart condition	Tenho problemas cardíacos	Te-nyoo pro-ble-mas kar-jee-a-kos

I am diabetic	Sou diabético	So jee-a-**be**-tee-koo
I suffer from asthma	Tenho asma	Te-nyoo **as**-ma
I've had a high temperature since yesterday	Estou com febre alta desde ontem	**Es**-toh koⁿ **fe**-bre **al**-ta **des**-je oⁿ-teⁿ
I've a pain in my right arm	Estou com dor no braço direito	**Es**-toh koⁿ dor noo **bra**-soo jee-**ray**-too
My wrist hurts	Meu pulso está doendo	**May**-oo **pool**-soo es-**ta** doo-eⁿ-doo
I think I've sprained/broken my ankle	Penso que torci/quebrei o tornozelo	**Payⁿ**-soo ke **tor**-see/ke-**brey** oo tor-noo-**zay**-loo
I fell down and hurt my back	Caí e as minhas costas estão doendo	Ka-**ee** e as **mee**-nyas **kos**-tas es-**towⁿ** doo-eⁿ-doo
My foot is swollen	Meu pé está inchado	**May**-oo peh es-**ta** eeⁿ-**sha**-doo
I've burned/cut/bruised myself	Eu me queimei/cortei/machuquei	**Ay**-oo me **kay**-may/**koor**-tay/ma-**shoo**-kay
I think it is infected	Creio que está infeccionado	**Kray**-oo ke es-**ta** eeⁿ-**fek**-seeo-**na**-doo
I've developed a rash/an inflammation	Minha pele está com alergia/inflamada	**Mee**-nya **pe**-le es-**ta** koⁿ a-ler-**zhee**-a/eeⁿ-fla-**ma**-da
My stomach is upset	Estou mal do estômago	**Es**-toh mal doo es-**to**-ma-goo
My appetite's gone	Não tenho apetite	Nowⁿ **te**-nyoo a-pe-**tee**-te
I've got indigestion	Estou com indigestão	**Es**-toh koⁿ eeⁿ-jee-zhes-**towⁿ**

I have diarrhoea	Estou com diarréia	Es-toh ko^n jee-a-**hey**-a
I think I've got food poisoning	Penso que estou intoxicado	**Pay**^{n}-soo ke es-toh ee^n-tok-see-**ka**-doo
I can't eat/sleep	Não consigo comer/dormir	Now^n kon-**see**-goo koo-**mer**/door-**meer**
My nose keeps bleeding	Meu nariz está sangrando	**May**-oo na-**rees** es-ta sa^n-**gra**^{n}-doo
I have difficulty breathing	Tenho dificuldade em respirar/Não respiro bem	Te-nyoo dee-fee-kool-**da**-je e^n hes-pee-**rar**/now^n res-**pee**-roo be^n
I feel dizzy/sick	Estou com tontura/enjôo	Es-toh ko^n to^n-**too**-ra/e^n-zhoo
I feel shivery	Estou com tremor	Es-toh ko^n tre-**mor**
I keep vomiting	Estou vômitando	Es-toh vo-mee-ta^n-doo
I think I've caught 'flu	Penso que estou com gripe	**Pay**^{n}-soo ke es-toh ko^n **gree**-pe
I've got a cold	Estou com resfriado	Es-toh ko^n hes-free-a-doo
I've had it since yesterday/for a few hours	Estou resfriado desde ontem/há algumas horas	Es-toh hes-free-a-doo **des**-je o^n-tay^n/ah al-**goo**-mas **o**-ras
abscess	o abcesso	ab-**se**-soo
ache	a dor	dor
allergy	a alergia	a-ler-**zhee**-a
appendicitis	a apendicite	a-pe^n-jee-**see**-te
asthma	a asma	as-ma
back pain	a dor nas costas	dor nas **kos**-tas

blister	a bolha	**bo**-lya
boil	o furúnculo	foo-**roo**[n]-koo-loo
bruise	a contusão/o machucado	ko[n]-too-**zow**[n]/ma-shoo-**ka**-do
burn	a queimadura	kay-ma-**doo**-ra
cardiac condition	o problema cardíaco	pro-**ble**-ma kar-**jee**-a-ko
chill, cold	o resfriado	hes-free-**a**-doo
constipation	a prisão de ventre	pree-**zow**[n] je **ve**[n]-tre
cough	a tosse	**tos**-se
cramp	a câimbra	**ka**-ee[n]-bra
diabetic	o diabético	jee-a-**be**-tee-koo
diarrhoea	a diarréia	jee-a-**hey**-a
earache	a dor de ouvidos	dor je oh-**vee**-doos
epilepsy	a epilepsia	e-pee-lep-**see**-a
fever	a febre	**fe**-bre
food poisoning	a intoxicação alimentar	ee[n]-tok-see-ka-**sow**[n] a-lee-me[n]-**tar**
fracture	a fratura	fra-**too**-ra
hay fever	a febre do feno	**fe**-bre doo **fay**-noo
headache	a dor de cabeça	dor je ka-**bay**-sa
heart attack	o ataque cardíaco/o infarte	a-**ta**-ke kar-**jee**-a-koo/ee[n]-**fah**-te
heart condition	o problema cardíaco	pro-**ble**-ma kar-**jee**-a- ko

high blood pressure	a pressão arterial alta	pres-**sow**n ar-te-ree-**aw al**-ta
ill, sick	doente	doo-e n te
illness	a doença	doo-e n-sa
indigestion	a indigestão	ee n-jee-zhes-**tow**n
infection	a infecção	ee n-fe-**sow**n
Influenza	a gripe	**gree**-pe
insect bite	a picada de inseto	pee-**ka**-da je ee n-se-too
insomnia	a insônia	ee n-**so**-nee-a
itch	a coceira	ko-**sey**-ra
nausea	a náusea	now-zee-a
nose bleed	o sangramento nasal	sa n-gra **me**n-too na-saw
pain	a dor	dor
rheumatism	o reumatismo	hee-oo-ma-**tees**-moo
sore throat	a dor de garganta	dor je gar-**ga**n ta
sprain	a distensão	jees-te n-**sow**n
sting	o ferrão de inseto	fe-**how**n je ee n-se-too
stomach ache	a dor de estômago	dor je es-**to** ma-goo
sunburn	a queimadura de sol	kny ee ma-**doo**-ra je sol
sunstroke	a insolação	ee n-soo-la-**sow**n
swelling	o inchaço	ee n-**sha**-soo
tonsillitis	amigdalite	a-meeg-da-**lee**-te

toothache	**a dor de dente**	dor je de^n-te
ulcer	**a úlcera**	**ool**-se-ra
wound	**a ferida**	fe-**ree**-da

Diagnosis and treatment

Where does it hurt?	***Onde dói?**	O^n-je doy
Have you a pain here?	***Aqui dói?**	A-**kee** doy
How long have you had the pain?	***Há quanto tempo você sente dor?**	Ah **kwa**^{n}-too **tay**^{n}-poo vo-seh **se**^{n}-te dor
Does that hurt?	***Dói?**	Doy
A lot?	***Muito?**	**Mwee**-too
A little?	***Um pouco?**	Oo^n **po**-koo
Open your mouth	***Abra a boca**	A-bra a **bo**-ka
Put out your tongue	***Ponha a língua para fora**	**Po**-nya a **lee**^{n}-gwa **pa**-ra **fo**-ra
Breathe in	***Respire fundo**	Hes-**pee**-re **foo**^{n}-doo
Breathe out	***Expire**	Es-**pee**-re
You're hurting me	**Você está me machucando**	**Vo**-seh es-**ta** me ma-shoo-**ka**^{n}-do
Please lie down	***Deite-se, por favor**	**Day**-te-se poor fa-**vor**
I will need a urine specimen	***Preciso de uma amostra de urina**	Pre-**see**-zoo **joo**-ma a-**mos**-tra je oo-**ree**-na
You must have a blood test	**Você tem que fazer um exame de sangue**	**Vo**-seh te^n ke fa-**zair** oo^n e-**za**-me je **sa**^{n}-ghe

What medicines have you been taking?	*Que remédios tem tomado?	Ke he-**me**-jee-oos te^n too-**ma**-doo
I am pregnant	**Estou grávida**	**Es**-toh **gra**-vee-da
I am allergic to ...	**Sou alérgico a ...**	So a-**ler**-zhee-koo a
I'll give you ...	***Vou lhe dar ...**	Vo lye dar
an antibiotic	**um antibiótico**	oo^n a^n-tee-bee-**o**-tee-koo
a sedative	**um sedativo**	oo^n se-da-**tee**-voo
some medicine	**uns remédios**	oo^{n}s he-**me**-jee-oos
some pills	**uns comprimidos**	oo^{n}s ko^n-pree-**mee**-doos
Take this prescription to the chemist's	***Leve esta receita à farmácia**	**Le**-ve es-ta he-**say**-ta ah far-**ma**-see-a
Take this three times a day	***Tome isto três vezes ao dia**	To-me ees-too trays **vay**-zes a-oo jee-a
I'll give you an injection	***Vou lhe dar uma injeção**	Vo lye dar **oo**-ma ee^n-zhe-**sow**^{n}
I'll put you on a diet	***Vou lhe dar uma dieta**	Vo lye dar **oo**-ma jee-e-ta
You must be X-rayed	***Tem que tirar uma radiografia**	Te^n ke tee-**rar** oo-ma ha-jee-oo-gra-**fee**-a
You must go to hospital	***Tem que ir a um hospital/a uma clínica**	Te^n ke eer a oo^n ōs-pee-taw/a oo-ma **klee**-nee-ka
You've pulled a muscle	***Você distendeu um músculo**	Vo-seh jees-te^n-de-oo oo^n **moos**-koo loo
You have a fracture/ sprain	***Você tem uma fratura/ distensão**	Vo-seh te^n oo-ma fra-**too**-ra/jees te^n-**sow**^{n}

You need a few stitches	*Você precisa de alguns pontos	**Vo**-seh pre-**see**-sa je al-**goo**ⁿs poⁿ-tos
You must stay in bed	*Tem de ficar de cama	Teⁿ je fee-**kar** je **ka**-ma
Come and see me again in two days' time	*Volte dentro de dois dias	**Vol**-te **day**ⁿ-troo je **do**-ees **jee**-as
Will you call again?	Você voltará?	**Vo**-seh vol-ta-**ra**
Is it serious/contagious?	É grave/contagioso?	Eh **grah**-ve/koⁿ-ta-**zheo**-soo
Nothing to worry about	*Nada para se preocupar	**Nah**-da **pa**-ra se pray-o-koo-**par**
I feel better now	Eu me sinto melhor agora	**Ay**-oo me **see**ⁿ-too me-**lyor** a-**go**-ra
When can I travel again?	Quando posso viajar de novo?	**Kwa**ⁿ-doo **pos**-soo vee-a-**zhar** je **no**-voo
You should not travel until ...	*Não deve viajar até ...	Nowⁿ **de**-ve vee-a-**zhar** a-**te**
How much do I owe you?	Quanto lhe devo?	**Kwa**ⁿ-too lye **de**-voo
I'd like a receipt for the health insurance	Queria um recibo para o seguro de saúde	Ke-**ree**-a ooⁿ re-**see**-boo **pa**-ra oo se-**goo**-roo de sa-**oo**-je
ambulance	a ambulância	aⁿ-boo-**la**ⁿ-see-a
anaesthetic	a anestesia	a-nes-**te**-zee-a
aspirin	a aspirina	as-pee-**ree**-na
bandage	a atadura	a-ta-**doo**-ra
chiropodist	o quiropodista	kee-ro-po-**dees**-ta

first aid station/A&E	o pronto-socorro	pro[n]-too-so-**ko**-ho
hospital	o hospital	os-pee-**taw**
injection	a injeção	ee[n]-zhe-**sow**[n]
laxative	o laxante	la-**sha**[n]-te
nurse	a enfermeiro(a)	e[n]-fer-**may**-roo(a)
operation	a operação	o-pe-ra-**sow**[n]
optician	o oculista	o-koo-**lees**-ta
osteopath	o osteopata	os-te-o-**pa**-ta
pill	a pílula	**pee**-loo-la
(adhesive) plaster	o bandcide/o esparadrapo	ha[n]-de-**ee**-je/es-pa-ra-dra-poo
prescription	a receita	he-**say**-ta
X-ray	a radiografia/ o raio-x	ha-jee-oo-gra-**fee**-a/ ha-yo-xis

Optician

Key Phrases

| I have broken my glasses, can you repair them? | Quebrei meus óculos, pode consertá-los? | Ke-**brey** me-oos o-koo-loos; po-je ko[n]-ser-**ta**-los |
| Can you give me a new pair of glasses to the same prescription? | Pode me arranjar um novo par de óculos com a mesma receita? | Po-je me a-ha[n]-**zhar** oo[n] **no**-voo par je o-koo-loos ko[n] a **mez**-ma he-**say**-ta |

Can I have an eye test?	**Posso fazer um teste de visão?**	**Pos**-soo fa-**zair** oo^n **tes**-te je vee-**sow**^n
I am short-sighted	**Sou míope**	So **mee**-oo-pe
I am long-sighted	**Não vejo bem de perto**	Now^n **ve**-zhoo bay^n je **per**-too
I have broken the frame/arm	**Quebrei a armação/ perna dos óculos**	Ke-**brey** a ar-ma-**sow**^n/**per**-na doos o-koo-los
When will they be ready?	**Quando estarão prontos**	**Kwa**^n-doo es ta-**raw**^n **pro**^n-toos
I have difficulty with reading/with long distance vision	**Tenho dificuldade em ler/ver de longe**	**Te**-nyoo dee-fee-kool-**da**-je ay^n ler/ver je **lo**^n-zhe
I have lost one of my contact lenses	**Perdi uma das minhas lentes de contato**	Per-**jee** oo-ma das **mee**-nyas **le**^n-tes je ko^n-**ta**-too
I should like to have contact lenses	**Queria lentes de contato**	Ke-**ree**-a **le**^n-tes je ko^n-**ta**-too
My vision is blurred	**A minha visão é embaçada**	A **mee**-nya vee-**sow**^n eh e^n-ba-**sa**-da
I can't see clearly	**Não consigo ver claramente**	Now^n ko^n-**see**-goo ver kla-ra-**me**^n-te

Parts of the Body

ankle	**o tornozelo**	tor-noo-**ze**-loo
arm	**o braço**	**bras**-soo
artery	**a artéria**	ar-**te**-ree-a

back	as costas	**kos**-tas
bladder	a bexiga	be-**shee**-ga
blood	o sangue	sa^n-ghe
body	o corpo	**kor**-poo
bone	o osso	**os**-soo
bowel	o intestino	ee^n-tes-**tee**-noo
brain	o cérebro	se-re-broo
breast	o seio	**say**-oo
cheek	a bochecha	bo-**she**-sha
chest	o peito	**pay**-too
chin	o queixo	**kay**-shoo
collar-bone	a clavícula	kla-**vee**-koo-la
ear *(facial/ hearing organ)*	a orelha/ o ouvido	o-re-lya /oh-**vee**-doo
elbow	o cotovelo	koo-too-**vay**-loo
eye	o olho	o lyoo
eyelid	a pálpebra	**pal**-pe-bra
face	a cara/o rosto	ka-ra/**hos**-too
finger	o dedo	de-doo
foot	o pé	peh
forehead	a testa	**tes**-ta
gum	a gengiva	zhe^n-zhee-va
hand	a mão	mow^n
head	a cabeça	ka-**bay**-sa

heart	o coração	koo-ra-sow[n]
heel	o calcanhar	kal-ka-nyar
hip	o quadril	ka-dreew
jaw	a mandíbula	ma[n]-jee-boo-la
joint	a articulação	ar-tee-koo-la-sow[n]
kidney	o rim	hee[n]
knee	o joelho	zhoo-ay-lyoo
knee-cap	a rótula	ho-too-la
leg	a perna	per-na
lip	o lábio	la-bee-oo
liver	o fígado	fee-ga-doo
lung	o pulmão	pool-mow[n]
mouth	a boca	bo-ka
muscle	o músculo	moos-koo-loo
nail	a unha	oo-nya
neck	o pescoço	pes-ko-soo
nerve	o nervo	nair-voo
nose	o nariz	na-rees
pelvis	o pélvis	pel-vees
pulse	o pulso	pool-so
rib	a costela	koos-te-la
shoulder	o ombro	o[n]-broo
skin	a pele	pe-le

spine	a espinha/a coluna	es-**pee**-nya/ko-**loo**-na
stomach	o estômago	es-**to**-ma-goo
thigh	a coxa	**ko**-sha
throat	a garganta	gar-**ga**^{n}-ta
thumb	o polegar	po-le-**gar**
toe	o dedo do pé	**de**-doo doo peh
tongue	a língua	**lee**^{n}-gwa
tonsils	as amígdalas	a-**meeg**-da-las
tooth	o dente	**de**^{n}-te
vein	a veia	**vay**-ya
wrist	o pulso	**pool**-soo

MEETING PEOPLE

Introductions

Key Phrases		
Glad to meet you	Muito prazer em conhecê-lo/la	**Mwee**-too pra-**zer** ay^n koo-nye-**say**-lo/la
How are you?	Como está/estão?	**Ko**-moo es-**ta**/es-**tow**^{n}
My name is . . .	O meu nome é . . .	Oo **may**-oo **no**-me eh
I'm on holiday/a business trip	Estou de férias/a negócios	**Es**-toh je **fe**-ree-as/a ne-**go**-see-oos
What is your telephone number?	Qual é o seu número de telefone?	Kwal eh oo **say**-oo **noo**-me-roo je te-le-**fo**-ne
Thanks for the invitation	Obrigado (a) pelo convite	O-bree-**ga**-doo (a) **pe**-lo ko^n-**vee**-te
Yes, I'd like to come	Gostaria muito de ir	Goos-ta-**ree**-a **mwee**-too je eer
I'm sorry, I can't come	Desculpe, mas não posso ir	Des-**kool**-pe mas now^n **pos**-soo eer

May I introduce . . . ?	Posso apresentar . . . ?	**Pos**-soo a-pre-say^n-**tar**
Have you met . . . ?	Você já conhece . . . ?	**Vo**-seh zha ko-**nye**-se
How are things?	Como estão as coisas?	**Ko**-moo es-**tow**^{n} as **koy**-zas

Fine, thanks, and you?	Bem, obrigado (a), e você?	Be^n o-bree-**ga**-doo (a) e **vo**-seh
What is your name?	Como se chama?	**Ko**-moo se **sha**-ma
This is . . .	Este (a) é . . .	**Es**-te (a) eh
Am I disturbing you?	Estou te incomodando?	**Es**-toh te ee^n-ko-mo-**da**^{n}-doo
Sorry to have troubled you	Desculpe ter te incomodado	Jes-**kool**-pe ter te ee^n-ko-mo-**da**-doo
Leave me alone	Deixe-me só (em paz)	**De**-she-me soh (e^n paz)

Getting Acquainted

Are you on holiday?	Você está de férias?	**Vo**-seh es-**ta** je fe-ree-as
I'm on holiday/a business trip	Estou de férias/ viajando a negócios	**Es**-toh je fe-ree-as / vee-a-**zha**^{n}-doo a ne-**go**-see-oos
Do you live/are you staying here?	Vive/está vivendo aqui?	**Vee**-ve/es-**ta** vee-**ve**^{n}-doo a-**kee**
Do you travel a lot?	Viaja muito?	Vee-**a**-zha **mwee**-too
We've been here for a week	Estamos aqui há uma semana	Es-**ta**-moos a-**kee** ah oo ma se-**ma** na
Is this your first time here?	É a primeira vez que você vem aqui?	Eh a pree-**may**-ra vezh ke **vo**-seh ve^n a-**kee**
Do you like it here?	Gosta daqui?	**Gos**-ta da-**kee**
Are you on your own?	Está sozinho (a)?	Es-**ta** so-**zee**-nyoo (a)
I am travelling alone	Viajo sozinho (a)	Vee-a-**zhoo** so-**zee**-nyoo (a)

Where do you come from?	De onde você é?	Je o^n-je vo-seh eh
I come from ...	Venho de ...	Ve-nyoo je
Have you been to England/USA?	Já esteve na Inglaterra/Estados Unidos?	Zhah es-tay-ve na een-gla-te-ha/es-ta-dos oo-nee-dos
It's been nice talking to you	Foi um prazer falar com você	Fo-ee oo^n pra-zer fa-lar ko^n vo-seh
I hope to see you again	Espero vê-lo de novo	Es-pe-roo vay-loo je no-voo

Personal Information

I am with ...	Estou com	Es-toh ko^n
a colleague	um colega	oo^n ko-le-ga
a friend	um(a) amigo(a)	oo^n/oo-ma a-mee-goo (a)
my family	a minha família	a mee-nya fa-mee-lee-a
my husband	o meu marido	oo may-oo ma-ree-doo
my parents	os meus pais	oos may-oos pa-ees
my wife	a minha esposa	a mee-nya es-po-za
I have a boyfriend/ girlfriend	Eu tenho um namorado/ namorada	Ay-oo te-nyoo oo^n na-mor-a-doo/ na-mor-a-da
I live with my partner	Eu vivo com meu parceiro (a)	Ay-oo vee-vo ko^n may-oo par-sey-roo (a)

I am separated/ divorced	Sou separado (a)/ divorciado (a)	So se-pa-**ra**-doo (a) /jee-vor-see-**a**-doo (a)
I am a widow(er)	Sou viúvo (a)	So vee-**oo**-voo (a)
Are you married/ single?	É casado(a)/ solteiro(a)?	Eh ka-**za**-doo(a)/sol-**tay**-ee-roo(a)
Do you have children/ grandchildren?	Tem filhos/netos?	Te^n **fee**-lyoos/**ne**-tos
What do you do?	O que você faz?	Oo ke **vo**-seh faz
I work for ...	Eu trabalho para ...	**Ay**-oo tra-**ba**-lyo **pa**-ra
I work freelance	Eu sou freelancer	**Ay**-oo so freelancer
I'm a consultant	Sou consultor	So ko^n-sool-**tor**
We're retired	Nós somos aposentados	Nohs so-**moos** a po-ze^n ta-dos
What are you studying?	O que é que você está estudando?	Oo ke eh ke **vo**-seh es-ta es-too-**da**^{n}-do
What do you do in your spare time?	O que você faz no seu tempo livre?	Oo ke **vo**-seh faz noo **say**-oo te^n-poo lee-vre
I like sailing/ swimming/walking	Eu gosto de velejar/ nadar/andar	**Ay**-oo gos-tou je ve-le zhar/na-dar/a^n-dar
I don't like cycling	Eu não gosto de andar de bicicleta	**Ay**-oo now^n gos-too je a^n-dar je bee-see-kle-ta
I don't like (playing) tennis	Eu não gosto de (jogar) tênis	**Ay**-oo now^n gos-tóo je (zho-gar) te-nees
I'm interested in art/ music	Eu gosto de arte/ música	**Ay**-oo gos-too je ar te/ moo-see-ka

Going Out[1]

Could we have coffee/a drink somewhere?	*Poderíamos tomar um café/uma bebida em algum lugar?	Po-de-**ree**-a-moos too-**mar** oo^n ka-**fe/oo**-ma be-**bee**-da e^n al-**goo**^{n} loo-**gar**
Can I get you a drink?	Posso te comprar uma bebida?	**Pos**-soo te ko^n-**prar oo**-ma be-**bee**-da
I'd like ... please	Gostaria de ... por favor	Gos-ta-**ree**-a je ... poor fa-**vor**
No thanks, I'm all right	Não obrigado (a)	Now^n o-bree-**ga**-doo (a)
Cheers!	Saúde!	Sa-**oo**-je
Would you like to have lunch with us tomorrow?	Gostaria de almoçar com a gente amanhã?	Gos-ta-**ree**-a je al-mo-**sar** ko^n a **zhe**^{n}-te a-ma-**nya**^{n}
Can you come to dinner/for a drink?	Pode vir jantar/ tomar uma bebida?	**Po**-je veer zha^n-**tar**/ to-**mar oo**-ma be-**bee**-da
We're giving/There is a party. Would you like to come?	Vamos dar uma festa/ Vai ter uma festa. Gostaria de vir?	**Va**-moos dar **oo**-ma **fes**-ta/ Vy ter **oo**-ma **fes**-ta. Gos-ta-**ree**-a je veer
May I bring a (girl) friend?	Posso trazer um amigo (uma amiga)?	**Pos**-soo tra-**zer** oo^n a-**mee**-goo (**oo**-ma a-**mee**-ga)
Shall we go to the cinema/theatre/beach?	*Vamos ao cinema/ teatro/à praia?	**Va**-moos a-oo see-**nay**-ma/te-**a**-troo/ah **pry**-a
Shall we go for a walk?	Quer dar uma caminhada?	Ker dar **oo**-ma kam-ee-**nya**-da

1. See also Entertainment (pp. 125–129).

Would you like to go dancing/for a drive?	*Quer ir dançar?/dar uma volta de carro?	Ker eer da^n-sar/dar oo-ma vol-ta je ka-ho
Do you know a good disco/restaurant?	Conhece uma discoteca boa/um restaurante bom?	Koo-nye-se oo-ma jees-ko-teh-ka boa/oo^n res-tow-ra^n-te bo^n
Are you doing anything tonight/tomorrow afternoon?	Vai fazer alguma coisa hoje à noite/ amanhã à tarde?	Vy fa-zer al-goo-ma koy-sa o-je ah no-ee-te/ a-ma-nya^n ah tar-je
Let's go to a gay bar	Vamos para um bar GLS	Va-moos pa-ra oo^n bar je-ele-ese

Arrangements

Where shall we meet?	Onde vamos nos encontrar?	O^n-je va-moos nos ay^n-ko^n-trar
What time shall I/we come?	A que horas devo/ devemos vir?	A ke o-ras de-vo/de-vay-moos veer
I could pick you up at …	Eu poderia ir te buscar às …	Ay-oo po-dee-ree-a eer te boos-kar ahs
Could you meet me at … (time)?	Poderia me encontrar às … ?	Pu-de-ree-a me ay^n-ko^n-trar ahs
May I see you home?	Posso levá lo (a) a casa?	Pos-soo le-vah-loo (a) a ka-za
Can I give you a lift home/to your hotel?	Posso te dar uma carona para casa/ para o hotel?	Pos-soo te dar oo-ma ka-ro-na pa-ra ka-za/pa-ra oo o-tew
Where do you live?	Onde você mora?	O^n-je vo-seh mo-ra
What is your telephone number?	Qual é o número do seu telefone?	Kwal eh oo noo-me-roo doo say-oo te-le-fo-ne

Hope to see you again soon	Espero revê-lo/la em breve	Es-**pe**-roo he-**ve**-loo/la e^n **bre**-ve
See you soon/later/tomorrow	Até mais/até logo/até amanhã	A-**teh** my-**ees**/a-**teh** lo-goo/a-**teh** a-ma-**nya**^{n}
Are you free this weekend?	Está livre no fim de semana?	Es-**ta** lee-vre no fee^n je se-**ma**-na

Accepting, thanking and declining

Thanks for the invitation	Obrigado (a) pelo convite	O-bree-**ga**-doo (a) **pe**-lo ko^n-**vee**-te
Yes, I'd like to come	Sim, gostaria muito de ir	See^n gos-ta-**ree**-a mwee-too je eer
Did you enjoy it?	Você gostou?	**Vo**-seh **gos**-to
It was lovely	Foi agradável	**Fo**-ee a-gra-**da**-vel
I've enjoyed myself very much	Eu me diverti muito	**Ay**-oo me jee-ver-**tee** **mwee**-too
It was interesting/funny/fantastic	Foi interessante/engraçado/fantástico	Foy ee^n-te-res-**sa**^{n}-te / e^n-gra-**sa**-doo/ fa^n- **tas**-tee-koo
Thanks for the evening/nice time	Obrigado (a) pela noite/pela diversão	O-bree-**ga**-doo (a) **pay**-la no-ee-te/**pe**-la jee-ver-**sow**^{n}
Thanks for the drink/ride	Obrigado (a) pela bebida/pelo passeio	O-bree-**ga**-doo (a) **pe**-la be-**bee**-da/**pe**-lo pas-**say**-ee-oo
I'm sorry, I can't come	Desculpe, mas não posso ir	Des-**kool**-pe mas now^n **pos**-soo eer
Maybe another time	Talvez em uma outra oportunidade	Tal-**vez** e^n **oo**-ma **o**-tra o-por-too-nee-**da**-je

No thanks, I'd rather not	**Não obrigado (a), prefiro não**	Now[n] o-bree-**ga**-doo (a) pre-**fee**-roo now[n]
Go away	**Vá embora**	Va ay[n]-**bo**-ra
Leave me alone	**Deixe-me só (em paz)**	**De**-she-me soh (e[n] pazh)

MONEY

Key Phrases

Where is the nearest ATM?	**Onde fica o caixa eletrônico mais próximo?**	O^n-je **fee**-ka o **kay**-sha e-le-**tro**-nee-koo my-**ees pro**-see-moo
Do you take credit cards?	**Aceita cartão de crédito?**	A-**say**-ta kar-**tow**^{n} je **kreh**-jee-too
Is there a bank/ exchange bureau near here?	**Tem algum banco/casa de câmbio aqui perto?**	Te^n al-**goo**^{n} **ba**^{n}-koo/ **ka**-za je **ka**^{n}-bee-oo a-**kee per**-too
Can you give me some small change?	**Pode me dar alguns trocados?**	**Po**-je me dar al-**goo**^{n}s tro-**ka**-doos
I want to open a bank account	**Quero abrir uma conta bancária**	**Ke**-roo a-**breer oo**-ma **ko**^{n}-ta ba^n-**ka**-ree-a

Credit and Debit cards

I'll pay with a credit card	**Vou pagar com cartão de crédito**	Vo pa-**gar** ko^n kar-**tow**^{n} je **kreh**-jee-too
I'd like to get some cash with my	**Eu gostaria de retirar dinheiro com meu**	**Ay**-oo gos-ta-**ree**-a je re-tee-**rar** jee-**nyay**-roo ko^n **me**-oo
credit card	**cartão de crédito**	kar-**tow**^{n} je **kreh**-jee-too
debit card	**cartão de débito**	kar-**tow**^{n} je de-bee-too

| Please enter your PIN | **Por favor digite sua senha** | Poor fa-**vor** jee-**zhee**-te **soo**-a se-nya |
| The ATM has swallowed my card | **O caixa automático engoliu meu cartão** | Oo ka-**ee**-sha ow-to-**ma**-tee-koo e^n-**go**-lee-oo me-oo kar-**two**^{n} |

Exchange

| Do you cash traveller's cheques? | **Trocam cheques de viagem?** | Tro-ka^n **sheh**-kes je vee-a-zhe^n |
| Where can I cash traveller's cheques? | **Onde posso trocar cheques de viagem?** | O^n-je **pos**-soo troo-**kar** **sheh**-kes je vee-a-zhe^n |

I want to change some English/ American money	**Quero trocar dinheiro inglês/ americano**	Ke-roo tro-**kar** jee-**nyay**-roo ee^n-**glays**/a-me-ree-ka-noo
Your passport, please	*Por favor seu passaporte	Poor fa-**vor** se-oo pas-sa-por-te
Where do I sign?	**Onde é que assino?**	O^n je eh ke as-see-noo
Sign here, please	*Assine aqui, por favor	As-see-ne a-**kee** poor fa-**vor**
Go to the cashier	*Vá ao caixa	Va ow kay-sha
What is the current rate of exchange?	**Qual e a taxa de câmbio atual?**	Kwal eh a **ta**-shu je ku^n bee-oo a-too-aw
Can you give me some small change?	**Pode me dar alguns trocados?**	Po-je me dar al **goo**^{n}s tro-**ka**-doos

General Banking

I arranged for money to be transferred from England. Has it arrived yet?	**Mandei transferir dinheiro da Inglaterra; já chegou?**	Ma^n-**day** tra^{n}s-fe-**reer** jee-**nyay**-roo da ee^n-gla-**te**-ha; zhah she-**go**
I want to open a bank account	**Quero abrir uma conta bancária**	**Ke**-roo a-**breer** oo-ma ko^n-ta ba^n-**ka**-ree-a
Please credit this to my account	**Por favor credite na minha conta**	Poor fa-**vor** kre-**jee**-te na **mee**-nya ko^n-ta
I'd like to withdraw some cash with my debit card	**Gostaria de tirar dinheiro com meu cartão de débito**	Gos-ta-**ree**-a je tee-**rar** jee-**nyay**-roo ko^n **me**-oo kar-**tow**^{n} je **de**-bee-too
I want to make a transfer	**Quero fazer uma transferência**	**Ke**-roo fa-**zer** oo-ma trans-fe-re^n-sya
balance	**saldo**	**sal**-doo
bank card	**cartão de banco**	kar-**tow**^{n} je **ba**^{n}-koo
cheque book	**talão de cheques**	ta-**low**^{n} je **sheh**-kes
current account	**conta corrente**	**ko**^{n}-ta koo-**hay**^{n}- te
foreign currency	**moeda estrangeira**	mo-**e**-da es-tra ^{n}-**zhay**-ra
savings account	**conta-poupança**	**ko**^{n}-ta po-**pa**^{n}-sa
statement	**extrato bancário**	es-**tra**-too ba ^{n}-**ka**-ree-oo

SHOPS[1] AND SERVICES

Where to go

antique shop	a loja de antiguidades	lo-zha je a^n-tee-gwee-da-jes
audio-equipment shop	a loja de equipamento áudio	lo-zha je e-kee-pa-me^n-too ow-jyoo
bakery	a padaria	pa-da-ree-a
bank	o banco	ba^n-koo
barber (see pp. 179–180)	a barbearia	bar-bee-a-ree-a
beauty and spa treatments (see p. 168)	spa e tratamentos estéticos	spa e tra-ta-me^n-tos es-te-tee-kos
bicycle repair shop (see p. 186)	a loja de conserto de bicicletas	lo-zha je ko^n-ser-too je bee-see-kle tas
bookshop (see pp. 169–170)	a livraria	lee vra ree-a
building supplies (see pp. 180–183)	a loja de materiais de construção	lo-zha je ma-te-ree-ais je ko^n-stroo-sow^n
butcher (see pp. 177–178)	o açougue	a-soo-ghe
cake shop (see pp. 177–178)	a confeitaria	ko^n-fey ta ree-a
camping equipment (see pp. 180–182)	o equipamento de camping	ay-kee-pa-may^n-too je ka^n-peeng

1. See tables (p. 175–176) for continental sizes in clothing.

carpenter	o carpinteiro	kar-pee^n-**tay**-roo
chemist's (see pp. 171–173)	a farmácia	far-**ma**-see-a
confectioner (see pp. 177–178)	a confeitaria	kon-fay-ta-**ree**-a
consulate	o consulado	ko^n-soo-**la**-doo
craft shop	a loja de artesanato	**lo**-zha je ar-te-za-**na**-too
decorator, painter	o decorador, o pintor	de-ko-ra-**dor**, pee^n-**tor**
delicatessen	a loja de frios e laticínios	**lo**-zha je **free**-os e la-tee-**see**-nee-os
dentist (see pp. 130–131)	o dentista	day^n-**tees**-ta
department store (see pp. 173–176)	a loja de departmento / o magazine	**lo**-zha je je-part-**me**^{n}-too / ma-ga-**zee**-ne
DIY store (see pp. 180–181)	a loja de bricolage	**lo**-zha je bree-ko-**la**-zhe
doctor (see pp. 132–140)	o medico	**me**-jee-koo
dry cleaner (see pp. 182–184)	a lavagem a seco	la-va-**zhe**^{n} a **say**-koo
electrical appliances	os eletrodomésticos	ee-le-tro-do-**mes**-tee-koos
electrician	o eletricista	ee-le-tree-**sees**-ta
embassy	e embaixada	e^n-bay-**sha**-da
fishmonger (see pp. 177–178)	a peixaria	pey-sha-**ree**-a
florist	a florista	flo-**rees**-ta

furniture shop	a loja de móveis	lo-zha je mo-vays
garden centre	a loja de jardinagem	lo-zha je zhar-jee-na-zhe^n
gardener	o jardineiro	zhar-jee-nay-roo
gift shop	a loja de presentes	lo-zha je pre-ze^n-tes
greengrocer's (see pp. 177–178)	a mercearia	mer-se-a-ree-a
grocery	o armazém	ar-ma-ze^n
haberdashery (for fabrics, see pp. 165–166)	o armarinho	ar-ma-ree-nyo
hairdresser (see pp. 179–180)	o cabeleireiro	ka-be-lay-ray-roo
hardware store (see p. 180–182)	a loja de ferragens	lo-zha je fe-ha-zhay^{n}s
health-food shop	a loja de alimentos naturais	lo-zha je a-lee-me^n-tos na-too-rays
home-entertainment shop	a loja de entretenimento doméstico	lo-zha je e^n-tre-te-nee-me^n too do-mes-tee-koo
interior design shop	a loja de design de interiores	lo-zha je design jee^n-te-ree-or-es
ironmonger (see Hardware and Outdoors, pp. 180–182)	o ferreiro	fe-hay-roo
jeweller	a joalheria	zho-a-lye-ree-a
kitchen shop	a loja de utensílios para cozinha	lo-zha je oo-te^n-see-lyos pa-ra ko-zee-nya
launderette	a lavanderia	la-va^n-de-ree-a

laundry (see pp. 182–184)	a lavanderia	la-va^n-de-**ree**-a
light-fittings shop	a loja de iluminação	**lo**-zha je ee-loo-mee-na-**sow**^{n}
liquor/wine store (see pp. 96/115)	a loja de bebidas	**lo**-zha je be-**bee**-das
market (see p. 184)	o mercado	mer-**ka**-doo
mobile/cell phone shop (see p. 81)	a loja de celular	**lo**-zha je se-loo-**lar**
newsagent (see p. 169)	banca de jornal/ de revista	**ba**^{n}-ka je zhor-**nal**/je he-**vees**-ta
optician (see p. 141)	o oculista	o-koo-**lees**-ta
outdoor equipment shop (see p. 180)	a loja de equipamentos outdoor	**lo**-zha je e-kee-pa-**me**^{n}-tos outdoor
pastry shop (see p. 177)	a pastelaria (*Portugal*)	pas-te-la-**ree**-a
photographer	o fotógrafo	foo-**to**-gra-foo
photographic equipment (see p. 185)	a loja de equipamentos fotográficos	**lo**-zha je e-kee-pa-**me**^{n}-tos fo-to-**gra**-fee-kos
plasterer	o estucador	es-too-ka-**dor**
plumber (for plumbing problems, see p. 167)	o encanador/ canalizador	e^n- ka-na-**dor**/ka-na-lee-za-**dor**
police (see p. 118)	a polícia	po-**lee**-see-a
post office (see p. 80)	o correio	ko-**hay**-oo

shoemaker, cobbler	o sapateiro	sa-pa-**tay**-roo
shoe repairs (see p. 186)	o sapateiro	sa-pa-**tay**-roo
shoe shop (for shoe sizes, see p. 173)	a sapataria	sa-pa-ta-**ree**-a
souvenir shop	a loja de lembrancinhas	lo-zha je leⁿ-braⁿ-**see**-nyas
sports shop	a loja de artigos esportivos	lo-zha je ar-**tee**-goos es-poor-**tee**-voos
stationer's (see p. 169)	a papelaria	pa-pe-la-**ree** a
supermarket (see p. 177)	o supermercado	soo-per-mer-**ka**-doo
tobacconist	a tabacaria	ta-ba-ka-**ree** a
tourist information office	o posto de informações turísticas	**pos**-too je eeⁿ-for-ma-soⁿ-ees too-**rees**-tee-kas
toy shop	a loja de brinquedos	lo-zha je breeⁿ-**kay**-doos
travel agency	a agência de viagens	a-zhayⁿ-see-a je vee-a-zhayⁿs
travel goods shop	a loja de artigos de viagem	lo-zha je ar-tee-gos je vee-a zhayⁿ
wine merchant	o comerciante/ negociante de vinhos	ko-mer-see-aⁿ-te /ne go-see-anⁿ-te je vee-nyoos

In the Shop

Key Phrases

Which is the best...?	Qual é o melhor...?	Kwal eh oo me-**lyor**
Where is the nearest...?	Onde é o mais próximo...?	O[n]-je eh oo **ma**-ees **pro**-see-moo
Can you recommend...?	Pode recomendar...?	Po-je he-ko-may[n]-**dar**
Where is the market?	Onde é o mercado?	O[n]-je eh oo mer-**ka**-doo
Is there a market every day?	Há mercado todos os dias?	Ah mer-**ka**-doo to-doos oos **jee**-as
Where can I buy...?	Onde posso comprar...?	O[n]-je **pos**-soo ko[n]-**prar**
When are the shops open?	Quando abrem as lojas?	**Kwa**[n]-doo a-**bray**[n] as **lo**-zhas

checkout/cash desk	* caixa	**kay**-sha
manager	o gerente	zhe-**ray**[n]-te
sale (clearance)	* a liquidação	lee-kee-da-**sow**[n]
self-service	* auto-serviço	ow-to-sair-**vee**-soo
shop assistant	o(a) vendedor(a)	ve[n]-de-**dor**(a)
Where can I get a trolley?	Onde posso pegar um carrinho?	O[n]-je **pos**-so pe-**gar** oo[n] kar-**hee**-nyo
Can I help you?	* Posso ajudar?	**Pos**-soo a-zhoo-**dar**

I want to buy . . .	Quero comprar . . .	Ke-roo ko^n-prar
Do you sell . . . ?	Você vende . . . ?	Vo-seh vay^n-de
I'm just looking round	Só estou dando uma olhada	Soh es-to da^n-do oo-ma o-lya-da
I don't want to buy anything now	Não quero comprar nada agora	Now^n ke-roo ko^n-prar na-da a-go-ra
Could you show me . . . ?	Pode me mostrar. . . ?	Po-je me mos-trar
We do not have that	*Nós não temos isso	Nohs now^n tay-moos ee-soo
You'll find them at that counter	*Você os encontrará no balcão	Vo-seh oos e^n-ko^n tra-ra noo bow-kow^n
We've sold out but we'll have more tomorrow	Está esgotado, mas teremos mais amanhã	Es-ta ezh-goo-ta-doo mas te re-moos ma-ees a-ma-nya^n
Anything else?	*Mais alguma coisa?	Ma-ees al-goo-ma ko-ee-za
That will be all	É tudo	Eh too-doo
Will you take it with you?	*Você irá levá-lo?	Vo-seh ee-ra le-va-lo
I will take it with me	Vou levá-lo comigo	Vo le-va-loo koo-mee-goo
Will you gift wrap it?	Você pode embalar para presente?	Vo-seh po-je e^n-ba-lar pa-ra pre-se^n-te

Choosing

I like the one in the window	Eu gostaria daquele que está na vitrine	Ay-oo gos-ta-**ree**-a da-**ke**-le ke es-**ta** na vee-**tree**-ne
Could I see that one, please?	Posso ver aquele, por favor?	**Pos**-soo ver a-**ke**-le poor fa-**vor**
Is it handmade?	É feito à mão?	Eh **fay**-too ah mow^n
What's it made of?	Do que é feito?	Doo ke eh **fay**-too
I like the colour but not the style	Gosto da cor mas não do estilo	**Gos**-too da kor mas now^n do es-**tee**-loo
I want a darker/ lighter shade	Quero um tom mais escuro/leve	**Ke**-roo oo^n to^n **ma**-ees es-**koo**-roo/**le**-ve
Do you have one in another colour/size?	Tem outro em outra cor/tamanho?	Te^n **o**-troo e^n **o**-tra kor/ ta-**ma**-nyoo
It's for a three-year-old	É para uma criança de três anos	Eh **pa**-ra **oo**-ma kree-a^n-sa je trays **a**-noos
Have you anything better/cheaper?	Tem algo melhor/ mais barato?	Te^n **al**-goo me-**lyor**/**ma**-ees ba-**ra**-too
How much is this?	Quanto custa isto?	Kwa^n-too **koos**-ta **ees**-too
That is too much for me	É muito (caro) para mim	Eh **mwee**-too (**ka**-ro) **pa**-ra mee^n

Colours

beige	bege	**bey**-zhe
black	preto	**pray**-too
blue	azul	a-**zool**

brown	marrom	ma-ho^n
gold	dourado	do-ra-doo
green	verde	vayr-je
grey	cinza	see^n-za
mauve	violeta	vee-o-le-ta
orange	laranja	la-ra^n-zha
pink	rosa	ho-za
purple	roxo	ho-shoo
red	vermelho	ver-may-lyoo
silver	prateado	pra-te-a-doo
white	branco	bra^n-koo
yellow	amarelo	a-ma-re-loo

Materials

canvas	a lona/ a tela	lo-na/te-la
cotton	o algodão	al-goo-dow$^{\prime\prime}$
glass	o vidro	vee-dro
lace	a renda	he^n-da
leather	o couro	koo-ro
linen	o linho	lee^n nyoo
muslin	a musselina	moo-se-lee-na
plastic	o plastico	plas-lee-koo
silk	a seda	say-da
suede	a camurça	ka-moor-sa

synthetic	o sintético	seeⁿ-**te**-tee-koo
velvet	o veludo	ve-**loo**-do
wood	a madeira	ma-**dey**-ra
wool	a lã	laⁿ

Paying

How much is this?	Quanto custa?	Kwaⁿ-too **koos**-ta
That's ... reais/euros	*São ... reais/euros	Sowⁿ ... he-ay-ees/**ay**-oo-ros
They are ... reais/euros each	*São ... reais/euros cada	Sowⁿ ... he-ay-ees/**ay**-oo-ros
It's too expensive	É muito caro	Eh **mwee**-too **ka**-roo
Is that your best price?	É o melhor preço que você pode fazer?	Eh oo me-**lyor pre**-so ke vo-seh **po**-je fa-**zair**
Can you give me a discount?	Pode me dar um desconto?	**Po**-je me dar ooⁿ des-**ko**ⁿ-too
How much does that come to?	Qual é o total da conta?	Kwal eh oo to-**taw** da **ko**ⁿ-ta
That will be ...	*O total é ...	Oo to-**taw** eh
How would you like to pay?	Como você gostaria de pagar?	Ko-moo **vo**-seh gos-ta-**ree**-a je pa-gar
Cash only, please	Só aceitamos dinheiro	Soh a-say-**ta**-mos jee-**nyay**-roo
Do you take credit cards?	Aceitam cartão de crédito?	A-say-taⁿ kar-**tow**ⁿ je **kreh**-jee-too
Do I have to pay VAT?	Tenho que pagar IVA?	Te-nyoo ke pa-**gar ee**-va

Please pay the cashier	*Pague na caixa, por favor	Pa-ghe na kay-sha poor fa-vor
May I have a receipt, please	Gostaria de ter a nota fiscal, por favor	Gos-ta-ree-a je ter a no-ta fees-kaw poor fa-vor
You've given me the wrong change	O troco não está certo	Oo tro-koo nown es-ta ser-too

Complaints

I want to see the manager	Quero falar com o gerente	Ke-roo fa-lar kon oo zhe-rayn-te
I bought this yesterday	Comprei isto ontem	Kon-pray ees-too on-tayn
It doesn't work/fit	Não funciona/cabe	Nown foon-see-o-na/ka-be
This is ...	Está ...	Es-ta
bad	mau/má	maw/mah
broken	quebrado	ke-bra-doo
cracked	rachado	ra-sha-doo
dirty	sujo	soo-zhoo
stained	manchado	man-sha-doo
torn	rasgado	ras-ga-doo
I'd like to return this	Quero devolver isto	Ke-roo de-vol-vayr ees-too
Will you change it, please?	Pode trocá-lo, por favor?	Po-jen tro-ka-loo poor fa-vor

| Will you refund my money? | **Pode me devolver o dinheiro?** | Po-je me de-**vol**-vayr oo dee-**nyay**-roo |
| Here is the receipt | **Aqui está a nota fiscal** | A-**kee** es-**ta** a **no**-ta fees-**kaw** |

Beauty and Spa Treatments

I'd like a manicure/ pedicure	**Eu gostaria de fazer a mão/ o pé**	Ay-oo gos-ta-**ree**-a je fa-**zair** a mow^n/oo peh
I'd like a facial/ massage	**Eu gostaria de um tratamento facial/ uma massagem**	Ay-oo gos-ta-**ree**-a je oo^n tra-ta-**me**^n-too fa-see-al/ oo-ma mas-**sa**-zje^n
Do you do waxing?	**Vocês fazem depilação?**	**Vo**-sehs fa-ze^n de-pee-la-**sow**^n
I'd like my eyebrows shaped	**Quero fazer minha sobrancelha**	**Ke**-roo fa-**zair** me-nya so-bra^n-**se**-lya
Do you do aromatherapy?	**Vocês fazem aromaterapia?**	**Vo**-sehs fa-ze^n a-ro-ma-te-ra-**pee**-a
Is there a sauna/ steam room?	**Há uma sauna/ banho turco?**	Ah oo-ma sow-na/**ba**-nyo **toor**-koo
What spa packages are available?	**Quais são os pacotes disponíveis no spa?**	**Kwa**-ees sow^n oos pa-ko-tes jees-po-**nee**-veys no spa
How much does it cost?	**Quanto custa?**	**Kwa**^n-too **koos**-ta

Books, Newspapers and Stationery

Do you sell English/American newspapers/ magazines?	Vendem jornais/ revistas ingleses(as)/ americanos(as)?	Vayⁿ-dayⁿ zhoor-na-ees/ he-vees-tas eeⁿ-glay-zes(as)/a-me-ree-ka-noos(as)
Can you get . . . magazine for me?	Podem me arranjar a revista . . . ?	Po-dayⁿ me a-haⁿ-zhar ah re-vees-ta
Where can I get the . . . ?	Onde eu consigo o . . . ?	Oⁿ je ay-oo koⁿ-see-goo oo
I'd like a map of the city/road map of . . .	Quero um mapa da cidade/um mapa rodoviário	Ke-roo ooⁿ ma-pa da see-da-je/ooⁿ ma-pa ho-do-vee-a-ree-oo
I'd like an entertainment guide	Quero um guia de entretenimento	Ke-roo ooⁿ ghee-a je eⁿ-tre-te-nee-meⁿ too
Do you have any books in English?	Tem livros em inglês?	Teⁿ lee-vroos ayⁿ eeⁿ-glays
Have you any books by . . . ?	Tem algum livro de . . . ?	Teⁿ al-gooⁿ lee-vroo je
I want some postcards	Quero alguns cartões postais	Ke-roo al-gooⁿs kar-toyⁿs pos-tais
Do you sell souvenirs/toys?	Vende suvenires/ lembrancinhas/ brinquedos?	Vayⁿ je soo-ve-nee-res/ leⁿ-braⁿ-see-nyas/breeⁿ kay-doos
ballpoint pen	a caneta esferográfica	ka-ne-ta es-fe-ro-gra-fee-ka
calculator	a calculadora	kal-koo-la-do-ra

card	o cartão	kar-tow[n]
dictionary	o dicionário	jee-syo-**nah**-ryoo
drawing paper	o papel de desenho	pa-**pew** je de-ze-nyoo
drawing pin	a tachinha/o percevejo	ta-**shee**-nya/per-se-ve-zhoo
elastic band	o elástico	e-**las**-tee-koo
envelope	o envelope	e[n]-ve-**lo**-pe
felt-tip pen	a caneta hidrográfica	ka-**nay**-ta ee-dro-**gra**-fee-ka
glue/paste	a cola/a massa	**koh**-la/**mas**-sa
guide book	o guia de viagem	**ghee**-a je vee-a-**zhe**[n]
ink	a tinta	**tee**[n]-ta
notebook	o caderno de notas	ka-**der**-noo je **no**-tas
paperclip	o clipe de papel	**klee**-pe je pa-**pew**
pen	a caneta	ka-**ne**-ta
pen cartridge	a carga de caneta	**kar**-ga je ka-**ne**-ta
(coloured) pencil	o lápis de cor	**lah**-pees je cor
pencil sharpener	o apontador de lápis	a-po[n]-ta-**dor** je **lah**-pees
postcard	o cartão postal	kar-**tow**[n] pos-**taw**
rubber	a borracha	bo-**ha**-sha
sellotape	a fita adesiva	**fee**-ta a-de-**zee**-va
string	o cordão	kor-**dow**[n]
sketch pad	o bloco de desenho	**blo**-koo je de-ze-nyoo
wrapping paper	o papel de presente	pa-**pew** je pre-**ze**[n]-te

CDs/DVDs

Can you recommend any CDs of local music?	Você pode me recomendar algum CD de música local?	Vo-sch po-je me he-ko-me^n-dar al-goo^n CD je moo-see-ka lo-kaw
Are there any new CDs by ...?	Você tem algum CD novo do ...?	Vo-seh te^n al-goo^n CD no-voo doo
Have you any CDs by ...?	Você tem algum CD do ...?	Vo-seh te^n al-goo^n CD doo
I'm looking for DVDs of ...	Eu estou procurando DVDs de...	Ay-oo es-toh pro-koo-ra^n-doo DVDs je

Chemist[1]

Can you prepare a prescription, please?	Pode fazer uma receita médica, por favor?	Po-je fa zair oo-ma he-say-ta me-jee-ka poor fa-vor
Have you a small first-aid kit?	Tem um kit de primeiros socorros?	Te^n oo^n kit je pree-may-roos so-ko hoos
I want ...	Quero ...	Ke-roo
a pack of adhesive plasters	uma caixa de curativos adesivos	oo-ma kay-sha je koo-ra-tee-vos a-de-zee-vos
an antiseptic cream	creme antiséptico	kre-me a^n-tee-se tee koo
some aspirin	algumas aspirinas	al goo-mas as-pee-ree-nas
a disinfectant	desinfetante	de-see^n-fe-ta^n-te

1. See also DOCTOR (pp. 132–141).

a mosquito repellent	repelente de mosquitos	re-pe-le^n-te je mos-kee-toos
a mouthwash	antiséptico bucal	a^n-tee-se-tee-koo boo-kaw
some nose drops	descongestionante nasal	des-ko^n-zhes-tyo-na^n-te na-zaw
paracetamol	paracetamol	paracetamol
sun cream (for children)	protetor solar (para crianças)	pro-te-tor so-lar (pa-ra kree-a^n-sas)
throat lozenges	pastilhas para a garganta	pas-tee-lyas pa-ra a gar-ga^n-ta
Can you give me something for	Pode me dar alguma coisa para . . .	Po-je me dar al-goo-ma koy-za pa-ra
constipation?	prisão de ventre?	pree-zow^n je vay^n-tre
diarrhoea?	diarréia?	jee-a-hay-a
indigestion?	indigestão?	ee^n-jee-zhes-tow^n
insect sting	picada de inseto?	pee-ka-da je een-se-too
jellyfish sting	queimadura de água-viva?	key-ma-doo-ra je a-gwa-vee-va
stomach ache	dor de estômago?	dor je es-to-ma-goo
sunburn	queimadura de sol?	key-ma-doo-ra je sol
Do you sell . . .	Vende . . .	Vay^n-je
condoms?	camisinha/ preservativo?	ka-mee-zee-nya/pre-zer-va- tee-voo
contraceptive pills?	pílula contraceptiva?	pee-loo-la ko^n-tra-sep-tee-va

cotton wool?	algodão?	al-goo-**dow**ⁿ
sanitary towels?	absorventes femininos?	ab-sor-**ve**ⁿ-tes fe-mee-nee-noos
tampons?	tampões?	taⁿ-**poy**ⁿs
I need something for ...	Preciso de algo para ...	Pre-**see**-zoo je al-goo pa-ra
a hangover	ressaca	hes-**sa**-ka
a headache	dor de cabeça	dor je ka-**be**-sa
travel sickness	enjôo	ayⁿ-**zho**-oo

Clothes, Shoes and Accessories[1]

I'd like a hat/sunhat	Quero um chapéu/chapéu de sol	Ke-roo ooⁿ sha-pe-oo/sha-pe-oo je sol
Where are the beach clothes?	Onde está a roupa de praia?	Oⁿ-je es-ta a ho-pa je pray-a
I'd like a short-/long sleeved shirt	Quero uma camisa de manga curta/comprida	Ke-roo oo-ma ka-**mee**-za je maⁿ-ga koor-ta/koⁿ-**pree**-da
Where can I find ...	Onde posso comprar ...	Oⁿ-je pos-soo koⁿ-**prar**
socks?	meias?	**may**-as
tights?	meia-calça?	**may**-a-**kal**-sa
I am looking for ...	Estou à procura ...	Es-**toh** ah pro-**koo**-ra

1. For sizes see pp. 175–176.

a blouse	duma blusa	**doo**-ma **bloo**-za
a bra	dum sutiã	doo^n soo-tee-a^n
a dress	dum vestido	doo^n ves-**tee**-doo
a sweater	dum pulover	doo^n pool-**o**-ver
I need . . .	Preciso de . . .	Pre-**see**-zo je
a coat	um casaco	oo^n ka-**za**-koo
a raincoat	uma capa de chuva	**oo**-ma ka-pa je **shoo**-va
a pair of trousers	calças	**kal**-sas
Do you have other colours?	Você tem em outra cor?	**Vo**-seh te^n e^n o-tra kor
I need it to match this	Preciso que combine com isto	Pre-**see**-zoo ke ko^n-**bee**-ne ko^n **ees**-too
What size is this?	Que medida é esta?	Ke me-**jee**-da eh **es**-ta
I take size . . .	Eu visto o tamanho . . .	**Ay**-oo **vees**-too oo ta-**ma**-nyoo
Can you measure me?	Pode tirar as minhas medidas?	**Po**-je tee-**rar** as mee-nyas me-**jee**-das
May I try it on?	Posso provar?	**Pos**-soo pro-**var**
Is there a mirror?	Tem um espelho?	Te^n oo^n es-**pay**-lyoo
This doesn't fit	Isto não serve	**Ees**-too now^n **ser**-ve
It's too . . .	É muito . . .	Eh **mwee**-too
long	comprido	ko^n-**pree**-doo
loose	largo	**lar**-goo

short	**curto**	**koor**-too
tight	**apertado**	a-per-**ta**-doo
Have you a larger/ smaller one?	**Tem um maior/ menor?**	Te^n oo^n may-**or**/me-**nor**
I need something warmer/thinner	**Quero algo mais quente/leve**	**Ke**-roo **al**-goo ma-ees **kay**^{n}-te/**le**-ve
Is it colour fast?	**Desbota?**	Des-**bo**-ta
Is it machine washable?	**Pode lavar na máquina?**	**Po** je la-**var** na ma-**kee**-na
Will it shrink?	**Encolhe?**	Λy^n ko **lye**
I'd like a pair of ...	**Quero um par de ...**	**Ke**-roo oo^n par je
black shoes	**sapatos pretos**	sa-**pa**-tos **pre**-tos
boots	**botas**	**bo**-tas
sandals	**sandálias**	san-**da**-lee-as
trainers	**tenis**	**te**-nees
walking shoes	**sapatos confortáveis**	sa-**pa**-toos ko^n-foor-**ta**-vay-ees

Clothing sizes

Women's clothing

Coats, dresses, shirts, tops, trousers

Brazil		40	42	44	46	48	50
UK/Australia		8	10	12	14	16	18
USA/Canada		6	8	10	12	14	16
Europe		38	40	42	44	46	48

Shoes

Brazil	35	36	37	38	39	40	41
UK	4	5	6	7	8	9	10
USA/Canada	$5^{1}/_2$	$6^{1}/_2$	$7^{1}/_2$	$8^{1}/_2$	$9^{1}/_2$	$10^{1}/_2$	$11^{1}/_2$
Europe	37	38	39/40	41	42	43	44

Men's clothing

Suits and coats

UK/USA/Canada	36	38	40	42	44	46
Europe	46	48	50	52	54	56

Shirts

UK/USA/Canada	14	$14^{1}/_2$	15	$15^{1}/_2$	16	$16^{1}/_2$	17
Europe	36	37	38	39	40	41	42

Shoes

Brazil	41	42	43	44	45
UK	$9^{1}/_2$	10	$10^{1}/_2$	11	$11^{1}/_2$
USA/Canada	10	$10^{1}/_2$	11	$11^{1}/_2$	12
Europe	43	44	44	45	45

Food[1]

Give me a kilo/half a kilo of . . . please	Um quilo/meio quilo de . . . por favor	Ooⁿ kee-loo/**may**-oo kee-loo je . . . poor fa-**vor**
100 grammes of sweets, please	Cem gramas de balas/ bombons, por favor	Sayⁿ **gra**-mas je ba-las/ boⁿ-**bo**ⁿs poor fa-**vor**
A bottle of . . .	Uma garrafa de . . .	Oo-ma ga-**ha**-fa je
beer	cerveja	ser-**ve**-zha
mineral water	água mineral	**a**-gwa mee-ne-**raw**
wine	vinho	**vee**-nyoo
A litre of semi-skimmed/whole milk, please	Um litro de leite semi-desnatado/ integral, por favor	Ooⁿ **lee**-troo je ley-te se-mee-des-na-ta-doo/eeⁿ-te-graw poor fa-**vor**
A carton of plain yoghurt	Um pote de iogurte natural	Ooⁿ po-te je yo-**goor**-te na-too-**raw**
A dozen/half a dozen eggs	Uma dúzia/meia dúzia de ovos	Oo-ma **doo**-zee a/**may**-a **doo**-zee-a je o-vos
I'd like . . .	Quero . . .	**Ke**-roo
a jar of . . .	uma jarra de . . .	oo-ma **zha**-ha je
a packet of . . .	um pacote de . . .	ooⁿ pa-**ko**-te je
a tin (can) of . . .	uma lata de . . .	oo-ma **la** ta je
. . . slices of ham	. . . fatias de presunto	fa-**tee**-as je pre-**soo**ⁿ-too

1. See also the various MENU sections (p. 103 onwards) and WEIGHTS AND MEASURES (pp. 229–233).

300 grammes of cheese	**trezentas gramas de queijo**	tre-**ze**^{n}-tas **gra**-mas je **ke**-zhoo
Do you sell frozen foods?	**Vende alimentos congelados?**	Vay^n-de a-lee-**may**^{n}-toos ko^n-zhe-**la**-doos
These pears are too hard/soft	**Estas peras estão muito duras/ maduras**	Es-tas **pay**-ras es-**tow**^{n} mwee-too **doo**-ras/ma-**doo**-ras
Is it fresh?	**É fresco?**	Eh **frays**-koo
Are they ripe?	**Estão maduros?**	Es-**tow**^{n} ma-**doo**-roos
This is bad	**Isto não está bom**	**Ees**-too now^n es-**ta** bo^n
A loaf of bread, please	**Um pão, por favor**	Oo^n pow^n poor fa-**vor**
How much a kilo/ bottle?	**Quanto custa um quilo/uma garrafa?**	**Kwa**^{n}-too **koos**-ta oo^n **kee**-loo/**oo**-ma ga-**ha**-fa
A kilo of sausages	**Um quilo de salsichás/ linguiça**	Oo^n **kee**-loo je saw-**see**-chas/lee^n-**gwee**-sa
Four pork chops	**Quatro costeletas de porco**	**Kwa**-troo kos-te-**le**-tas je **por**-koo
Will you mince the meat?	**Pode moer a carne?**	**Po**-je mo-**er** a **kar**-ne
Will you bone it?	**Pode tirar os ossos?**	**Po**-je tee-**rar** oos **o**-soos
Will you clean the fish?	**Pode limpar o peixe?**	**Po**-je lee^n-**par** oo **pay**-she
Please fillet the fish	**Corte o peixe em fatias**	**Kor**-te oo **pay**-she ay^n fa-**tee**-as
Is there any shellfish?	**Tem marisco?**	Te^n ma-**rees**-koo
Shall I help myself?	**Posso me servir?**	**Pos**-soo me ser-**veer**

Hairdresser and Barber

May I make an appointment for this morning/tomorrow afternoon?	Posso marcar hora para esta manhã/ para amanhã à tarde?	Pos-soo mar-**kar** o-ra pa-ra es-ta ma-**nya**^{n}/**pa**-ra a-ma-**nya**^{n} ah **tar**-je
What time?	A que horas?	A ke **o**-ras
I'd like my hair cut	Quero cortar meu cabelo	**Ke**-roo kor-**tar may**-oo ka-**be**-loo
I'd like my hair cut/ trimmed	Quero cortar/aparar o meu cabelo	**Ke**-roo kor-**tar**/a-pa-**rar** oo **may**-oo ka-**be**-loo
Not too short at the sides	Não muito curto dos lados	Now^n **mwee**-too **koor** too doos **la**-doos
I'll have it shorter at the back/on top	Mais curto atrás/em cima	**Ma**-ees **koor**-too a-tras e^n **see**-ma
That's fine	Está bem	Es-**ta** bay^n
I want a shave	Quero fazer a barba	**Ke**-roo fa-**zair** a **bar**-ba
Could you trim my beard/moustache?	Pode aparar a barba/o bigode?	**Pô** je a pa-**rar** a **bar**-ba/ oo bee-**go**-je
My hair is oily/dry	Meu cabelo é oleoso/ seco	**May**-oo ka-**be**-loo eh o-le-o-**zoo**/se koo
I'd like a shampoo	Quero lavar a cabeça	**Ke**-roo la-**var** a ka-**be**-sa
Please use conditioner	Por favor use o condicionador	Poor fa-**vor** oo-ze oo ku^n-jee-syo-na-**dor**
I'd like my hair washed and blow-dried	Quero lavar e secar o cabelo	**Ke**-roo la-**var** e se-**kar** oo ka-**be**-loo

Please do not use any hairspray	Por favor não use spray fixador/ laquê	Poor fa-**vor** now[n] **oo**-ze spray feek-sa-**dor**/la-ke
I want a colour rinse	Quero passar shampoo tonalizante	Ke-roo pas-**sar** sha[n]-**poo** to-na-lee-**za**[n]-te
May I see a colour chart	Gostaria de ver o catálogo de cores	Goos-ta-**ree**-a je vayr oo ka-**ta**-loo-goo je **ko**-res
I'd like a darker/ lighter hade	Quero um tom mais escuro/mais claro	Ke-roo oo[n] to[n] ma-ees es-**koo**-roo/**ma**-ees **kla**-roo
I'd like a tint/ highlights	Quero fazer uma pintura/fazer luzes	Ke-roo fa-**zair** oo-ma pee[n]-**too**-ra/fa-**zair** **loo**-zes
The water is too cold	A água está muito fria	A **ah**-gwa es-**ta** mwee-too **free**-a
The dryer is too hot	O secador está muito quente	Oo se-ka-**dor** es-**ta** mwee-too kay[n]- te
Thank you, I like it very much	Obrigado (a), está muito bem	O-bree-**ga**-doo (a) es-**ta** mwee-too bay[n]
I'd like a manicure	Quero fazer a mão	Ke-roo fa-**zair** a mow[n]

Hardware and Outdoors

| Where is the camping equipment? | Onde está o equipamento para camping? | O[n]-je es-**ta** oo ay-kee-pa-**may**[n]-too **pa**-ra ka[n]-peeng |
| Do you have a battery for this? | Tem uma bateria para isto? | Te[n] **oo**-ma ba-te-**ree**-a **pa**-ra **ees**-too |

Where can I get butane gas?	Onde posso obter gás butano?	On-je pos-soo ob-tayr gas boo-ta-noo
I need a . . .	Preciso de um . . .	Pre-see-zoo je oon
bottle opener	abridor de garrafas	a-bree-dor je ga-ha-fas
corkscrew	saca-rolhas	sa-ka-ro-lyas
a small/large screwdriver	uma chave de fenda pequena/grande	oo-ma sha-ve je fen-da pe-ke-na/gran-de
tin opener	abridor de latas	a-bree-dor je la-tas
I want . . .	Eu quero . . .	Ay-oo ke-roo
candles/matches	velas/fósforos	ve-las/fos-foo-roos
a pair of scissors	uma tesoura	oo-ma te-zo-ra
a pen knife	um canivete	oon ka-nee-ve-te
a torch	uma lanterna	oo-ma lan-ter-na
Do you sell string/rope?	Você vende cordão/barbante?	Vo-seh ven-je kor-down/bar-ban-te
Where can I find	Onde posso encontrar . . .	On-je pos-soo ayn kon trar
a dishcloth?	o pano de prato?	pa-noo je pra-too
scouring powder?	o pó de arear?	poh je a-ree ar
a scrubbing sponge?	a escova de esfregar?	es-ko-va je es-fre-gar
washing-up liquid?	o detergente?	de-ter-rhen to
I need . . .	Preciso de . . .	Pre-see-zoo je
a bucket	um balde	oon bow-je
a brush	uma escova	oo-ma es-ko-va
a frying pan	uma frigideira	oo-ma free-zhee-day-ra

a groundsheet	uma lona	oo-ma lo-na
I want to buy a barbecue	Quero comprar uma churrasqueira	Ke-roo kon-prar oo-ma shoo-has-key-ra
Do you sell charcoal?	Vende carvão?	Ven-je kar-vown
adaptor	o adaptador	a-dap-ta-dor
basket	o cesto	says-too
duster	o espanador de pó	es-pa-na-dor je poh
electrical flex	o fio eléctrico	fee-oo ee-le-tree-koo
extension lead	o fio de extensão/ derivador	fee-oo je es-tayn-sown/ de-ree-va-dor
fuse	o fusível	foo-zee-vel
insulating tape	a fita de isolamento	fee-ta je ee-zo-la-men-too
light bulb	a lâmpada	lan-pa-da
plug (*bath*)	tampão	tan-pown
plug (*electric*)	a tomada	to-ma-da

Laundry and Dry Cleaning

Where is the nearest launderette?	Onde é a lavanderia mais próxima?	On-je eh a la-van-de-ree-a ma-ees pro-see-ma
I'd like to have this washed/cleaned	Quero isto lavado/ limpo	Ke-roo ees-too la-va-doo/leen-poo
Can you get this stain out?	Pode tirar esta mancha?	Po-je tee-rar es-ta man-sha

It is . . .	É . . .	Eh . . .
coffee	café	ka-feh
grease	gordura	gor-doo-ra
wine	vinho	vee-nyoo
These stains won't come out	*Estas manchas não saem	Es-tas ma^n-shas now^n sy-e^n
It only needs to be pressed	Só falta passar	Soh fal-ta pa-sar
This is torn. Can you mend it?	Isto está rasgado. Você pode costurá-lo?	Ees-too es-ta ras-ga-doo. Voh-se po-je kos-too-ra-loo
There's a button missing	Falta um botão	Fal ta oo^n bo-tow^n
Will you sew on another one, please?	Pode costurar outro, por favor?	Po-je kos-too-rar o-troo poor fa-vor
When will it be ready?	Quando ficará/ estará pronto?	Kwa^n-doo fee-ka-ra/es-ta-ra pro^n-too
I need it by this evening/tomorrow	Preciso disso para esta noite/para amanhã	Pre-see-zoo Jees-so pa-ra es-ta no-ee-te/pa-ra a-ma-nya^n
Call back at five o'clock	*Volte às cinco horas	Vol-te ahs see^n-koo o-ras
We can't do it until Tuesday	*Não podemos fazê-lo antes de quinta-feira	Now^n po-day-moos fa zay loo a^n-tes je kee^n-ta-fey-ra
It will take three days	*Ficará/ estará pronto em três dias	Fee-ka-ra/Es-ta-ra pro^n-too e^n trays jee-as
This isn't mine	Isto não é meu	Ees-too now^n eh may-oo
I've lost my ticket	Perdi o meu ticket	Per-jee oo may-oo ticket

Household laundry

bath towel	a toalha de banho	too-a-lya je ba-nyoo
(woollen) blanket	o cobertor (de lã)	koo-ber-tor (je la^n)
napkin	o guardanapo	gwar-da-na-poo
pillowcase	a fronha	fro-nya
sheet	o lençol	lay^n-sol
tablecloth	a toalha de mesa	too-a-lya je may-za
tea towel	o pano de secar a louça	pa-noo je se-kar a lo-sa

Markets

Which day is market day?	Que dia é o mercado?	Ke jee-a eh oo mer-ka-doo
Where is the market held?	Onde fica o mercado?	O^n-je fee-ka oo mer-ka-doo
Is it a permanent/ covered market?	O mercado é permanente/ coberto?	Oo mer-ka-doo eh per-ma-ne^n- te/ko-ber-too
What time does it start?	Que horas começa?	Ke or-as ko-me-sa
When does it finish?	Que horas termina/ acaba?	Ke or-as ter-mee-na/a-ka-ba
Is there a market today in a nearby town?	Há algum mercado em uma cidade aqui perto?	Ah al-goo^n mer-ka-doo e^n oo-ma see-da-je a-kee per-too

Photography

I'd like to buy . . .	Quero comprar . . .	Ke-roo kon-prar
a camcorder	uma filmadora	oo-ma feel-ma-do-ra
a digital camera	uma máquina digital	oo-ma ma-kee-na jee-zhee-taw
a disposable camera	uma máquina descartável	oo-ma ma-kee-na jes-kar ta-vew
Do you have a memory card for this camera?	Você tem um cartão de memória para esta máquina?	Vo-seh ten oon kar-town je me-mor-ee-a pa-ra es-ta ma-kee-na
Can you print photos from this card/ disk/USB?	Você pode imprimir as fotos deste cartão/ disco/ pen drive?	Vo-seh po-je een-pree-meer as fo-tos des-te kar-town/jees-koo/pen drive
I'd like . . . prints of this image	Quero . . .cópias desta imagem	Ke-roo ko-pee-as des-ta ee-ma-zhen
I'd like to enlarge the image	Gostaria de aumentar a imagem	Gos-ta-ree-a je ow-men-tar a ee ma-zhen
I'd like the express service, please	Quero serviço expresso, por favor	Ke-roo ser ver-soo es-pres-so poor fa-vor
When will it be ready?	Quando estará pronto?	Kwan-doo es-ta-ra pron-too
Will it be done tomorrow?	Estará pronto amanhã?	Es-ta ra pron-too a-ma-nyan
My camera's not working. Can you check it/mend it?	A minha máquina fotográfica não funciona, podem vê-la/consertá-la?	A mee-nya ma-kee-na fo-to-gra-fee-ka nown foon-see-o-na po-deyn vay-la/kon-ser-ta-la
You will have to leave the camera for a few days	Você deve deixar a máquina fotográfica por alguns dias	Vo-seh de ve de-shar a ma-kee-na fo-to-gra-fee-ka poor al-goons jee-as

Repairs

This is broken; could you mend it?	Isto está quebrado; pode consertar?	Ees-too es-ta ke-bra-doo; po-je kon-ser-tar
Could you do it while I wait?	Pode consertar enquanto eu espero?	Po-je kon-ser-tar en-kwan-too ay-oo es-pe-roo
When should I come back for it?	Quando posso vir buscá-lo/a?	Kwan-doo pos-soo veer boos-ka-loo/a
I'd like these shoes soled (with leather)	Quero solas (em couro) nestes sapatos	Ke-roo so-las (ayn ko-ro) nes-tes sa-pa-toos
I'd like them heeled (with rubber)	Quero saltos (em borracha) nestes sapatos	Ke-roo sal-toos (ayn boo-ha-sha) nes-tes sa-pa-toos
Do you sell shoelaces?	Você vende cadarços?	Vo-seh ven-je ka-dar-sos
My watch is broken	Meu relógio está quebrado	May-oo re-lo-zhee-oo es-ta ke-bra-doo
I have broken the glass/strap	Eu quebrei o vidro/a tira	Ay-oo ke-brey oo vee-droo/a tee-ra
Could you mend my bag?	Pode consertar minha bolsa?	Po-je kon-ser-tar mee-nya bol-sa
Could you put in a new zipper?	Você poderia colocar um zíper novo?	Vo-seh po-de-ree-a ko-lo-kar oon zee-per no-voo
The stone/charm/screw has come loose	A pedra/o amuleto/o parafuso está solto (a)	A pe-dra/oo a-moo-lay-too/oo pa-ra-foo-zoo es-ta sol-too (a)
The fastener/clip/chain is broken	O fecho/a mola/o colar/a corrente está partido (a)	Oo fay-shoo/a mo-la/oo koo-lar/a ko-hen-te es-ta par-tee-doo (a)

It can't be repaired	*Não tem conserto	Now[n] tay[n] ko[n]-**ser**-too
You need a new one	*Necessita um novo/ uma nova	Ne-se-**see**-ta oo[n] **no**-voo/**oo**-ma no-va
How much would a new one cost?	Quanto custaria um novo?	Kwa[n]-too koos-ta-**ree**-a oo[n] **no**-voo

Toiletries[1]

A packet of razor blades, please	Um pacote de lâminas de barbear, por favor	Oo[n] pa-**ko**-te je la-**mee**-nas je bar-bee-**ar** poor fa-**vor**
How much is this aftershave lotion?	Quanto custa esta loção de barba?	Kwa[n]-loo koos-ta es-ta lo-**sow**[n] je bar-ba
a tube of toothpaste	um tubo de pasta de dentes	oo[n] **too**-boo je **pas**-ta je **day**[n]-tes
a box of paper handkerchiefs	uma caixa de lenços de papel	**oo**-ma ka-ee-sha je **lay**[n]-soos je pa-**pew**
a roll of toilet paper	papel higiénico	pa-**pew** ee-zhee-e-nee-koo
I'd like some eau-de-cologne/perfume	Quero um frasco de água de colónia/ perfume	**Ke**-roo oo[n] **fras**-koo je **a**-gwa je ko-lo-**nee**-a/ per-**foo**-me
May I try it?	Posso experimentar?	Pos-**soó** es-pe-ree-may[n]-tar
a shampoo for dry/ greasy hair	um shampoo para cabelo seco/oleoso	Oo[n] **sha**[n] poo pa-ra ka-he-**loo** say-koo/ o-lee **o**-zoo
I'd like ...	Queria ...	Ke-**ree**-a

1. See **CHEMIST**, pp. 171–173.

a bar of soap	um sabonete	oo^n sa-bo-**ne**-te
cleansing cream/ lotion	creme /loção de limpeza	**kre**-me /lo-**sow**^{n} je lee^n-**pay**-za
hair conditioner	condicionador de cabelo	ko^n-jee-see-o-na-**dor** je ka-**be**-loo
hand cream	creme para as mãos	**kre**-me **pa**-ra as mow^{n}s
lip salve	creme para os lábios	**kre**-me **pa**-ra oos la-bee-oos
moisturizer	creme hidratante	**kre**-me ee-dra-**ta**^{n}-te

SIGHTSEEING[1]

Key Phrases

Where is the tourist office?	Onde é o posto de informações turísticas?	Oⁿ-je eh oo pos-too je eeⁿ-for-ma-soyⁿs too-rees-tee-kas
Is there a map/plan of the places to visit?	Há um mapa/plano dos locais/lugares para visitar?	Ah ooⁿ ma-pa/pla-no doos lo-ka-ees/loo-ga-res pa-ra vee-zee-tar
Is there a good sightseeing tour?	Há alguma boa excursão turística?	Ah al-goo-ma bo-a es-koor sowⁿ too-rees-tee-ka
How much does the tour cost?	Quanto custa a excursão?	Kwaⁿ-too koos-ta a es-koor-sowⁿ
Is there access for wheelchairs?	Há acesso para cadeira de rodas?	Ah a-se-soo pa-ra ka-dey-ra je ho das
Is there an audio guide in English?	Há um áudio-guia em inglês?	Ah ooⁿ ow jee-o ghee-a eⁿ eeⁿ-glays

What should we see here?	Que lugares devemos visitar aqui?	Ke loo-ga-res de-ve-mos vee zee-tar a-kee
I want a guide book	Quero um guia de viagem	Ke-roo ooⁿ ghee-a je vee-a-zheⁿ
Is there a guided walking tour of the town?	Há um passeio com guia pela cidade?	Ah ooⁿ pas-say-oo koⁿ ghee-a pe-la see da-je

1. See also Getting Around (p.12) and Directions (p. 48).

Can you suggest an interesting half-day excursion?	Você pode sugerir uma excursão de meio período?	Vo-seh po-je soo-zhe-reer oo-ma es-koor-sow^n je me-yo pe-ree-oo-do
Can we take a boat cruise/balloon flight?	Podemos fazer um passeio de barco/ voo de balão?	Po-de-mos fa-zer oo^n pas-say-oo je bar-koo/ voo je ba-low^n
We want to go hiking	Nós queremos fazer uma caminhada	Nohs ke-re-mos fa-zer oo-ma ka-mee-nya-da
Do we need a guide?	Precisamos de um guia?	Pre-see-za-moos je oo^n ghee-a?
It's ...	É ...	Eh
beautiful	bonito	bo-nee-too
funny	engraçado	e^n-gra-sa-doo
impressive	impressionante	ee^n-pres-syo-na^n-te
romantic	romantico	ro-ma^n-tee-koo
stunning	deslumbrante	des-loo^n-bra^n-te
unusual	incomum	ee^n-ko-moo^n

Exploring

Where is the old part of the city?	Onde é a parte velha da cidade?	O^n-je eh a par-te ve-lya da see-da-je
I'd like to walk around the old town	Eu gostaria de passear na cidade velha	Ay-oo gos-ta-ree-a je pas-se-ar na see-da-je ve-lya
Is there a good street plan showing the monuments?	Há um bom mapa das ruas que mostra os monumentos?	Ah oo^n bo^n ma-pa das hoo-as ke mos-tra oos mo-noo-me^n-tos

Which bus goes to the castle?	**Qual é o ônibus para o castelo?**	Kwal eh oo **o**-nee-boos **pa**-ra oo kas-**te**-loo
We want to visit the ...	**Queremos visitar ...**	Ke-**ray**-moos vee-zee-**tar**
cathedral	**a catedral**	a ka-te-**draw**
cloister	**o claustro**	oo **klow**-stroo
fortress	**a fortaleza**	a for-ta-**lay**-za
library	**a biblioteca**	a bee-blee-oo-**te**-ka
monastery	**o mosteiro**	oo mos-**tay**-roo
palace	**o palácio**	oo pa-**la**-see-oo
ruins	**as ruínas**	as hoo-ee-nas
May we walk around the walls?	**Podemos andar em volta das muralhas?**	Po-de-moos an-dar en vol-ta das moo-ra-lyas
May we go up the tower?	**Podemos subir à torre?**	Po-de-moos soo-beer ah **to**-he
Where do we find antique shops/the flea market?	**Onde é a feira de antiguidades/ mercado das pulgas?**	On-je eh a **fay**-ee-ra je an-tee-gwee-da-jes/ mer-ka-doo das pool-gas
What's this building?	**O que é este prédio?**	On ke eh es-te pre-dee-oo
Which is the oldest building in the city?	**Qual é o prédio mais antigo na cidade?**	Kwal eh oo pre-dee-oo ma-ees an-tee-goo na see-da je
What's the name of this church?	**Qual é o nome desta igreja?**	Kwal eh oo no-me des-ta ee-gre-zha

Gardens, Parks and Zoos

Where is the botanic garden/zoo?	**Onde é o jardim botânico/zoológico?**	Oⁿ-je eh oo zhar-**jee**ⁿ bo-**ta**-nee-koo/zoo-oo-**lo**-zhee-koo
How do I get to the park?	**Como posso ir ao parque?**	**Ko**-moo **pos**-soo eer ow **par**-ke
Can we walk there?	**Pode-se ir a pé?**	**Po**-je-se eer a peh
Can we drive through the park?	**Pode-se dirigir no parque?**	**Po**-je-se jee-ree-**zheer** noo **par**- kee
Are the gardens open to the public?	**Os jardins estão abertos ao público?**	Oos zhar-**jee**ⁿs es-**tow**ⁿ a-**ber**-toos a-oo **poo**-blee-koo
What time do the gardens close?	**A que horas os jardins fecham?**	A ke **o**-ras oos zhar-**jee**ⁿs fe-**sha**ⁿ
Is there a plan of the gardens?	**Há um mapa dos jardins?**	Ah ooⁿ **ma**-pa dos zhar-**jee**ⁿs
Who designed the gardens?	**Quem criou os jardins?**	Kayⁿ kree-**o** oos zhar-**dee**ⁿs
Where is the tropical plant house/lake?	**Onde é a estufa de plantas tropicais/o lago?**	Oⁿ-je eh a es-**too**-fa je **pla**ⁿ-tas troo-pee-**ka**-ees/oo **la**-goo

Historic Sites

We want to visit . . . Can we get there by car?	**Nós queremos visitar . . . Podemos ir lá de carro?**	Nohs ke-**ray**-moos vee-zee-**tar** . . . Poo-**day**-moos eer la je **ka**-ho
Is it far to walk?	**É muito longe para ir andando?**	Eh **mwee**-too loⁿ-zhe **pa**-ra eer aⁿ-**dan**-doo

Is it an easy walk?	É fácil ir a pé?	Eh **fa**-seew eer a peh
Is there access for wheelchairs?	Há acesso para cadeira de rodas?	Ah a-**se**-soo **pa**-ra ka-**dey**-ra je **ho**-das
Is it far to the ...	É longe ...	Eh **lon**-zhe
aqueduct?	o aqueduto?	oo a-ke-**doo**-too
castle?	o castelo?	oo kas-**te**-loo
fort?	o forte?	oo **for**-te
fortifications?	as fortificações?	as for-tee-fee-ka-**soy**ⁿs
fountain?	a fonte?	a **fo**ⁿ-te
gate?	o portão?	oo por-**tow**ⁿ
ruins?	as ruínas?	as hoo-**ee**-nas
the walls?	as muralhas?	as moo-**ra**-lyas
When was it built?	Quando foi construído?	**Kwa**ⁿ-doo foy koⁿs-troo-**ee**-doo
Who built it?	Quem construiu?	Keⁿ koⁿs-troo-**yoo**
Where is the ...	Onde fica ...	**O**ⁿ je **fee**-ka
cemetery?	o cemitério?	oo se-mee-**te**-ree-oo
church?	a igreja?	a ee-**gre**-zha
house?	a casa?	a **ka**-za

Museums and Galleries

When is the museum open?	Quando abre o museu?	**Kwa**ⁿ-doo a-bre oo moo-**zay**-oo
Is it open every day?	Está aberto todos os dias?	Es-**ta** a-**ber**-too **to**-doos oos **jee**-as

The gallery is closed on Mondays	*A galeria está fechada às segundas-feiras	A ga-le-**ree**-a es-**ta** fe-**sha**-da as se-**goo**n-das-**fay**-ras
Is there wheelchair access?	Tem acesso para cadeira de rodas?	Te^n a-**ses**-soo **pa**-ra ka-**dey**-ra je **ho**-das
How much does it cost?	Quanto custa?	**Kwa**^{n}-too **koos**-ta
Are there reductions for . . .	Há descontos para . . .	Ah jes-**ko**^{n}-toos **pa**-ra
children?	crianças?	kree-**a**^{n}-sas
seniors?	idosos?	ee-do-**soos**
students?	estudantes?	es-too-**da**^{n}-tes
Is there a family ticket?	Há entrada para família	Ah e^n-**tra**-da **pa**-ra fa-**mee**-lya
Are admission fees reduced on any special day?	Há ingressos mais baratos em dias especiais?	Ah ee^n-**gre**-soos **ma**-ees ba-**ra**-toos e^n **jee**-as es-pe-see-**a**-ees
Admission free	*Entrada gratuita	E^n-**tra**-da gra-**twee**-ta
Have you got a ticket?	*Você tem o ingresso?	**Vo**-seh te^n oo ee^n-**gres**-soo
Where do I get tickets?	Onde posso comprar ingressos?	**O**^{n}-je **pos**-soo ko^n-**prar** ee^n-**gres**-soos
Are there guided tours of the museum?	Há visita com guia ao museu?	Ah vee-**zee**-ta ko^n **ghee**-a **a**-oo moo-**zay**-oo
Does the guide speak English?	O guia fala inglês?	Oo **ghee**-a **fa**-la ee^n-**glays**
Is there an audio guide in English?	Há um áudio-guia em inglês?	Ah oo^n **ow**-jee-o-**ghee**-a e^n ee^n-**glays**

We don't need a guide	**Nós não precisamos de guia**	Nohs nowⁿ pre-see-**za**-moos je **ghee**-a
I would prefer to go round alone; is that all right?	**Eu preferia visitar/ir sozinho; é possível?**	Ay-oo pre-fe **ree**-a vee-zee-**tar**/eer so-**zee**-nyoo; eh poo-**see**-vew
Where is the exhibition?	**Onde é a exposição?**	Oⁿ-je eh a es-po-zee-**sow**ⁿ
It's over there	*** É ali**	Eh a-**lee**
Please leave your bag in the cloakroom	***Por favor deixe a bolsa na chapelaria**	Poor fa-**vor de**-she a **bol**-sa na sha-pe-la-**ree**-a
Can I take photographs?	**Posso tirar fotografias/ fotos?**	**Pos**-sou tee-**rar** fo-to gra-**fee**-as/**fo**-tos
Photographs are prohibited	***Não é permitido tirar fotos**	Nowⁿ eh per-mee-**tee**-do tee-**rar fo**-tos
Where can I get a catalogue?	**Onde posso conseguir o catálogo?**	Oⁿ-je **pos**-so koⁿ-se-**gheer** oo ka-**ta**-loo-goo

Places of Worship

Where Is the . . .	**Onde fica . . .**	Oⁿ-je **tee**-ka
cathedral?	**a catedral?**	a ka-té-**draw**
Catholic church?	**a igreja católica?**	a ee-**gre**-zha ka-to-lee-ka
mosque?	**a mesquita?**	a mes-kee ta
Protestant church?	**a igreja protestante?**	a ee-**gre**-zha pro-tes-taⁿ-te
synagogue?	**a sinagoga?**	a see-na-**go**-ga
When is the mass/ service?	**Quando é a missa/ cerimônia?**	Kwaⁿ-doo eh a **mees**-sa/ se-ree-**mo**-nya

Tours

We'd like to take a coach tour round the sights	Gostaríamos de ir em uma excursão de ônibus pelos pontos turísticos	Gos-ta-**ree**-a-mos je eer e^n oo-ma es-koor-**sow**^{n} je o-nee-boos **pe**-los **po**^{n}-tos too-**rees**-tee-koos
Does the coach stop at ... hotel?	O ônibus pára no hotel ...?	Oo o-nee-boos **pa**-ra noo o-**tew** ...
Is there boat ride?	Há um passeio de barco?	Ah oo^n pas-**say**-oo je **bar**-koo
Is there an excursion to ... tomorrow?	Há uma excursão para ... amanhã?	Ah oo-ma es-koor-**sow**^{n} pa-ra ... a-ma-**nya**^{n}
Is there a walking tour of the town?	Há um passeio a pé pela cidade?	Ah oo^n pas-**say**-oo a peh **pe**-la see-**da**-je
How long does the tour take?	Quanto tempo leva a excursão?	Kwa^n-too **tay**^{n}-poo le-va a es-koor-**sow**^{n}
When does it leave?	A que horas sai?	Ah ke **o**-ras sy
When does it return?	A que horas volta?	Ah ke **o**-ras **vol**-ta
How much does the tour cost?	Quanto custa a excursão?	Kwa^n-too **koos**-ta a es-koor-**sow**^{n}
Are all admission fees included?	Estão incluídas todas as entradas?	Es-**tow**^{n} ee^n-kloo-**ee**-das **to**-das as e^n-**tra**-das
Does it include lunch?	Está incluído o almoço?	Es-**ta** ee^n-kloo-**ee**-doo o al-**mo**-soo
Could we stop here ...	Poderíamos parar aqui ...	Po-de-**ree**-a-mos pa-**rar** a-**kee**
to buy souvenirs?	para comprar suvenirs/ lembrancinhas?	pa-ra ko^n-**prar** soo-ve-**neers**/le^n-bra^n-**see**-nyas

to get a bottle of water?	**para pegar água?**	**pa**-ra pe-**gar a**-gwa
to take photographs?	**para tirar fotos?**	**pa**-ra tee-**rar fo**-tos
to use the toilet?	**para ir ao banheiro?**	**pa**-ra eer ow ba-**nyer**-oo
How long do we stay here?	**Por quanto tempo podemos ficar aqui?**	Poor **kwan**-too **ten**-poo po-**de**-mos fee-**kar** a-**kee**

SPORTS AND LEISURE[1]

Where is the nearest tennis court/golf course?	Onde fica a quadra de tênis/campo de golfe mais próximo?	On-je fee-ka a kwa-dra je te-nees/kan-poo je golf ma-ees pro-see-moo
Is there a gym/ running track?	Há uma sala de ginástica/ uma pista de corrida?	Ah oo-ma sa-la je jee-na-stee-ka/oo-ma pees-ta je ko-hee-da
What is the charge per . . .	Quanto custa por . . .	Kwan-too koos-ta poor
day?	dia?	jee-a
game?	jogo?	zho-goo
hour?	hora?	o-ra
Is it a club?	É um clube?	Eh oon kloo-be
Do I need temporary membership?	Preciso ser sócio temporário?	Pre-see-zoo sayr so-see-oo tayn-poo-ra-ree-oo
Where can we go fishing?	Onde podemos ir pescar?	On-je po-de-moos eer pes-kar
Can I hire . . .	Posso alugar . . .	Pos-soo a-loo-gar
clubs?	tacos de golf?	ta-koos je golf
fishing gear?	artigos de pesca?	ar-tee-goos je pes-ka
a racket?	uma raquete?	oo-ma ha-ke-te
I want to go fishing. Do I need a permit?	Quero ir pescar. Preciso de autorização?	Ke-roo eer pes-kar. Pre-see-zoo je ow-to-ree-za-sown

1. See also by Bike or Moped (p. 43).

Where do I get a permit?	**Onde obtenho uma autorização?**	O^n-je ob-**tay**^{n}-nyoo **oo**-ma ow-too-ree-za-**sow**^{n}
Is there a skating rink?	**Há uma pista de patinação?**	Ah **oo**-ma **pees**-ta je pa-tee-na-**sow**^{n}
Can I hire skates?	**Posso alugar patins?**	**Pos**-soo a-loo-**gar** pa-**tee**^{n}s
I'd like to ride	**Gostaria de andar a cavalo**	Gos-ta-**ree**-a je a^n-**dar** a ka-**va**-loo
Is there a stable nearby?	**Há um estábulo aqui perto?**	Ah oo^n es-ta-boo-lo a-**kee per**-too
Do you give riding lessons?	**Oferecem lições de equitação?**	O-fe-re-se^n lee-**soy**^{n}s je e-kee-ta-**sow**^{n}
I am an inexperienced/a good rider	**Sou um cavaleiro inexperiente/um bom cavaleiro**	So oo^n ka-va-**lay**-roo ee-nes-pe-ree-**ay**^{n}-te/óo^n bo^n ka-va-**lay**-roo

At the Beach

Which is the best beach?	**Qual é a melhor praia?**	Kwal eh a me-**lyor pry**-a
Is there a quiet beach near here?	**Há por aqui alguma praia sossegada?**	Ah poor a-**kee** al-goo-ma **pry**-a sos-se-**ga**-da
Is it far to walk?	**Dá para ir a pé?**	Dah pa-ra eer a peh
Is there a bus to the beach?	**Há ônibus para a praia?**	Ah o-nee-boos pa-ra a **pry**-a
Is it a sandy/pebbly/rocky beach?	**A praia é de areia ou de pedras?**	A **pry**-a eh jé a **ray**-a o je pe-dras
Is it safe for swimming?	**Pode-se nadar sem perigo?**	Po-je-se na-**dar** se^n pe-**ree**-goo

Is it safe for small children?	**Não tem perigo para crianças?**	Nowⁿ tayⁿ pe-**ree**-goo **pa**-ra kree-aⁿ-sas
Is there a lifeguard?	**Há um salva-vidas?**	Ah ooⁿ **sal**-va-**vee**-das
Bathing prohibited	***Proibida entrada na água**	Proo-ee-**bee**-da eⁿ-**tra**-da na **a**-gwa
It's dangerous	***É perigoso**	Eh pe-ree-**go**-zoo
Is the tide rising/ falling?	**A maré está subindo/baixando?**	A ma-**reh** es-**ta** soo-**bee**ⁿ-doo/by-**sha**ⁿ-doo
I'd like to hire a cabin for . . .	**Quero alugar uma barraca . . .**	Ke-roo a-loo-**gar oo**-ma ba-**ha**-ka
the day	**para todo o dia**	**pa**-ra **to**-do oo **jee**-a
the morning	**pela manhã**	**pe**-la ma-**nya**ⁿ
two hours	**por duas horas**	poor **doo**-as **o**-ras
I'd like to hire a deckchair/sunshade	**Podemos alugar uma cadeira/um guarda-sol?**	Po-**de**-moos a-loo-gar-**oo**-ma ka-**day**-ra/ ooⁿ **gwar**-da-sow
Where can I buy . . .	**Onde posso comprar . . .**	Oⁿ-je **pos**-soo koⁿ-**prar**
a bucket and spade?	**um balde e pá?**	ooⁿ **baw**-je e pah
flippers?	**pés-de-pato?**	pehs-je-**pa**-too
a snorkel?	**um snorkel?**	ooⁿ snorkel
ball	**a bola**	**bo**-la
beach bag	**a bolsa de praia**	**bol**-sa je **pry**-a
boat	**o barco**	**bar**-koo

motor	a motor	a mo-tor
pedal	a pedais	a pe-da-ees
rowing	a remo	a heh-moo
sailing	à vela	ah ve-la
crab	o caranguejo	ka-ran-gay-zhoo
first aid	primeiros socorros	pree-may-ee-roos soo-ko-hoos
jellyfish	a medusa/a água-viva	me-doo-za/a-gwa-vee-va
lifeguard	o salva-vidas	sal-va-vee-das
lifejacket	o colete salva-vidas	ko-le-te sal-va-vee-das
lighthouse	o farol	fa-rol
outboard motor	o barco com motor de popa	bar-koo ko^m mo tor je po-pa
rock	a rocha	ho sha
rockpool	a piscina rochosa	pee-see-na ho-sho za
sand	a areia	a-ray-a
sandbank	o banco de areia	ba^n-koo je a ray-a
sandcastle	o castelo de areia	kas-te-loo je a-ray-a
shell	a concha	ko^n-sha
suncream	o protetor solar	pro-te-tor so-lar
sunglasses	os óculos de sol	oh-koo-loos je sow
sunshade	o guarda-sol	gwar-da-sow
swimming trunks	os calções de banho	kal-soy^{n}s je ba-nyoo

swimsuit	o maiô de banho	ma-**yo** je **ba**-nyoo
towel	a toalha	to-**a**-lya
wave	a onda	o^n-da

Swimming

Is there an indoor/outdoor swimming pool?	Há uma piscina coberta/ao ar livre?	Ah **oo**-ma pee-**see**-na ko-**ber**-ta/a-oo ahr **lee**-vre
Is it heated?	É aquecida?	Eh a-ke-**see**-da
Is the water cold?	A água está fria?	A **a**-gwa es-**ta free**-a
It's warm	Está morna	Es-**ta mor**-na
Is it fresh or salt water?	É água doce ou salgada?	Eh a-gwa **do**-se o sal-**ga**-da
Can one swim in the lake/river?	Pode-se nadar no lago/rio?	**Po**-je-se na-**dar** noo **la**-goo/**hee**-oo
There's a strong current here	*A corrente aqui é forte	A ko-**he**^{n}-te a-**kee** eh **for**-te
Are you a strong swimmer?	*Você nada bem?	**Vo**-seh **na**-da be^n
Is it deep?	É fundo?	Eh **foo**^{n}-doo
Are there showers?	Há chuveiros?	Ah shoo-**vey**-roos
No lifeguard on duty	*Não há salva-vidas de plantão	Now^n ah **sal**-va-**vee**-das je pla^n-**tow**^{n}
armbands	as boias de braço	**boy**-as je **bra**-soo

| goggles | os óculos de natação | o-koo-loos je na-ta-sow[n] |
| rubber ring | a boia circular | boy-a seer-koo-lar |

Watersports

Can we water ski here?	Podemos fazer esqui aquático aqui	Po-de-mos fa-zer es-kee a-kwa-tee-koo a-kee
I've never waterskied before	Nunca fiz esqui aquático	Noo[n]-ka fees es-kee a-kwa-tee-koo
Can I rent/borrow a wetsuit?	Posso alugar/pedir emprestada uma roupa de neoprene?	Pos-soo a-loo-gar/pe-jeer e[n]-pres-ta-da oo-ma ho-pa je ne-o-pre-ne
Should I wear a life jacket?	Devo usar colete salva-vidas?	De-voo oo-zar ko-le-te sal-va-vee-das
Can I hire ...	Posso alugar ...	Pos-soo a-loo-gar
diving equipment?	equipamento de mergulho?	e-kee-pa-me[n]-too je mer-goo-lyo
a jet ski?	um jet ski?	oo[n] zhet-skee
a motor boat?	um barco a motor?	oo[n] bar-koo a mo-tor
a rowing boat?	um barco a remo?	oo[n] bar-koo a hay-moo
a sailing boat?	um barco à vela	oo[n] bar-koo ah ve-la
a surf board?	uma prancha de surf?	oo-ma pra[n]-sha je surf
waterskis?	um esqui aquático?	oo[n] es-kee a-kwa-tee-koo
a windsurfer?	uma prancha de windsurf?	oo-ma pra[n]-sha je windsurf

Do you have a course on windsurfing for beginners?	Vocês tem um curso de windsurf para iniciantes?	Vo-sehs te^n oo^n koor-soo je windsurf pa-ra ee-nee-see-a^n-tes
Is there a map of the river?	Há um mapa do rio?	Ah oo^n ma-pa doo hee-oo
Are there many locks to pass?	Tem que passar por muitas comportas?	Te^n ke pas-sar poor mwee-tas ko^n-por-tas
Can I get fuel here?	Posso abastecer aqui?	Pos-soo a-bas-te-ser a-kee
Where's the harbour?	Onde é o porto?	O^n-je eh oo por-too
Can we go out in a fishing boat?	Podemos sair num barco de pesca?	Po-de-moos sa-eer noo^n bar-koo je pes-ka
What does it cost by the hour?	Quanto custa por hora?	Kwa^n-too koos-ta poor o-ra

Walking[1]

I'd like a map of the area showing walking trails	Gostaria de um mapa da área que mostre as trilhas de caminhadas	Gos-ta-ree-a je oo^n ma-pa da ah-ree-a ke mos-tre as tree-lyas je ka-mee-nya-das
Can we walk?	Podemos ir a pé?	Po-de-moos eer a peh
How long is the walk to...?	Quanto devemos caminhar até...	Kwa^n-too de-ve-mos ka-mee-nyar a-teh
It's an hour's walk to...	*É uma hora de caminhada até...	Eh oo-ma o-ra je ka-mee-nya-da a-teh
How far is the next town?	A que distância fica a próxima cidade?	A ke jees-ta^n-see-a fee-ka a pro-see-ma see-da-je

1. See also Directions (p. 48).

Which way is ...	Qual é o caminho para...	Kwal eh oo ka-**mee**-nyo **pa**-ra
the lake?	o lago?	oo la-goo
the nature reserve?	a reserva natural?	a he-**ser**-va na-too-**raw**
the waterfall?	a cachoeira?	a ka-shoo-**ey**-ra
Is there a scenic walk to ...?	Há uma rota cénica para ...?	Ah oo-ma **ho**-ta se-nee-ka **pa**-ra
Is it steep/far/difficult?	É íngreme/longe/difícil?	Eh een-gre-me/lon-zhe/jee-fee-seew
Is there a footpath to ...?	Há um caminho público para ...?	Ah oon ka-**mee**-nyoo poo-blee-koo **pa**-ra
Is there a short cut?	Há um atalho?	Ah oon a-**ta**-lyoo
Is there a bridge across the stream/river?	Há uma ponte por cima da corrente/rio?	Ah oo-ma pon-te poor see-ma da koo-**hayn**-te/**hee**-oo
Can you give me a lift to ...?	Pode me dar uma carona até ...?	Po-je me dar oo-ma ka-ro-na a-teh

Spectator Sports and Indoor Games

We want to go to a football match/tennis tournament	Queremos ir a uma partida de futebol/a um torneio de ténis	Kerray moos eer a oo-ma par-tee-da je foo-te-bow/a oon toor-**nay**-oo je te-nees
Where is the stadium?	Onde fica o estádio?	On-je fee-ka oo es-ta-jee-oo

Are there any seats left in the grandstand?	**Há lugares na arquibancada?**	Ah loo-**ga**-res na ar-kee-ba^n-**ka**-da
Can you get us tickets?	**Pode conseguir ingressos?**	Po-je ko^n-se-**gheer** ee^n-**gres**-soos
How much are the cheapest seats?	**Quanto custam os assentos mais baratos?**	**Kwa**^{n}-too **koos**-ta^n oos as-**se**^{n}-tos **ma**-ees ba-ra-toos
Who's playing?	**Quem joga?**	Kay^n **zho**-ga
When does it start?	**A que horas começa?**	A ke **o**-ras ko-**me**-sa
What is the score?	**Qual é o resultado?**	Kwal eh oo he-zool-**ta**-doo
Who's winning?	**Quem está ganhando?**	Kay^n es-**ta** ga-**nya**^{n}-doo
Where's the race course?	**Onde fica a pista de corrida?**	O^n-je **fee**-ka a **pees**-ta je ko-**hee**-da
When's the next meeting?	**Quando é o próximo encontro?**	**Kwa**^{n}-doo eh oo **pro**-see-moo e^n-**ko**^{n}-tro
Which is the favourite?	**Qual é o favorito?**	Kwal eh oo fa-vo-**ree**-too
What are the odds?	**Qual é a probabilidade?**	Kwal eh a pro-ba-bee-lee-**da**-je
Where can I place a bet?	**Onde posso apostar?**	O^n-je **pos**-soo a-pos-**tar**
Do you play cards?	**Sabe jogar baralho?**	**Sa**-be zho-**gar** ba-**ra**-lyo
Would you like a game of chess?	**Quer jogar xadrez?**	Ker zho-**gar** **sha**-drayz

TRAVELLING WITH CHILDREN

Key Phrases

Are children allowed?	É permitida a entrada de crianças?	Eh per-mee-tee-da a e^n-tra-da je kree-a^n-sas
Is there a lower price for children?	Há descontos para crianças?	Ah jes-ko^n-toos pa-ra kree-a^n-sas
Are there any organized activities for children?	Há atividades organizadas para crianças?	Ah a-tee-vee-da-jes or-ga-nee za-das pa-ra kree-a^n-sas
Can you put a child's bed/cot in our room?	Pode pôr uma cama/berço no quarto?	Po-je por oo-ma ka-ma/bayr-soo noo kwar-too
Where can I feed/change my baby?	Onde posso dar comida/trocar o meu bebé?	O^n-je pos-soo dar ku-mee-da/tro-kar oo may-oo be-be
My son/daughter is missing	O meu filho/a minha filha se perdeu	Oo may-oo fee-lyoo/a mee-nya fee-lya se per de-oo

Out and About[1]

Is there . . .	Há . . .	Ah
an amusement park?	**um parque de diversões?**	oo^n **par**-ke je jee-ver-**soy**^n s
a children's swimming pool?	**uma piscina para crianças?**	**oo**-ma pee-**see**-na **pa**-ra kree-**a**^n-sas
a games room?	**Uma sala/um salão de jogos?**	**oo**-ma **sa**-la/oo^n sa-**low**^n je **zho**-goos
a toyshop?	**uma loja de brinquedos?**	**oo**-ma **lo**-zha je bree^n-**kay**-doos
a park?	**um parque?**	oo^n **par**-ke
a playground?	**um playground/ um parquinho?**	oo^n playground/oo^n par-**kee**-nyo
a zoo?	**um zoológico?**	oo^n zo-o-**lo**-zhee-koo
Where is the aquarium?	**Onde fica o aquário?**	**O**^n-je **fee**-ka oo a-**kwa**-ree-oo
Is the beach safe for children?	**A praia é segura para crianças?**	A **pry**-a eh se-**goo**-roo **pa**-ra kree-**a**^n-sas
Can we hire a canoe/ paddle boat?	**Podemos alugar uma canoa/um pedalinho?**	Po-**de**-moos a-loo-**gar oo**-ma ka-**no**-a/oo^n pe-da-**lee**-nyo
Are there snorkelling/ riding lessons for children?	**Oferecem aulas de mergulho com snorkel/equitação para crianças?**	O-fe-**re**-se^n **ow**-las je mer-**goo**-lyo ko^n snorkel/ e-kee-ta-**sow**^n **pa**-ra kree-**a**^n-sas
I'd like . . .	**Queria . . .**	Ke-**ree**-a

1. See also At the Beach (p. 199).

a doll	uma boneca	oo-ma boo-ne-ka
roller skates	patins	pa-tee^{n}s
some playing cards	um baralho	oo^n ba-ra-lyo
He has lost his toy	Ele perdeu o brinquedo	E-le per-de-oo oo bree^n-kay-doo
I'm sorry if they have bothered you	Desculpe se eles o incomodaram	Des-kool-pe se ay-les oo ee^n-ko-mo-da-ra^n

Everyday Needs

Can you put a child's bed/cot in our room?	Pode pôr uma cama/ berço no quarto?	Po-je por oo-ma`ka-ma/bayr-soo noo kwar-too
Can you give us adjoining rooms?	Pode nos dar quartos conjugados?	Po-je noos dar kwar-toos ko^n-zhoo-ga-dos
Does the hotel have a babysitting service?	O hotel tem serviço de babá?	Oo o-tew te^n ser-vee-soo je ba-ba
Can you find me a babysitter?	Pode me arranjar uma babá?	Po-je me a-ha^n zhar oo-ma ba-ba
We shall be out for a couple of hours	Vamos sair por algumas horas	Va-moos sa-eer poor al goo mas o-ras
We shall be back at . . .	Nós voltamos às . . .	Nohs vol-ta-moos ahs
You can reach me at this number	Você pode entrar em contato comigo neste número	Vo-seh po-je e^n-trar e^n ko^n-ta-too ko-mee-goo nes-le noo-me-róõ

This is my mobile (cell) number	Este é o meu número de celular	Es-te eh oo me-oo noo-me-roo je se-loo-lar
Is there a children's menu?	Há um menu infantil?	Ah oo^n me-noo ee^n-fa^n-teew
Do you have half portions for children?	Tem meias porções para crianças?	Te^n may-as por-soy^n s pa-ra kree-a^n-sas
Have you got a high chair?	Tem uma cadeira de alimentação?	Te^n oo-ma ka-dey-ra je a-lee-me^n-ta-sow^n
Where can I feed/ change my baby?	Onde posso dar comida /trocar o meu bebê?	O^n-je pos-soo dar ko-mee-da/tro-kar oo may-oo be-be
Can you heat this bottle for me?	Pode aquecer esta mamadeira?	Po-je a-ke-sayr es-ta ma-ma-day-ra
I need ...	Preciso de ...	Pre-see-zoo je
baby food	comida de bebé	ko-mee-da je be-be
baby wipes	lenços umedecidos	le^n-sos oo-me-de-see-dos
a bib	um babador	oo^n ba-ba-dor
disposable nappies	fraldas descartáveis	fraw-das jes-kar-ta-vays
a feeding bottle	uma mamadeira	oo-ma ma-ma-day-ra

Health and Emergencies[1]

| My daughter suffers from travel sickness | A minha filha sofre de enjôo durante viagens | A mee-nya fee-lya so-kre je e^n-zhoo doo-ra^n-te vee-a-zhe^{n}s |
| She has hurt herself | Ela se machucou | E-la se ma-shoo-ko |

1. See also Doctor (p. 132).

My son is ill	Meu filho está doente	Me-oo fee-lyoo es-ta doo-ay^n-te
He is allergic to ...	Ele é alérgico a ...	E-le eh a-ler-zhee-koo a
My son/daughter is missing	O meu filho/a minha filha desapareceu	Oo me-oo fee-lyoo/a mee-nya fee-lya de-za-pa-re-sew
He/she is ... years old	Ele/ela tem ... anos	E-le/e-la te^n... a-nos
He/she is wearing ...	Ele/ela está vestindo ...	E-le/e-la es-ta ves-tee^n-doo

WORK[1]

I'm here on business	**Venho a negócios**	**Vay**ⁿ-nyoo a ne-**go**-see-oos
Where is the conference centre/ exhibition centre?	**Onde fica o centro de convenções/ exibições?**	Oⁿ-je **fee**-ka oo **se**ⁿ-troo je koⁿ-veⁿ-**soy**ⁿs/e-zee-bee-**soy**ⁿs
I'm here for the … trade fair	**Eu estou aqui para a feira de …**	**Ay**-oo es-**to** a-**kee** pa-ra a **fey**-ra je
I'm here for a conference/seminar/ congress	**Estou aqui para uma conferência/ um seminário/um congresso**	Es-**to** a-**kee** pa-ra **oo**-ma koⁿ-fe-**re**ⁿ-see-a/ooⁿ se-mee-**na**-ree-oo/ooⁿ koⁿ-**gres**-soo
This is my colleague	**Este é o meu colega**	Es-te eh oo **may**-oo ko-**le**-ga
I have a meeting with …	**Tenho uma reunião com …**	**Te**ⁿ-nyoo **oo**-ma he-oo-nee-**ow**ⁿ koⁿ
Here is my card	**Aqui está o meu cartão**	A-**kee** es-**ta** oo **may**-oo kar-**tow**ⁿ
Can you provide an interpreter?	**Pode arranjar um intérprete?**	**Po**-je a-haⁿ-**zhar** ooⁿ eeⁿ-**ter**-pre-te

1. See also Telephones, mobiles and SMS (p. 81).

TIME AND DATES[1]

Telling the Time

What time is it?	**Que horas são?**	Ke o-ras sowⁿ
It's . . . one o'clock	**É . . . uma hora**	Eh **oo**-ma o-ra
two o'clock	**São duas horas**	Sowⁿ **doo**-as o-ras
five past eight[1]	**oito e cinco**	o-ee-too e seeⁿ-koo
quarter past five	**cinco e um quarto**	seeⁿ-koo e ooⁿ **kwar**-too
twenty-five past eight	**oito e vinte cinco**	o-ee-too e veeⁿ-te seeⁿ-koo
half past four	**quatro e meia**	kwa-troo e **may**-a
twenty to three	**vinte para as três**	veeⁿ-te pa-ra as trays
quarter to ten	**quinze para as dez**	keeⁿ-ze pa-ra as des
hour	**a hora**	o-ra
minute	**o minuto**	mee-noo-too
second	**o segundo**	se-gooⁿ-doo
It's early/late	**É cedo/tarde**	Eh say-doo/tar-je
My watch is slow/fast	**O meu relógio está atrasado/adiantado**	Oo may-oo he-lo-zhee-oo es-ta a-tra-za-doo/a-jee-aⁿ-**ta**-doo

| The clock has stopped | **O relógio parou** | Oo he-**lo**-zhee-oo pa-**ro** |
| Sorry I'm late | **Desculpe o atraso** | Des-**kool**-pe oo a-**tra**-zoo |

Days of the Week

Monday	**a segunda-feira**	se-**goo**ⁿ-da-**fay**-ra
Tuesday	**a terça-feira**	**tair**-sa-**fay**-ra
Wednesday	**a quarta-feira**	**kwar**-ta-**fay**-ra
Thursday	**a quinta-feira**	**kee**ⁿ-ta-**fay**-ra
Friday	**a sexta-feira**	**says**-ta-**fay**-ra
Saturday	**o sábado**	**sa**-ba-doo
Sunday	**o domingo**	doo-**mee**ⁿ-goo

Months of the Year

January	**Janeiro**	Zha-**nay**-roo
February	**Fevereiro**	Fe-ve-**ray**-roo
March	**Março**	**Mar**-soo
April	**Abril**	A-**breew**
May	**Maio**	**My**-oo
June	**Junho**	**Zhoo**-nyoo
July	**Julho**	**Zhoo**-lyoo
August	**Agosto**	A-**gos**-too

September	**Setembro**	Se-te[n]-broo
October	**Outubro**	O-**too**-broo
November	**Novembro**	No-**ve**[n]-broo
December	**Dezembro**	De-**ze**[n]-broo

Seasons

spring	a primavera	pree-ma-**vai**-ra
summer	o verão	ve **row**[n]
autumn	o outono	o-to-noo
winter	o inverno	ee[n]-**vair**-noo

Periods of time

morning	a manhã	**ma**-nya[n]
this morning	esta manhã	es-ta ma-nya[n]
in the morning	pela manhã	pe-la ma-nya[n]
midday, noon	o meio-dia	may-oo-jee-a
at noon	ao meio-dia	ow may-oo-jee-a
afternoon	a tarde	**tar**-je
tomorrow afternoon	amanhã à tarde	a-ma-nya[n] ah tar-je
evening	o anoitecer/início da noite	a-no-ee-te-sair/ee-nee-syo da no-ee-te
night	a noite	a no-ee-te

midnight	a meia-noite	may-a-no-ee-te
tonight	hoje à noite	o-zhe ah no-ee-te
last night	ontem à noite	on-ten ah no-ee-te
day	o dia	jee-a
today	hoje	o-zhe
by day	de dia	je jee-a
yesterday	ontem	on-ten
day before yesterday	anteontem	an-te-on-ten
two days ago	dois dias atrás	do-ees jee-as a-tras
tomorrow	amanhã	a-ma-nyan
day after tomorrow	depois de amanhã	de-po-ees je a-ma-nyan
in ten days' time	dentro de dez dias	den-troo je dez jee-as
on Tuesday	na terça-feira	na tair-sa-fay-ra
on Sundays	aos domingos	a-os doo-meen-goos
week	a semana	se-ma-na
weekend	o fim de semana	feen je se-ma-na
weekdays	o dia de semana	jee-a je se-ma-na
working day	o dia útil	jee-a oo-teew
every week	todas as semanas	to-das as se-ma-nas
once a week	uma vez por semana	oo-ma vez por se-ma-nas
fortnight	a quinzena	keen-zay-na
month	o mês	mes
in March	em março	en mar-soo

since June	desde junho	des-je zhoo-nyoo
year	o ano	a-no
this year	este ano	ays-te a-noo
last year	o ano passado	oo a-noo pas-sa-doo
next year	o próximo ano	oo pro-see-moo a-noo
in spring	na primavera	na pree-ma-vair-a
during the summer	durante o verão	doo-ra^n-te oo ve-row^n
sunrise	o nascer do sol	na-sayr doo sow
dawn	a madrugada	ma-droo-ga-da
sunset	o pôr do sol	por doo sow
dusk, twilight	o crepúsculo	kre-poos-koo-lo

Dates

What's the date?	Que dia é hoje?	Ko jee-a eh n-zhe
It's 9th December	Hoje é dia nove de dezembro	O-zhe eh jee-a no-ve je de-zay^n-broo
We're leaving on 5th January	Partimos dia cinco de janeiro	Par-tee-moos jee-a seen-koo je zha-nay-roo
We got here on 27th July	Chegámos dia vinte e sete de julho	She-ga-moos jee-a veen-te e se-te je zhoo-lyoo

Public Holidays

Brazil

1 January (New Year's Day)	O Dia de Ano Novo
21 April (Tiradentes Day)	O Dia de Tiradentes
1 May (Labour Day)	O Dia do Trabalho
7 September (Independence Day)	O Dia da Independência
12 October (Our Lady of Aparecida)	Nossa Senhora Aparecida
2 November (All Souls' Day)	O Dia de Finados
15 November (Republic Day)	A Proclamação da República
25 December (Christmas Day)	O Natal

Portugal

1 January (New Year's Day)	O Dia de Ano Novo
25 April (Freedom Day)	O Dia da Liberdade
1 May (Labour Day)	O Primeiro de Maio/Dia do Trabalhador
10 June (Portuguese National Day)	O Dia de Camões/Portugal
Corpus Christi (Thursday of 8th week after Easter)	O Dia do Corpo de Deus
15 August (The Assumption)	O Dia da Assunção
5 October (Republic Day)	O Dia da República
1 November (All Saints' Day)	O Dia de Todos os Santos

1 December (Restauration of Independence)	O Dia da Restauração da Independência
8 December (Immaculate Conception)	O Dia da Imaculada Concepção
25 December (Christmas)	O Natal

Apart from these holidays every town and village celebrates its own holiday, which usually coincides with the day of its patron saint. Although not official holidays, many businesses, shops, etc. are closed on Shrove Tuesday, Good Friday and Maundy Thursday.

WEATHER

What is the weather forecast?	**Qual é a previsão do tempo?**	Kwal eh a pre-vee-**zow**ⁿ doo **te**ⁿ-poo
What is the temperature?	**Qual é a temperatura?**	Kwal eh a teⁿ-pe-ra-**too**-ra
It's going to be hot/ cold today	**Vai estar calor/frio hoje**	Vy es-**tar** ka-**lor**/**free**-oo **o**-zhe
It's ...	**Está ...**	Es-**ta**
cloudy	**nublado**	noo-**bla**-do
misty/foggy	**nebuloso**	ne-boo-**lo**-zoo
sunny	**ensolarado**	eⁿ-so-la-**ra**-do
windy	**com muito vento**	koⁿ **mwee**-to **ve**ⁿ-to
The mist will clear later	**A neblina vai clarear mais tarde**	A ne-**blee**-na vy kla-ree-ar **ma**-ees **tar**-je
Will it be fine tomorrow?	**Estará bom amanhã?**	Es-ta-**ra** boⁿ a-ma-**nya**ⁿ
What lovely/awful weather	**Que tempo bom/ ruim**	Ke **te**ⁿ-poo boⁿ/rwee**ⁿ**
Do you think it will rain/snow?	**Você acha que vai chover/nevar?**	**Vo**-seh **a**-sha ke vy sho-**ver**/ne-**var**
frost	**a geada**	zhe-**a**-da
hail	**o granizo**	gra-**nee**-zoo

humid *adj*	**úmido**	**oo**-mee-doo
ice	**o gelo**	**zhe**-lo
storm	**a tempestade/o temporal**	te^n-pe-**sta**-je/te^n-po-**ral**

OPPOSITES

before/after	**antes/depois**	a^n-tes/de-**po**-ees
early/late	**cedo/tarde**	**say**-doo/**tar**-je
first/last	**primeiro/último**	pree-**may**-roo/**ool**-tee-moo
now/later	**agora/mais tarde**	a-**go**-ra/**ma**-ees **tar**-je
far/near	**longe/perto**	lo^n-zhe/**per**-too
here/there	**aqui/ali**	a-**kee**/a-**lee**
in/out	**entrada/saída**	e^n-**tra**-da/sa-**ee**-da
inside/outside	**dentro/fora**	de^n-troo/**fo**-ra
under/over	**debaixo/em cima**	de-**bay**-shoo/ay^n **see**-ma
big, large/small	**grande/pequeno**	gra^n-de/pe-**kay**-noo
deep/shallow	**fundo/raso**	foo^n-doo/**ra**-soo
empty/full	**vazio/cheio**	va-**zee**-oo/**shay**-oo
fat/lean	**gordo/magro**	**gor**-doo/**ma**-groo
heavy/light	**pesado/leve**	pe-**za**-doo/**le**-ve
high/low	**alto/baixo**	**al**-too/**bay**-shoo
long, tall/short	**comprido, alto/ baixo**	ko^n-**pree**-doo, **al**-too/**bay**-shoo
narrow/wide	**estreito/largo**	es-**tray**-too/**lar**-goo

thick/thin	grosso/fino	gros-soo/fee-noo
least/most	o menos/o mais	oo me^n-noos/oo ma-ees
many/few	muitos/poucos	mwee-toos/po-koos
more/less	mais/menos	ma-ees/me-noos
much/little	muito/pouco	mwee-too/po-koo
beautiful/ugly	bonito, belo/feio	boo-nee-too, be-loo/fay-oo
better/worse	melhor/pior	me-lyor/pee-or
cheap/dear	barato/caro	ha-ra-too/ka-roo
clean/dirty	limpo/sujo	lee^n-poo/soo-zhoo
cold/hot, warm	frio/quente, morno	free-oo/ke^n-te, mor noo
easy/difficult	fácil/difícil	fa-seew/jee-fee-seew
fresh/stale	fresco/rançoso, estragado	frays-koo/ra^n-so-zoo, es-tra-ga-doo
good/bad	bom/mau	bo^n/ma-oo
new, young/old	novo, jovem/velho	no voo, zho-vay^n/ve-lyoo
nice/nasty	bonito, agradável, simpático/desagradável, antipático	boo-nee-too, a-gra-da-vew, see^n-pa-tee koo/de-za-gra-da-vew, a^n-lee-pa-tee-koo
open/closed, shut	aberto/fechado, encerrado	a-ber-too/te-sha-doo, e^n-se-ha-doo
quick/slow	rápido/lento	ha-pee-doo/le^n-too

quiet/noisy	calado, silencioso/ barulhento, ruidoso	ka-la-doo, see-le^n-see- o-zoo/ba-roo-lye^n-too, rwee-do-zoo
right/left	direita/esquerda	jee-rey-ta/es-ker-da
right/wrong	certo/errado	sayr-too/ay-ha-doo
sharp/blunt	agudo, afiado/ brusco, embotado	a-goo-doo, a-fee-a- doo/broo-skoo, e^n-boo- ta-doo

NUMBERS

Cardinal

0	zero	**zeh**-roo
1	um, uma	oo^n, **oo**-ma
2	dois, duas	**do**-ees, **doo**-as
3	três	trays
4	quatro	**kwa**-troo
5	cinco	**see**^{n}-koo
6	seis	**say**-ees
7	sete	**se**-te
8	oito	o-**ee**-to
9	nove	**no**-ve
10	dez	des
11	onze	**o**^{n}-ze
12	doze	**do**-ze
13	treze	**tray**-ze
14	catorze	ka-**tor**-ze
15	quinze	**kee**^{n}-ze
16	dezesseis	de-ze-**sais**
17	dezessete	de-ze-**se**-te

18	dezoito	de-**zoy**-too
19	dezenove	de-ze-**no**-ve
20	vinte	**vee**^{n}-te
21	vinte e um, uma	**vee**^{n}-te ee oo^n, **oo**-ma
22	vinte e dois, duas	**vee**^{n}-te ee **do**-ees, **doo**-as
30	trinta	**tree**^{n}-ta
31	trinta e um, uma	**tree**^{n}-ta ee oo^n, **oo**-ma
32	trinta e dois, duas	**tree**^{n}-ta ee **do**-ees, **doo**-as
40	quarenta	kwa-**re**^{n}-ta
41	quarenta e um, uma	kwa-**re**^{n}-ta ee oo^n, **oo**-ma
50	cinquenta	see^n-**kwen**-ta
51	cinquenta e um, uma	see^n-**kwen**-ta ee oo^n, **oo**-ma
60	sessenta	se-**se**^{n}-ta
61	sessenta e um, uma	se-**se**^{n}-ta ee oo^n, **oo**-ma
70	setenta	se-**te**^{n}-ta
71	setenta e um, uma	se-**te**^{n}-ta ee oo^n, **oo**-ma
80	oitenta	oy-**te**^{n}-ta
81	oitenta e um, uma	oy-**te**^{n}-ta ee oo^n, **oo**-ma
90	noventa	no-**ve**^{n}-ta
91	noventa e um, uma	no-**ve**^{n}-ta ee oo^n, **oo**-ma
100	cem	se^n
101	cento e um, uma	**se**^{n}-too ee oo^n, **oo**-ma

200	duzentos, duzentas	doo-ze^n-toos, doo-ze^n-tas
500	quinhentos, quinhentas	kee-nye^n-tos, kee-nye^n-tas
700	setecentos, setecentas	se-te-se^n-tos, se-te-se^n-tas
1,000	mil	meew
2,000	dois mil	do-ees meew
1,000,000	um milhão	oo^n mee-lyow^n

Ordinal

1st	primeiro, -a	pree-may roo
2nd	segundo, -a	se-goo^n-doo
3rd	terceiro, -a	ter-say-roo
4th	quarto, -a	kwar-too
5th	quinto, -a	kee^n-too
6th	sexto, -a	says-too
7th	sétimo, -a	se-chee-moo
8th	oitavo, -a	oy-ta-voo
9th	nono, -a	no-noo
10th	décimo, -a	de-see-moo
11th	décimo-primeiro	de-see-moo pree-may-roo
12th	décimo-segundo	de-see-moo se-goo^n-doo
13th	décimo-terceiro	de-see-moo ter-say-roo

14th	décimo-quarto	de-see-moo kwar-too
15th	décimo-quinto	de-see-moo keeⁿ-too
16th	décimo-sexto	de-see-moo says-too
17th	décimo-sétimo	de-see-moo se-chee-moo
18th	décimo-oitavo	de-see-moo oy-ta-voo
19th	décimo-nono	de-see-moo no-noo
20th	vigésimo	vee-zhe-zee-moo
21st	vigésimo-primeiro	vee-zhe-zee-moo pree-may-roo
30th	trigésimo	tree-zhe-zee-moo
40th	quadragésimo	kwa-dra-zhe-zee-moo
50th	quinquagésimo	keeⁿ-kwa-zhe-zee-moo
60th	sexagésimo	say-sa-zhe-zee-moo
70th	setuagésimo	se-too-a-zhe-zee-moo
80th	octogésimo	ok-to-zhe-zee-moo
90th	nonagésimo	no-na-zhe-zee-moo
100th	centésimo	seⁿ-te-zee-moo
1,000th	milésimo	mee-le-zee-moo
half	meio, -a/metade	may-oo/me-ta-je
quarter	um quarto	ooⁿ kwar-too
three-quarters	três quartos	trays kwar-toos
a third	um terço	ooⁿ ter-soo
two-thirds	dois terços	do-ees ter-soos

WEIGHTS AND MEASURES

Distance

kilometres – miles

km	*miles or km*	miles		km	*miles or km*	miles
1.6	1	0.6		14.5	9	5.6
3.2	2	1.2		16.1	10	6.2
4.8	3	1.9		32.2	20	12.4
6.4	4	2.5		40.2	25	15.3
8	5	3.1		80.5	50	31.1
9.7	6	3.7		160.9	100	62.1
11.3	7	4.4		402.3	250	155.3
12.9	8	5		804.7	500	310.7

A rough way to convert from miles to kilometres: divide by 5 and multiply by 8; from kilometres to miles: divide by 8 and multiply by 5.

Length and Height

centimetres – inches

cm	*inches or cm*	inches	cm	*inches or cm*	inches
2.5	1	0.4	17.8	7	2.7
5.1	2	0.8	20.0	8	3.2
7.6	3	1.2	22.9	9	3.5
10.2	4	1.6	25.4	10	3.9
12.7	5	2.0	50.8	20	7.9
15.2	6	2.4	127.0	50	19.7

A rough way to convert from inches to centimetres: divide by 2 and multiply by 5; from centimetres to inches: divide by 5 and multiply by 2.

metres – feet

m	*ft or m*	ft	m	*ft or m*	ft
0.3	1	3.3	2.4	8	26.3
0.6	2	6.6	2.7	9	29.5
0.9	3	9.8	3.0	10	32.8
1.2	4	13.1	6.1	20	65.6
1.5	5	16.4	15.2	50	164.0
1.8	6	19.7	30.5	100	328.1
2.1	7	23.0	304.8	1,000	3,280

A rough way to convert from feet to metres: divide by 10 and multiply by 3; from metres to feet: divide by 3 and multiply by 10.

metres – yards

m	*yds or m*	yds	m	*yds or m*	yds
0.9	1	1.1	7.3	8	8.8
1.8	2	2.2	8.2	9	9.8
2.7	3	3.3	9.1	10	10.9
3.7	4	4.4	18.3	20	21.9
4.6	5	5.5	45.7	50	54.7
5.5	6	6.6	91.4	100	109.4
6.4	7	77	457.2	500	546.8

A rough way to convert from yards to metres: subtract
10 per cent from the number of yards; from metres to yards:
add 10 per cent to the number of metres.

Liquid Measures

litres   gallons

litres	*galls or litres*	galls	litres	*galls or litres*	galls
4.6	1	0.2	36.4	8	1.8
9.1	2	0.4	40.9	9	2.0
13.6	3	0.7	45.5	10	2.2
18.2	4	0.9	90.9	20	4.4
22.7	5	1.1	136.4	30	6.6
27.3	6	1.3	181.8	40	8.8
31.8	7	1.5	227.3	50	11.0

1 pint = 0.6 litre; 1 litre = 1.8 pints

A rough way to convert from gallons to litres: divide by 2 and multiply by 9; from litres to gallons: divide by 9 and multiply by 2.

Temperature

Centigrade (°C)	Fahrenheit (°F)
°C	°F
−10	14
−5	23
0	32
5	41
10	50
15	59
20	68
25	77
30	86
35	95
37	98.4
38	100.5
39	102
40	104
100	180

To convert °F to °C: deduct 32, divide by 9, multiply by 5; to convert °C to °F: divide by 5, multiply by 9 and add 32.

Weight

kilograms – pounds

kg	*lb or kg*	lb	kg	*lb or kg*	lb
0.5	*1*	2.2	3.2	*7*	15.4
0.9	*2*	4.4	3.6	*8*	17.6
1.4	*3*	6.6	4.1	*9*	19.8
1.8	*4*	8.8	4.5	*10*	22.1
2.3	*5*	11.0	9.1	*20*	44.1
2.7	*6*	13.2	22.7	*50*	110.2

A rough way to convert from pounds to kilograms: divide
by 11 and multiply by 5; from kilograms to pounds: divide by 5
and multiply by 11.

grams – ounces

grams	oz	oz	grams
100	3.5	2	57.1
250	8.8	4	114.3
500	17.6	8	228.6
1,000 (1kg)	35.0	16 (1lb)	457.2

BASIC GRAMMAR

Nouns

Nouns in Portuguese are either masculine or feminine.

Nouns denoting males, and most nouns ending in **-o** (except **-ção -são**) are masculine.

e.g. **o tio** – uncle; **o castelo** – castle.

Nouns denoting females, and those ending in **-a, -ção, -são, -dade** are feminine.

e.g. **a tia** – aunt; **a cidade** – city.

There are exceptions to these rules.

e.g. **o coração** – heart.

Plural

The plural is formed by adding **-s** if the word ends in a vowel.

Most words ending in a consonant add **-es** to form the plural.

e.g. **mulher** (woman) – **mulheres**; **luz** (light) – **luzes**.

As a general rule nouns ending in **-al** become **-ais** in the plural.

e.g. **metal** (metal) – **metais**; **material** (material) – **materiais**.

Nouns ending in **-ão** have varied forms in the plural.

e.g. **limão** (lemon) – **limões**; **instrução** (instruction) – **instruções**; but **pão** (bread) – **pães**; **cão** (dog) – **cães**.

Definite Article

o before a masculine singular noun	**o banco** (the bank)
os before a masculine plural noun	**os bancos**
a before a feminine singular noun	**a mulher** (the woman)
as before a feminine plural noun	**as mulheres**

Indefinite Article

um before a masculine singular noun	**um barco** (a ship)
uns before a masculine plural noun	**uns barcos** (some ships)
uma before a feminine singular noun	**uma cadeira** (a chair)
umas before a feminine plural noun	**umas cadeiras** (some chairs)

Adjectives

Adjectives agree in gender and number with the noun.

Those ending in **-o** change to **-a** in the feminine.

e.g. **fresco – fresca** (fresh, cool); **cansado** *of a man* – **cansada** *of a woman* (tired).

Those ending in **-e** and most of those ending in a consonant are the same in the masculine and the feminine.

e.g. **o castelo grande; a cadeira grande.**

The plural is formed by adding **-s** if the word ends in a vowel, and **-es** in most cases when it ends in a consonant.

e.g. **fresco – frescos; grande – grandes; inglês – ingleses.**

Adjectives ending in **-l** change the **-l** to **-is** or **-eis**.

e.g. **subtil – subtis** (subtle).

The comparative and superlative are formed by putting **mais** before the adjective.

um hotel barato	a cheap hotel
um hotel mais barato	a cheaper hotel
o hotel mais barato	the cheapest hotel

There are, however, exceptions to this rule; e.g. **grande** (big, great) becomes **maior** (bigger, greater).

Possessive Adjectives

	m s	m pl	f s
my	meu	meus	minha
your *fam.*	teu	teus	tua
his, hers	seu/dele	seus/deles	sua/dela
our	nosso	nossos	nossa
your *fam.*	vosso	vossos	vossa
their, your *polite*	seu	seus	sua

These adjectives agree with the thing possessed, e.g. **meu pai** (my father); **meus pais** (my parents); **minha casa** (my house), **minhas casas** (my houses); **vosso livro** (your book); **vossas cartas** (your letters).

Personal Pronouns

	subject	object
I	eu	me
you *fam.*	tu	te
you *polite*	você	o *m* and a *f*
he	ele	o
she	ela	a
we	nós	nos
you	vós	vos
they *m*	eles	os
they *f*	elas	as

In Brazil, the use of the two forms of 'you' (**você** and **tu**) depends on geographical regions. In order to show respect when addressing someone, Brazilians adopt '**senhor**' and '**senhora**'. In Brazil the pronoun **vós** and the possessive adjective **vosso** are no longer used.

In Portugal, when speaking to strangers always use the form **o senhor, a senhora** and **os senhores, as senhoras**, with the verb in the third person. **Tu** and **você** are used to close friends and to children.

Personal pronouns are usually omitted before the verb.

e.g. **vou** – I go; **vem** – he (or she) comes.

In Brazilian Portuguese, the direct and indirect object pronouns are usually placed before the verb. In European Portuguese they are usually placed after.

e.g. **o tenho** (Brazil) **tenho-o** (Portugal) – I have it.

Indirect object pronouns are the same as direct object pronouns except that **lhe** is used to mean to it, to him, to her, to you (*polite*), and **lhes** means to them, to you (*polite*). The third person reflexive pronoun is always **se**.

e.g. **dar-lhe** – to give to him, her; **dar-lhes** – to give to them.

If a direct and an indirect object pronoun are used together, the indirect one is placed first.

e.g. **damo-vo-lo** – we give it to you (**vos–o** becomes **vo-lo**).

Lhe and **lhes** combine with the direct object pronoun to give the forms **lho, lha, lhos, lhas.**

e.g. **dar-lho** – to give it to him, her, you (*polite*).

Demonstrative Pronouns

this one, that one

	m	f
this (*one*)	este	esta
these	estes	estas
that (*one*)	esse	essa
those	esses	essas
that (*one*) over there	aquele	aquela
those over there	aqueles	aquelas

They agree in gender and number with the nouns they represent.

e.g. *este é o meu bilhete* – this is my ticket.

quero *este* livro, *esse*, e *aquele* – I want this book, that one and that one over there.

The demonstrative adjectives have the same form as the pronouns.

Verbs

'To be' is translated by **ser** and **estar**.

When it is followed by a noun, or when it indicates an origin, or a permanent or inherent quality, **ser** is used.

a neve *é* fria e branca	snow is cold and white
sou Britânico	I am British
a Inglaterra *é* parte duma ilha	England is part of an island

When it indicates position or a temporary state, **estar** is used.

o carro *está* na rua principal	the car is in the main street
estamos no Brasil	we are in Brazil

Present tense of **ser** and **estar**

	ser	estar
I am	sou	estou
you are *fam.*	és	estás
you are *polite*	é	está
he, she is	é	está
we are	somos	estamos

you are	**sois**	**estais**
they, you are	**são**	**estão**

In Portuguese there are three types of regular verbs, distinguished by the endings of the infinitives.

-**ar** falar – to speak	-**er** vender – to sell
-**ir** partir – to leave, go away	

The **_present tense_** is formed as follows:

falar	vender	partir
fal**o**	vend**o**	part**o**
fal**as**	vend**es**	part**es**
fal**a**	vend**e**	part**e**
fal**amos**	vend**emos**	part**imos**
fal**ais**	vend**eis**	part**is**
fal**am**	vend**em**	part**em**

The **_imperfect past tense_**

falar		**vender**	
fal**ava**	_I spoke, have spoken, was speaking, etc._	vend**ia**	_I sold, have sold, was selling, etc._
fal**avas**		vend**ias**	
fal**ava**		vend**ia**	

falávamos	vendíamos
faláveis	vendíeis
falavam	vendiam

Verbs ending in **-ir** (partir) have the same endings in the imperfect as those in **-er** (vender).

The *irregular imperfect tense* of **ser** – to be

era
eras
era
éramos
éreis
eram

The present and imperfect tenses of some common irregular verbs:

dar – *to give*		**dizer** – *to say*		**fazer** – *to do, make*	
dou	dava	digo	dizia	faço	fazia
dás	davas	dizes	dizias	fazes	fazias
dá	dava	diz	dizia	faz	fazia
damos	dávamos	dizemos	dizíamos	fazemos	fazíamos
dais	dáveis	dizeis	dizíeis	fazeis	fazíeis
dão	davam	dizem	diziam	fazem	faziam

ir – *to go*		**poder** – *can, to be able*		**saber** – *to know*	
vou	ia	posso	podia	sei	sabia
vais	ias	podes	podias	sabes	sabias
vai	ia	pode	podia	sabe	sabia
vamos	íamos	podemos	podíamos	sabemos	sabíamos
ides	íeis	podeis	podíeis	sabeis	sabíeis
vão	iam	podem	podiam	sabem	sabiam

ter – *to have*		**ver** – *to see*		**vir** – *to come*	
tenho	tinha	vejo	via	venho	vinha
tens	tinhas	vês	vias	vens	vinhas
tem	tinha	vê	via	vem	vinha
temos	tínhamos	vemos	víamos	vimos	vínhamos
tendes	tínheis	vêdes	víeis	vindes	vínheis
têm	tinham	vêem	viam	vêm	vinham

The *future* is formed by adding the following endings to the infinitives of all regular verbs:

falar	vender	partir
falarei	venderei	partirei
falarás	venderás	partirás
falará	venderá	partirá
falaremos	venderemos	partiremos
falareis	vendereis	partireis
falarão	venderão	partirão

The present tense of **ir** – to go, can also be used to form the future, as in English.

e.g. **vou** comprar um guia – I'm going to buy a guide book, I shall buy a guide book.

The *negative* is formed by putting **não** before the verb.

e.g. **não** falo português – I don't speak Portuguese.

VOCABULARY

For additional words, please see the specific vocabulary lists elsewhere in the book:

A

a, an	um/uma	oo^n/oo-ma
be able (to)	poder	poo-dair
about	em torno de/ cerca de	e^n tor-no je/sair-ka je
above	em cima de/sobre	e^n see-ma je/so-bre
abroad	no exterior	noo es-te-ree-or
accept (to)	aceitar	a-say-tar
accident	o acidente	a-see-de^n-te
accommodation	a acomodação	a-ko-mo-da sow^n
account	a conta	ko^n-ta
ache (to)	doer	dwer

acquaintance	o conhecido	koo-nye-**see**-doo
across	através	a-tra-**ves**
act (to)	atuar/agir	a-**twar**/a-**zheer**
add (to)	adicionar	a-dee-see-o-**nar**
address	o endereço	eⁿ-de-re-**soo**
admire (to)	admirar	ad-mee-**rar**
admission	a admissão	ad-mee-**sow**ⁿ
adventure	a aventura	a-ven-**too**-ra
advertisement	o anúncio/o comercial	a-**noo**ⁿ-see-oo/ko-mer -**syaw**
advice	o conselho	koⁿ-**say**-lyoo
aeroplane	o avião	a-vee-**ow**ⁿ
afford (to)	comportar	koⁿ-por-**tar**
afraid (to be)	ter medo	ter **may**-doo
after	depois	de-**po**-ees
afternoon	a tarde	**tar**-jee
again	de novo	je **no**-vo
against	contra	**ko**ⁿ-tra
age	a idade	ee-**da**-jee
agree (to)	concordar	koⁿ-kor-**dar**
ahead	adiante	a-jee-**a**ⁿ-te
air	o ar	ahr
air conditioning	o ar condicionado	ahr koⁿ-jee-see-o-**na**-doo
alarm clock	o despertador	jes-per-ta-**dor**

alcoholic (drink)	a bebida alcoólica	be-**bee**-da al-koo-o-lee-ka
alike	igual/parecido	ee-gwal/pa-re-see-doo
all	todo(s)/tudo	**to**-doo(s)/**too**-doo
alive	vivo	**vee**-voo
allow (to)	permitir	per-mee-**teer**
all right	está bem	es-**ta** ben
almost	quase	**kwa**-zee
alone	só	soh
along	ao longo	ow lon-goo
already	já	zhah
also	também	tan-ben
alter (to)	alterar	al-te-rar
alternative	a alternativa	al-ter-na-**tee**-va
although	embora	en-**bo**-ra
always	sempre	**sen**-pre
ambulance	a ambulância	an-hoo-lan-see-a
American	o americano	a-me-ree-**ka**-noo
among	entre/no meio de	en-tre/noo **may**-oo je
amuse (to)	divertir/entreter	jee-ver-**teer**/en-tre-ter
amusing	divertido	jee-ver-**tee**-doo
ancient	antigo/ancião	an-**tee**-goo/an-see-own
and	e	ee
angry	furioso	foo-ree-o-zoo

animal	animal	a-nee-**maw**
anniversary	o aniversário	a-nee-ver-**sa**-ree-oo
annoyed	irritado	ee-hee-**ta**-doo
another	outro/mais um	**oh**-troo/**ma**-ees oo^n
answer	a resposta	hes-**pos**-ta
answer (to)	responder	hes-po^n-**der**
antique	antigo/a antiguidade	a^n-**tee**-goo/a^n-tee-gwee-**da**-je
any	qualquer/algum	kwal-ker/al-**goo**^{n}
anyone	qualquer um/ alguém	kwal-**ker** oo^n/al-**ghe**^{n}
anything	qualquer coisa/ nada *in a negative context: not anything*	kwal-**ker** ko-**ee**-sa/**na**-da
anyway	de qualquer jeito	je kwal-**ker** **zhey**-too
anywhere	qualquer lugar	kwal-**ker** loo-**gar**
apartment	o apartamento	a-par-ta-**me**^{n}-too
apologize (to)	pedir desculpas/ desculpar-se	pe-**jeer** des-**kool**-pa/des-kool-**par**-se
appetite	o apetite	a-pe-**tee**-te
appointment	a hora marcada	**o**-ra mar-**ka**-da
architect	o arquiteto	ar-kee-**te**-too
architecture	a arquitetura	ar-kee-te-**too**-ra
area	a área	**a**-ree-a
arm	o braço	**bra**-soo

armchair	a poltrona	pol-**tro**-na
army	o exército	e-**ser**-see-too
around	ao redor de/em volta de	a-oo he-**door** je/e^n **vol**-ta je
arrange (to)	arrumar/arranjar	a-hoo-**mar**/a-ha^n-**zhar**
arrival	a chegada	she-**ga**-da
arrive (to)	chegar	she-**gar**
art	a arte	**ar**-te
art gallery	a galeria de arte	ga-le-**ree**-a je **ar**-te
artist	o artista	ar-**tees**-ta
artificial	artificial	ar-tee-fee-see-**aw**
as	como	**ko**-mo
as much as	tanto . . . quanto	ta^n-too . . . kwa^n-too
as soon as	logo que/ assim que	lo-goo ke/a-see^n ke
as well/also	também	ta^n **be**^{n}
ashtray	o cinzeiro	see^n **zair**-oo
ask (to)	pedir	pe-**jeer**
asleep	adormecido/estar dormindo	a dor-me-see-doo/es-**tar** dor-**mee**^{n} doo
at *place*	em	e^n
at *time*	às	ahs
at last	finalmente	jee now-me^n-te
at once	de uma vez	je **oo**-ma vez
atmosphere	a atmosfera	at-mos-**fe**-ra

attention	a atenção	a-te^n-**sow**^{n}
attractive	atraente	a-tra-e^n-te
auction	o leilão	ley-**low**^{n}
audience	a audiência/o público/a platéia	ow-dee-**ay**^{n}-see-a/**poo**-blee-koo/pla-**te**-ya
aunt	a tia	**tee**-a
Australia	a Austrália	ows-**tra**-lee-a
Australian	australiano	ows-tra-lee-**a**-noo
Austria	a Áustria	**ows**-tree-a
Austrian	austríaco	ows-**tree**-a-koo
author	o autor	ow-**tor**
available	disponível	jees-po-**nee**-vel
avenue	a avenida	a-ve-**nee**-da
average (n)	a média	**me**-jee-a
awake	acordado	a-kor-**da**-doo
away	fora/ embora/ longe	**fo**-ra/e^n-**bo**-ra/lo^n-zhe
awful	péssimo	**pes**-see-moo

B

baby	o bebê/o nenê/o neném	be-**be**/ne-**ne**/ne-**ne**^{n}
baby food	a papinha de bebê	pa-**pee**-nya je be-**be**
babysitter	a babá	ba-**ba**

bachelor	o solteiro	sol-**tay**-roo
back	costas/ parte de trás	**kos**-tas/**par**-te je trahs
backpack	a mochila	mo-**shee**-la
bad	mau/ má	mow/mah
bag	a mala/ a sacola	**ma**-la/sa-**ko**-la
baggage	a bagagem	ba-**ga**-zhen
bait	a isca	**ees**-ka
balcony	o balcão/ a sacada	bow-**kown**/sa-**ka**-da
ball *sport*	a bola	**bo**-la
ballet	o balé	ba-**le**
band *music*	a banda	**ban**-da
bank	o banco	**ban**-koo
bare	nu/ pelado/ descoberto	noo/pe-**la**-doo/des-ko-**ber**-too
basket	a cesta	**ses**-ta
bath	a banheira	ba-**nye**-ra
bathe (to)	tomar banho	to-**mar ba**-nyo
bathing cap	a touca de banho	**to**-ka je **ba**-nyo
bathing suit	o maiô de banho	my-o je ba-nyo
bathing trunks	o calção/a sunga	kal-**sown**/**soon**-ga
bathroom	o banheiro	ba-**nye**-roo
battery	a bateria	ba-te-**ree**-a
bay	a baia	ba-**ee**-a

be (to) *permanent/ temporary*	**ser/ estar**	ser/es-**tar**
beach	**a praia**	**pry**-a
beard	**a barba**	**bar**-ba
beautiful	**bonito**	bo-**nee**-too
because	**porque**	**poor**-ke
become (to)	**tornar-se**	tor-**nar**-se
bed	**a cama**	**ka**-ma
bedroom	**o quarto**	**kwar**-too
before	**antes**	**an**-tes
begin (to)	**começar**	ko-me-**sar**
beginning	**começo/ início**	ko-**may**-soo/ee-**nee**-syo
behind	**atrás**	a-**tras**
believe (to)	**acreditar**	a-kre-jee-**tar**
bell (*door bell*)	**a campaínha/ o sino**	ka^n-**pay**-nya/**see**-noo
belong (to)	**pertencer**	per-te^n-**sair**
below	**abaixo**	a-**bay**-shoo
belt	**o cinto**	**see**^{n}-too
bench	**o banco**	**ba**^{n}-koo
bend (to)/ bend over (to)	**fazer uma curva/ inclinar-se**	fa-**zair** oo-ma **koor**-va/ee^n-klee-**nar**-se
beneath	**debaixo**	de-**bay**-shoo
beside	**ao lado de**	ow **la**-doo je
besides	**além disso/ além do mais**	a-**le**^{n} **jees**-so/a-**le**^{n} doo **my**-ees

best	o melhor	oo me-**lyor**
bet	a aposta	a-**pos**-ta
better	melhor	me-**lyor**
between	entre	e^n-tre
bicycle	a bicicleta	bee-see-**kle**-ta
big	grande	**gra**^{n}-je
bill	a conta	**ko**^{n}-ta
binoculars	o binóculo	bee-**no**-koo-loo
bird	a ave	a-ve
birthday	o aniversário	a-nee-ver-sa-ree-o
bite (to)	morder	mor-**dair**
bitter	amargo	a-**mar**-goo
blanket (woollen)	a manta/o cobertor (de lã)	**ma**^{n}-ta/ko-ber-**tor** (je la^n)
bleed (to)	sangrar	sa^n-**grar**
blind	cego	**se**-go
blond	loiro	**loy**-roo
blood	o sangue	**sa**^{n}-ghe
blouse	a blusa	**bloo**-za
blow (to)	soprar/ explodir	so-prar/es-plo-jeer
(on) board	a bordo	a bor-doo
boat	o barco	**bar**-koo
body	o corpo	**kor**-poo
bone	o osso	**os**-soo

book	o livro	**lee**-vroo
book (to)	reservar	he-zer-**var**
boot *shoe/car*	a bota/o porta-malas	**bo**-ta/**por**-ta **ma**-las
border	a fronteira	froⁿ-**tay**-ra
borrow (to)	pegar emprestado	pe-**gar** eⁿ-pres-**ta**-doo
both	ambos	aⁿ-boos
bottle	a garrafa	ga-**ha**-fa
bottle opener	o abridor de garrafas	a-bree-**dor** je ga-**ha**-fas
bottom	o fundo	**foo**ⁿ-doo
bowl	a tigela	tee-**ge**-la
box *container*	a caixa	**kay**-sha
theatre	o palco	**pal**-koo
box office	a bilheteria	bee-lye-te-**ree**-a
boy	o menino/o garoto	me-**nee**-noo/ga-**ro**-too
bracelet	o bracelete/a pulseira	bra-se-**le**-te/pool-**sey**-ra
brain	o cérebro	**se**-re-broo
branch	o galho	**ga**-lyoo
brand	a marca	**mar**-ka
Brazil	Brasil	Bra-**zeew**
Brazilian	brasileiro (a)	bra-zee-**ley**-roo (a)
brassière	o sutiã	soo-**tee**-aⁿ
break (to)	quebrar	ke-**brar**

breakfast	o café da manhã	ka-**feh** da ma-**nya**ⁿ
breathe (to)	respirar	hes-pee-**rar**
bridge	a ponte	poⁿ-te
briefs	a cueca	**kwe**-ka
bright	brilhante	bree-**lya**ⁿ-te
bring (to)	trazer	tra-**zair**
British	britânico	bree-**ta**-nee-koo
broadband	a banda larga	**ba**ⁿ-da **lar**-ga
broken	quebrado	ke-**bra**-doo
brooch	o broche	**bro**-she
brother	o irmão	eer-**mow**ⁿ
bruise (to)	machucar-se	ma-shoo-**kar**-se
brush	a escova	es-**ko**-va
brush (to)	escovar	es-ko-**var**
bucket	o balde	**bow**-je
buckle	a fivela	fee-**ve**-la
build (to)	construir	koⁿ stroo-**eer**
building	o prédio	**pre**-jee-oo
burn (to)	queimar	**key**-mar
burst (to)	estourar	es-to-**rar**
bus	o ônibus	o-nee-boos
bus stop	o ponto de ônibus	poⁿ-too je o-nee-boos
business	o negócio	ne-**go**-see-oo
busy	ocupado	o-koo-**pa**-doo

but	**mas**	mas
button	**o botão**	bo-**tow**ⁿ
buy (to)	**comprar**	koⁿ-**prar**
by	**ao lado/ por**	ow **la**-doo/poor

C

cabin	**a cabine**	ka-**bee**-ne
call *telephone*	**a chamada**	sha-**ma**-da
call (to) *summon*	**chamar**	sha-**mar**
name	**chamar-se**	sha-**mar**-se
telephone	**ligar**	lee-**gar**
visit	**visitar**	vee-see-**tar**
calm	**calmo**	**kal**-moo
camera *photographic device/ video camera*	**a máquina / a filmadora**	**ma**-kee-na/feel-ma-**do**-ra
camp (to)	**acampar**	a-kaⁿ-**par**
campsite	**o local de acampamento**	lo-**kaw** je a-kaⁿ-pa-**me**ⁿ-too
can (to be able)	**poder**	po-**der**
can *tin*	**a lata**	**la**-ta
Canada	**Canadá**	ka-na-**da**
Canadian	**canadense**	ka-na-**de**ⁿ-se
cancel (to)	**cancelar**	kaⁿ-se-**lar**
candle	**a vela**	**ve**-la

canoe	a canoa	ka-**no**-a
cap	o boné	bo-**neh**
capable	capaz	ka-**paz**
capital city	a capital	ka-pee-**tow**
car	o carro	**ka**-ho
car park	o estacionamento	es-ta-syo-na-**me**^{n}-too
caravan	o trailer	trailer
card	o cartão	kar-**tow**^{n}
care (to)	importar-se	ee^n-por-**tar**-se
careful	cuidadoso	kwee-da-**do**-zoo
careless	descuidado/ negligente	des-kwee-**da**-doo/ ne-glee-**zhe**^{n}-te
carry (to)	carregar	ka-he-**gar**
carnival	o carnaval	kar-na-**vow**
cash	o dinheiro	jee-**nyer**-oo
cashier	o caixa	**kay**-sha
casino	o casino	kas-**see**-noo
castle	o castelo	kas-**te**-loo
cat	o gato	**ga**-too
catalogue	o catálogo	ka-**la**-loo-goo
catch (to)	pegar	pe-**gar**
cathedral	a catedral	ka-te-**drow**
Catholic	católico	ka-**to**-lee-koo
cause	a causa	**kow**-za

cave	a caverna	ka-**ver**-na
cell phone	o celular	se-loo-**lar**
central	central	se^n-**trow**
centre	o centro	se^n-troo
century	o século	se-koo-loo
ceremony	a cerimónia	se-ree-**mo**-nee-a
certain *adj*	certo	**sair**-too
certain *pron*	alguns	al-**goo**^{n}**s**
certainly	certamente	ser-ta-**me**^{n}-te
chair	a cadeira	ka-**dey**-ra
chambermaid	a camareira	ka-ma-**rey**-ra
chance	a chance/ a sorte	sha^n-se/**sor**-te
(by) chance	por acaso	poor a-**ka**-soo
(small) change *money*	os trocados	tro-**ka**-doos
change (to)	mudar	**moo**-dar
charge	a cobrança/ a taxa	ko-**bra**^{n}-sa/**ta**-sha
charge (to) *money/ electronic device*	cobrar/carregar	ko-**brar**/ka-he-**gar**
cheap	barato	ba-**ra**-too
check (to)	checar/ verificar	she-**kar**/ve-ree-fee-**kar**
checkout/till	o caixa	**kay**-sha
cheque	o cheque	**she**-ke

child	a criança	kree-a^n-sa
china	a porcelana	por-se-la-na
choice	a escolha	es-**ko**-lya
choose (to)	escolher	es-ko-**lyer**
church	a igreja	ee-**gre**-zha
cigar	o charuto	sha-**roo**-too
cigarettes	os cigarros	see-**ga**-hos
cinema	o cinema	see-ne-ma
circus	o circo	**seer**-koo
city	a cidade	see-**da**-je
class	a classe	**klas**-se
clean	limpo	lee^n-poo
clean (to)	limpar	lee^n-par
clear	claro	**kla**-roo
cliff	o penhasco/a falésia	pe-**nyas**-koo/fa-**le**-see-a
climb (to)	escalar	es-ka-lar
cloakroom	a chapelaria	sha-pe-la-**ree**-a
clock	o relógio	he-lo-**zhee**-oo
close (to)	fechar	fe-**shar**
closed	fechado	fe-**sha**-doo
cloth	o pano	**pa**-noo
clothes	a roupa	**ho**-pa
cloud	a núvem	**noo**-ve^n
coach	o treinador	trey-na-**dor**

coast	o litoral	lee-to-**raw**
coat	o casaco	ka-**za**-koo
coathanger	o cabide	ka-**bee**-je
coin	a moeda	mo-e-da
cold	frio	**free**-oo
collar *of shirt or jacket*	o colarinho	ko-la-**ree**-nyoo
collect (to)	colecionar	ko-le-syo-**nar**
colour	a cor	kor
comb	o pente	**pe**^{n}-te
come (to)	vir	veer
come in (to)	entrar	e^n-**trar**
comfortable	confortável	ko^n-for-**ta**-vew
common	comum	ko-**moo**^{n}
company	a companhia/a empresa	ko^n-pa-**nyee**-a/e^n-**pre**-za
complain (to)	reclamar	he-kla-**mar**
complaint	a reclamação	he-kla-ma-**sow**^{n}
complete	completo	ko^n-**ple**-too
completely	completamente	ko^n-ple-ta-**me**^{n}-te
concert	o concerto	ko^n-**ser**-too
condition	a condição	ko^n-jee-**sow**^{n}
condom	o preservativo/a camisinha	pre-ser-va-**tee**-voo/ka-mee-**see**-nya
conductor *orchestra*	o maestro	**my**-stroo

congratulations	parabéns	pa-ra-be^{n}s
connect (to)	conectar	ko-nek-tar
connection *train, etc.*	a conexão/a baldeação	ko-ne-ksaw^n /bow-je-a-sow^n
consul	o cônsul	ko^n-sool
consulate	o consulado	ko^n-soo-la-doo
contain (to)	conter	ko^n-ter
convenient	conveniente	ko^n-ve-nee-e^n-te
conversation	a conversa/ a conversação	ko^n-ver-sa/ko^n-ver-sa-sow^n
cook	o cozinheiro	ko-zee-nye-roo
cook (to)	cozinhar	ko-zee-nyar
cool *temperature*	fresco	fres-koo
(interjection)	legal	le-gow
copy	a cópia	ko-pee-a
copy (to)	copiar	ko-pee-ar
cork	a rolha	ho-lya
corkscrew	o saca-rolhas	sa-ka-ho-lyas
corner	a esquina	es-kee-na
correct	correto	ko-he-too
corridor	o corredor	ko-he-dor
cosmetics	os cosméticos	kos-me-tee-koos
cost	o custo	koos-too
cost (to)	custar	koos-tar

cotton	o algodão	al-go-**dow**[n]
count (to)	contar	ko[n]-**tar**
country	o país	pa-**ees**
couple	o casal	ka-**zow**
course *dish*	o prato	**pra**-too
courtyard	o pátio	**pa**-tee-oo
cousin	o primo	**pree**-moo
cover	a capa	**ka**-pa
cover (to)	cobrir	ko-**breer**
cow	a vaca	**va**-ka
crash *collision*	a batida/a colisão	ba-**tee**-da/ko-lee-**zow**[n]
credit	o crédito	**kreh**-jee-too
credit card	o cartão de crédito	kar-**tow**[n] je **kreh**-jee-too
crew	a tripulação	tree-po-la-**sow**[n]
cross	a cruz	krooz
cross (to)	cruzar/ atravessar	kroo-**zar**/a-tra-ves-**sar**
crossroads	o cruzamento/a encruzilhada	kroo-za-**me**[n]-too/e[n]-kroo-zee-**lya**-da
crowd	a multidão	mool-tee-**dow**[n]
crowded	cheio/ lotado	**shey**-oo/lo-**ta**-doo
cry (to)	chorar	sho-**rar**
cup	a xícara	**shee**-ka-ra
cupboard	o armário	ar-**ma**-ree-oo
cure (to)	curar	koo-**rar**

curious	**curioso**	koo-ree-**o**-zoo
curl	**o cacho**	**ka**-shoo
current	**atual/ corrente**	a-too-**ow**/ko-**he**ⁿ-te
curtain	**a cortina**	kor-**tee**-na
curve	**a curva**	**koor**-va
cushion	**a almofada**	ow-mo-**fa**-da
customs	**a alfândega**	ow-**fa**ⁿ-je-ga
customs officer	**o aduaneiro**	a-dwa-**ney**-roo
cut	**o corte**	**kor**-te
cut (to)	**cortar**	kor-**tar**
cycling	**o ciclismo**	see-**klees**-moo
cyclist	**o ciclista**	see-**klees**-ta

D

daily *adj*	**diário**	jee-**a**-ree-oo
daily *adv*	**diariamente**	jee-a-ree-a-**me**ⁿ-te
damaged	**danificado**	da-nee-fee-**ka**-doo
damp	**úmido**	**oo**-mee-doo
dance	**a dança**	**da**ⁿ-sa
danger	**o perigo**	pe-**ree**-goo
dangerous	**perigoso**	pe-ree-**go**-zoo
dark	**escuro**	es-**koo**-roo
date *day/year*	**a data**	**da**-ta

appointment	a hora marcada	o-ra mar-**ka**-da
daughter	a filha	fee-lya
day	o dia	jee-a
dead	morto	**mor**-too
deaf	surdo	**soor**-doo
dear *expensive*	caro	**ka**-roo
decide (to)	decidir	de-see-**jeer**
deck	a plataforma/o convés	pla-ta-**for**-ma/ko^n-**ves**
deckchair	a espreguiçadeira	es-pre-ghee-sa-**dey**-ra
declare (to)	declarar	de-kla-**rar**
deep	profundo	pro-**foo**^{n}-doo
delay	o atraso	a-**tra**-zoo
deliver (to)	entregar	e^n-tre-**gar**
delivery	a entrega	e^n-**tre**-ga
dentist	o dentista	de^n-**tees**-ta
deodorant	o desodorante	de-zo-do-**ra**^{n}-te
depart (to)	partir	par-**teer**
department	o departamento	de-par-ta-**me**^{n}-too
department store	a loja de departamentos	**lo**-zha je de-par-ta-**me**^{n}-toos
departure	a partida	par-**tee**-da
dessert	a sobremesa	so-bre-**me**-za
detour	o desvio	jees-**vee**-oo

diamond	o diamante	jee-a-**ma**ⁿ-te
dice	o dado	**da**-doo
dictionary	o dicionário	jee-see-o-**na**-ree-oo
diet	a dieta	jee-**eh**-ta
diet (to)	fazer regime/ fazer dieta	fa-**zer** he-**zhee**-me/fa-**zer** jee-**eh**-ta
different	diferente	jee-fe-**re**ⁿ-te
difficult	difícil	jee-**fee**-seew
dine (to)	jantar	zhaⁿ-**tar**
dining room	a sala de jantar	**sa**-la je zhaⁿ-**tar**
dinner	o jantar	zhaⁿ-**tar**
direct	direto	jee-**re**-too
direction	a direção	Jee-re-**sow**ⁿ
dirty	sujo	**soo**-joo
disappointed	desapontado/ decepcionado	je-za-poⁿ-**ta**-doo/je-sep-syⁿ-**na**-doo
discount	o desconto	jes-**ko**ⁿ-too
dish	o prato	**pra**-too
disinfectant	o desinfetante	de-zeeⁿ-fe-**ta**ⁿ-te
distance	a distância	jee-**sta**ⁿ-see-a
disturb (to)	perturbar/ incomodar	per toor-**bar**/eeⁿ-ko-mo-**dar**
ditch	a valeta	va-**le**-ta
dive (to)	mergulhar	mer-goo-**lyar**
diving board	o trampolim	traⁿ-pu-**lee**ⁿ

divorced	divorciado	jee-vor-see-**a**-doo
do (to)	fazer	fa-**zer**
dock	a doca	**do**-ka
doctor	o médico	**me**-jee-koo
dog	o cachorro	ka-**sho**-ho
doll	a boneca	bo-**ne**-ka
door	a porta	**por**-ta
double	duplo	**doo**-ploo
double bed	a cama de casal	**ka**-ma je ka-**zow**
double room	o quarto com cama de casal	**kwar**-too ko^n **ka**-ma je ka-**zow**
down	para baixo	**pa**-ra **by**-shoo
downstairs	no andar de baixo	noo a^n-**dar** je **by**-shoo
dozen	a dúzia	**doo**-zee-a
drawer	a gaveta	ga-**ve**-ta
dream	o sonho	**so**-nyoo
dress	o vestido	ves-**tee**-doo
dressing-gown	o robe/ o roupão	**roh**-be/ro-**pow**^{n}
drink (to)	beber	be-**ber**
drinking water	a água de beber/a água potável	**a**-gwa je be-**ber**/**a**-gwa po-**ta**-vew
drive (to)	dirigir	jee-ree-**zheer**
driver	o motorista	mo-to-**rees**-ta
drop (to)	deixar cair	de-**shar** ka-eer

drunk	bêbado	be-ba-doo
dry	seco	se-koo
during	durante	doo-ra^n-te

E

each	cada	ka-da
early	cedo	se-doo
earrings	os brincos	bree^n-koos
east	o leste	les-te
easy	fácil	fa-seew
eat (to)	comer	ko-mer
edge	a beira/a beirada	bey-ra/bey-ra-da
elastic	o elástico	e-las-tee-koo
electric socket outlet	a tomada	to-ma-da
electricity	a eletricidade	e-le-tree-see da-je
elevator	o elevador	e-le-va-dor
embarrass (to)	envergonhar	e^n-ver-go-nyar
embassy	a embaixada	e^n-bay-sha-da
emergency exit	a saída de emergência	su-ee-dn je e-mer-zhe^n-see-a
empty	vazio	va-zee-oo
end	o fim	fee^n
engaged *to be married*	noivo	no-ee-voo

telephone	ocupado	o-koo-**pa**-doo
engine	o motor	mo-**tor**
England	Inglaterra	Een-gla-**te**-ha
English	inglês	een-**gles**
English (person)	o inglês/inglesa	een-**gles**/een-**gle**-za
enjoy (to)	aproveitar/curtir	a-pro-vey-**tar**/koor-**teer**
enough	bastante/suficiente	bas-**ta**^{n}-te/soo-fee-see-**e**^{n}-te
enter (to)	entrar	e^n-**trar**
entrance	a entrada	e^n-**tra**-da
envelope	o envelope	e^n-ve-**lo**-pe
equipment	o equipamento	e-kee-pa-**me**^{n}-too
escape (to)	escapar	es-ka-**par**
Europe	a Europa	E-oo-**ro**-pa
EU (European Union)	a UE (União Européia)	oo eh (oo-nee-**ow**^{n} e-oo-ro-**pey**-a)
even *not odd*	par	par
event	o evento	e-**ve**^{n}-too
ever *at any time/ always*	já /sempre	zhah/**se**^{n}-pre
every *each one/time*	todo /cada	**to**-doo/**ka**-da
everybody	todo mundo	**to**-doo **moo**^{n}-doo
everything	tudo	**too**-doo
everywhere	em todo lugar/por toda parte	e^n **to**-doo loo-**gar**/poor **to**-da **par**-te

example	o exemplo	e-zeⁿ-ploo
excellent	excelente	e-se-leⁿ-te
except	exceto	e-se-too
excess	o excesso	e-ses-soo
exchange bureau	a casa de câmbio	ka-za je kaⁿ-bee-oo
exchange rate	a taxa de câmbio	ta-sha je kaⁿ-bee-oo
excursion	a excursão	es-koor-sowⁿ
excuse	a desculpa	des-kool-pa
exhausted	exausto	e-zow-stoo
exhibition	a exibição	e-see-bee-sowⁿ
exit	a saida	sa-ee-da
expect (to)	esperar	es-pe-rar
expensive	caro	ka-roo
explain (to)	explicar	es-plee-kar
express train	o trem expresso	treⁿ es-pres-soo
extra	extra	e-stra

F

fabric	o tecido	te-see-doo
face	a face/a cara/o rosto	fa-se/ka-ra/hos-too
face cream	o hidratante/o creme facial	ee-dra-taⁿ-le/kre-me fa-see-ow
fact	o fato	fa-too

factory	**a fábrica**	**fa**-bree-ka
fade (to)	**sumir/desvanecer**	soo-**meer**/des-va-ne-**ser**
faint (to)	**desmaiar**	des-ma-**yar**
fair *colouring*	**claro**	**kla**-roo
fête	**a feira**	**fey**-ra
fall (to)	**cair**	ka-**eer**
family	**a família**	fa-**mee**-lee-a
far	**longe**	lo^n-zhe
fare	**a tarifa**	ta-**ree**-fa
farm	**a fazenda**	fa-**ze**^{n}-da
farmer	**o fazendeiro**	fa-ze^n-**dey**-roo
farther	**mais distante**	ma-**ees** jees-**ta**^{n}-te
fashion	**a moda**	**mo**-da
fast	**rápido**	**ha**-pee-doo
fat	**gordo**	**gor**-doo
father	**o pai**	pie
fault	**a culpa**	**kool**-pa
fear	**o medo**	**me**-doo
feed (to)	**alimentar**	a-lee-me^n-**tar**
feel (to)	**sentir**	se^n-**teer**
female *adj.*	**feminino**	fe-me-**nee**-noo
ferry	**a balsa**	**bow**-sa
fetch (to)	**ir buscar**	eer boos-**kar**

few	pouco	po-koo
fiancé(e)	noivo(a)	no-ee-voo (a)
field	o campo	kan-poo
fight (to)	brigar	bree-gar
fill (to)	encher	en-sher
film	o filme	feel-me
find (to)	achar	a-shar
fine	legal/ótimo	le-gow/oh-tee-moo
finish (to)	acabar/ terminar	a-ka-bar/ter-mee-nar
finished	acabado/terminado	a-ka-ba-doo/ter-mee-na-doo
fire	o fogo	fo-goo
fire escape	a escada de emergência	es-ka-da je e-mer-zhen-see-a
first	primeiro	pree-mey-roo
first aid	os primeiros socorros	pree-mey-roos so-ko-hoos
fish	o peixe	pe she
fish (to)	pescar	pes-kar
fisherman	o pescador	pes-ka-dor
fit healthy	em forma	en for-ma
fit (to)	servir/caber	ser-veer/ka-ber
flag	a bandeira	ban-dey-ra
flat adj	plano	pla-noo

noun	o apartamento	a-par-ta-**me**ⁿ-too
flight	o voo	**vo**-oo
flippers	os pés-de-pato	pehs-je-**pa**-too
float (to)	flutuar	floo-too-**ar**
flood	a enchente	eⁿ-**she**ⁿ-te
floor	o chão	showⁿ
storey	o piso/ o andar	**pee**-zoo/aⁿ-**dar**
floor show	o show	show
flower	a flor	flor
fly	a mosca	**mos**-ka
fly (to)	voar	vo-**ar**
fog	a bruma/o nevoeiro	**broo**-ma/ne-voo-**ey**-roo
fold (to)	dobrar	do-**brar**
follow (to)	seguir	se-**gheer**
food	a comida	ko-**mee**-da
foot	o pé	peh
football	o futebol	foo-te-**bow**
for	para	**pa**-ra
foreign	estrangeiro	es-traⁿ-**zhey**-roo
forest	a floresta	flo-**res**-ta
forget (to)	esquecer	es-ke-**ser**
fork	o garfo	**gar**-foo
forward *adv*	para a frente	**pa**-ra a **fre**ⁿ-te

forward (to)	encaminhar	e^n-ka-mee-**nyar**
fountain	a fonte	fo^n-te
fragile	frágil	fra-zheew
free	livre	lee-vre
fresh	fresco	fres-koo
fresh water	a água fresca	a-gwa fres-ka
friend	o amigo	a-**mee**-goo
friendly	simpático/amigável	see^n-**pa**-tee-koo/a-mee-ga-vew
from*starting point*	de/ desde	je/des-je
front	a frente	fre^n-te
frontier	a fronteira	fro^n-**tey**-ra
frozen	congelado	ko^n-zhe-la-doo
fruit	a fruta	**froo**-ta
full	cheio	**shey**-oo
fun	a diversão	jee-ver-suw^n
funny	engraçado	e^n-gra-**sa**-doo
fur	o pêlo	pe-loo
furniture	o móvel/a mobília	mo-vew/mo-bee-lee-a

G

gallery	a galeria	ga-le-**ree**-a
gamble (to)	apostar	a-pos-**tar**
game	o jogo	**zho**-goo

garage	**a garagem**	ga-ra-**zhe**ⁿ
garbage	**o lixo**	**lee**-shoo
garden	**o jardim**	zhar-**jee**ⁿ
gas	**o gás**	gas
gate	**o portão**	por-**tow**ⁿ
gentleman	**o cavalheiro/o senhor**	ka-va-**lyey**-roo/se-**nyor**
German *adj. and noun*	**alemão/o alemão**	a-le-**mow**ⁿ
Germany	**Alemanha**	A-le-**ma**-nya
get (to)	**pegar**	pe-**gar**
get off (to) *transport*	**descer/ sair/ desembarcar**	de-**ser**/ sa-**eer**/ de-zeⁿ-bar-**kar**
get on (to) *make progress*	**ir em frente**	eer eⁿ **fre**ⁿ-te
get on (with)	**dar-se bem (com)**	**dar**-se beⁿ (koⁿ)
gift	**o presente**	pre-**ze**ⁿ-te
girl	**a garota**	ga-**ro**-ta
give (to)	**dar**	dar
glad	**contente**	koⁿ-**te**ⁿ-te
glass	**o vidro**	vee-**droo**
glasses	**os óculos**	**o**-koo-loos
gloomy	**triste/melancólico**	**tree**-ste/me-laⁿ-**ko**-lee-koo
glorious	**glorioso**	glo-ree-**o**-zoo

glove	a luva	loo-va
go (to)	ir	eer
goal	o gol	gol
goal (to score a)	gol (fazer/marcar)	gol (fa-zer/mar-kar)
god	o deus	dey-oos
gold	o ouro	o-roo
good	bom	bon
government	o governo	go-ver-noo
granddaughter	a neta	ne-ta
grandfather	o avô	a-vo
grandmother	a avó	a-voh
grandson	o neto	ne-too
grass	a grama	gra-ma
grateful	grato/agradecido	gra-too/a-gra-de-see-doo
gravel	o cascalho/a pedra	kas-ka-lyo/pe-dra
great	ótimo	o-tee-moo
Great Britain	Grã-Bretanha	Gran-Bre-ta-nya
ground	o solo/o chão	so-loo/shown
grow (to)	crescer	kre-ser
guard	a defesa	de-fe-za
guest	o hóspede	os-pe-je

| guide | o guia | ghee-a |
| guide book | o guia de turismo/o guia de viagem | ghee-a je too-rees-moo/ ghee-a je vee-a-zhe^n |

H

hail	o granizo	gra-nee-zoo
hair	o cabelo	ka-be-loo
hair brush	a escova de cabelo	es-ko-va je ka-be-loo
hairpin	o grampo	gra^n-poo
half	a metade	me-ta-je
half fare	a meia-entrada	mey-a e^n-tra-da
hammer	o martelo	mar-te-loo
hand	a mão	mow^n
handbag	a bolsa	bow-sa
handkerchief	o lenço	le^n-soo
hang (to)	pendurar	pe^n-doo-rar
happen (to)	acontecer	a-ko^n-te-ser
happy	feliz	fe-leez
happy birthday	feliz aniversário	fe-leez a-nee-ver-sa-ree-oo
harbour	o porto	por-too
hard *solid*	duro	doo-roo
difficult	difícil	jee-fee-seew

hat	o chapéu	sha-**pe**-oo
have (to)	ter	ter
he	ele	**e**-le
health	a saúde	sa-**oo**-je
hear (to)	escutar/ouvir	es-koo-**tar**/o-**veer**
heart	o coração	ko-ra-**sow**^{n}
heat	o calor	ka-**lor**
heating	o aquecimento	a-ke-see-**me**^{n}-too
heavy	pesado	pé-**za**-doo
height	a altura	ow-**too**-ra
help	a ajuda	a **zhoo**-da
help (to)	ajudar	a-zhoo-**dar**
her/hers	dela	**de**-la
here	aqui	a-**kee**
high	alto	**ow**-too
hike (to)	caminhar	ka-mee-**nyar**
hill	a colina	ko-**lee**-na
him/to him	o /lhe	oo/lye
hire (to)	alugar	a-loo-**gar**
his	dele	**de**-le
hold (to)	segurar	se-goo-**rar**
hole	o buraco	boo-**ra**-koo
holiday	as férias	**feh**-ree-as

hollow	oco	o-koo
(at) home	em casa	e^n **ka**-za
honeymoon	a lua de mel	**loo**-a je mew
hope	a esperança	es-pe-**ra**^{n}-sa
hope (to)	esperar	es-pe-**rar**
horse	o cavalo	ka-**va**-loo
horse race	a corrida de cavalos	ko-**hee**-da je ka-**va**-loos
horse riding	o hipismo/a equitação	ee-**pees**-moo/e-kee-ta-**sow**^{n}
hospital	o hospital	os-spee-**tow**
host	o anfitrião	a^n-fee-tree-**ow**^{n}
hostess	a anfitriã	a^n-fee-tree-**a**^{n}
hot	quente	**ke**^{n}-te
hotel	o hotel	o-**tew**
hotel manager	o gerente do hotel	zhe-**re**^{n}-te doo o-**tew**
hot-water bottle	a bolsa de água quente	**bow**-sa je **a**-gwa **ke**^{n}-te
hour	a hora	**o**-ra
house	a casa	**ka**-za
how	como	**ko**-moo
how much/many?	quanto/quantos?	**kwa**^{n}-too/**kwa**^{n}-toos
hungry	com fome/faminto	ko^n **fo**-me/fa-**mee**^{n}-too
hurry (to)	apressar-se	a-pres-**sar**-se
hurt (to)	machucar	ma-shoo-**kar**
husband	o marido	ma-**ree**-doo

I

I	eu	ay-oo
if	se	se
immediately	imediatamente	ee-me-jee-a-ta-me^n-te
important	importante	ee^n-por-ta^n-te
in	em	e^n
include (to)	incluir	ee^n-kloo-eer
included	incluído	ee^n-kloo-ee-doo
inconvenient	inconveniente	ee^n-ko^n-ve-nee-e^n-te
incorrect	incorreto	ee^n-ko-he-too
indeed	de fato	je fa-too
indoors	interno	ee^n-ter-noo
information	a informação	ee^n for ma-sow^n
information bureau	o posto de informações	pos-too je ee^n-for-ma-soy^{n}s
ink	a tinta	tee^n-ta
inn	o hotel/a pousada	o-tew/po-za-da
insect	o inseto	ee^n-se-too
insect repellent	o repelente de inseto	re-pe-le^n-te je ee^n-se-too
insect sting	a picada de inseto	pee-ka-da je ee^n-se-too
inside	dentro	de^n-troo
instead of	em vez de	e^n vez je
instructor	o instrutor/o treinador/o professor	ee^n-stroo-tor/trey-na-dor/pro-fes-sor

insurance	o seguro	se-**goo**-roo
insure (to)	assegurar	as-se-goo-**rar**
interested	interessado	eeⁿ-te-res-**sa**-doo
interesting	interessante	eeⁿ-te-res-**sa**ⁿ-te
internet	a internet	internet
interpreter	o intérprete	eeⁿ-**ter**-pre-tee
into	para dentro	**pa**-ra **de**ⁿ-troo
introduce (to)	apresentar	a-pre-zeⁿ-**tar**
invitation	o convite	koⁿ-**vee**-te
invite (to)	convidar	koⁿ-vee-**dar**
Ireland	Irlanda	Eer-**la**ⁿ-da
Irish	irlandês	eer-laⁿ-**des**
iron (to) *clothes*	passar roupa	pas-**sar ho**-pa
island	a Ilha	**ee**-lya
it	ele *m*/ela *f*	**e**-le/**e**-la

J

jacket	a jaqueta	zha-**ke**-ta
jar	o jarro	**zha**-hoo
jelly fish	a água-viva	a-gwa **vee**-va
jewellery/costume jewellery	a jóia/a bijuteria	**zhoy**-a/bee-zhoo-te-**ree**-a
Jewish	judeu	zhoo-**dey**-oo

job	o emprego/o trabalho	eⁿ-**pre**-goo/tra-**ba**-lyoo
journey	a viagem/a jornada	vee-a-**zhe**ⁿ/zhor-**na**-da
jump (to)	pular	poo-**lar**

K

keep (to)	guardar/manter	gwar-**dar**/maⁿ-**ter**
key	a chave	**sha**-ve
kick (to)	chutar	shoo-**tar**
kind (friendly)	gentil	zheⁿ-**teew**
king	o rei	rey
kiss	o beijo	**bey**-zhoo
kiss (to)	beijar	bey-**zhar**
kitchen	a cozinha	ko-**zee**-nya
knife	a faca	**fa**-ka
knock (to)	bater	ba-**ter**
know (to) *fact*	saber	sa-**ber**
person	conhecer	ko-nye-**ser**

L

label	a etiqueta/ o rótulo	e-tee-**ke**-la/**ho**-too-loo
lace	a renda	**he**ⁿ-da
lady	a senhora	se-**nyo**-ra

lake	o lago	la-goo
lamp	a lâmpada	la^n-pa-da
land	a terra	te-ha
landlord	o proprietário da casa	pro-pree-e-**ta**-ree-oo da **ka**-za
language	a língua	lee^n-gwa
large	grande	gra^n-je
last	último	**ool**-tee-moo
late	atrasado	a-tra-**za**-doo
laugh (to)	rir	reer
launderette	a lavanderia	la-va^n-de-**ree**-a
law	a lei	lay
lawyer	o advogado	ad-vo-**ga**-doo
lead (to)	guiar/conduzir	ghee-**ar**/ko^n-doo-**zeer**
leader (to be)	liderar	lee-de-**rar**
leaf	a folha	**fo**-lya
leak (to)	vazar	va-**zar**
learn (to)	aprender	a-pre^n-**der**
least	mínimo	**mee**-nee-moo
(at) least	ao menos	ow **me**-noos
leather	o couro	**ko**-roo
leave (to) *abandon*	deixar	dey-**shar**
go away	sair/partir	sa-**eer**/par-**teer**

(on the) left	(à) esquerda	(ah) es-ker-da
lend (to)	emprestar	en-pres-tar
length	o comprimento	kon-pree-men-too
less	menos	me-nos
lesson	a lição	lee-sown
let (to) *rent*	alugar	a-loo-gar
allow	deixar	dey-shar
letter	a carta	kar-ta
library	a biblioteca	bee-blee o te-ka
licence	a licença	lee-sen-sa
life	a vida	vee-da
lift	o elevador	e-le-va-dor
light *colour*	claro	kla-roo
weight	leve	le-ve
noun	a luz	looz
lighthouse	o farol	fa-row
like (to)	gostar	gos-tar
line	a linha	lee-nya
linen *fibre*	o linho	lee-nyoo
household	a roupa de cama	ho-pa je ka-ma
lingerie	a lingerie	lingerie
lipstick	o batom	ba-ton
liquid *adj. and noun*	líquido/o líquido	lee-kee-doo

listen (to)	ouvir	o-**veer**
little	**pequeno/pouco**	pe-**ke**-noo/**po**-koo
live (to)	**viver**	vee-**ver**
loaf	**o pão**	pow^n
local	**o local**	lo-**kow**
lock	**o cadeado**	ka-je-a-doo
lock (to)	**trancar**	tra^n-**kar**
long	**longo**	lo^n-goo
look at (to)	**olhar**	o-**lyar**
look for (to)	**procurar**	pro-koo-**rar**
loose	**solto**	**sol**-too
lorry	**o caminhão**	ka-mee-**nyow**^{n}
lose (to)	**perder**	per-**der**
lost property office	**a seção de achados e perdidos**	se-**sow**^{n} je a-**sha**-doos ée per-**jee**-doos
lot	**muito**	**mwee**-too
loud	**barulhento**	ba-roo-**lyee**^{n}-too
love (to)	**amar**	a-**mar**
lovely	**amável**	a-**ma**-vew
low	**baixo**	**bay**-shoo
luggage	**a bagagem**	ba-ga-**zhe**^{n}
lunch	**o almoço**	ow-**mo**-soo

M

mad	louco *insane*/ furioso *angry*	lo-koo/foo-ree-o-zoo
magazine	a revista	re-vees-ta
maid	a empregada doméstica	en-pre-ga-da do-mes-tee-ka
mail	o correio	ko-hey-oo
main street	a rua principal	hoo-a preen-see-pow
make (to)	fazer	fa-zer
make-up	a maquiagem	ma-kee-a-zhen
male *adj.*	masculino	mas-koo-lee-noo
man	o homem	o-men
manage (to)	administrar	ad-mee-nees-trar
manager	o gerente	zhe-ren-te
manicure	a manicure	ma-nee-koo-re
many	muitos	mwee-toos
map	o mapa	ma-pa
market	o mercado	mer-ka-doo
married	casado	ka-za-doo
Mass	a missa	mees-sa
massage	a massagem	mas-sa-zhen
match *object*	o fósforo	fos-fo-roo
sport	a partida/o jogo	par-tee-da/zho goo

material	o material	ma-te-ree-**ow**
matinée	a matinê	ma-tee-**ne**
mattress	o colchão	kol-**show**^{n}
me	me/ mim	me/mee^n
meal	a refeição	he-fey-**sow**^{n}
measurements	as medidas	me-**jee**-das
meet (to)	encontrar	e^n-ko^n-**trar**
memory stick	a pen drive	pen drive
mend (to)	emendar/ consertar	e-me^n-**dar**/ko^n-ser-**tar**
mess	a bagunça	ba-**goo**^{n}-sa
message	a mensagem	me^n-sa-**zhe**^{n}
metal	o metal	me-**tow**
middle	o meio	**mey**-oo
middle-aged	a meia-idade	**mey**-a ee-**da**-je
mild	ameno/brando	a-**me**-noo/**bra**^{n}-doo
mine *pron.*	meu/minha	**may**-oo/**mee**-nya
minute	o minuto	mee-**noo**-too
mirror	o espelho	es-**pe**-lyoo
Miss	a senhorita	se-nyo-**ree**-ta
miss (to)	sentir falta/perder	se^n-**teer** fal-ta/per-**der**
mistake	o erro	**e**-hoo
mix (to)	misturar	mees-too-**rar**
mixed	misturado	mees-too-**ra**-doo

mobile phone	o celular	se-loo-**lar**
modern	**moderno**	mo-**der**-noo
moment	o momento	mo-**me**^{n}-too
money	o dinheiro	jee-**nyey**-roo
month	o mês	mes
monument	o monumento	mo-noo-**me**^{n}-too
moon	a lua	**loo**-a
more	mais	**ma**^{n}-ee
mosque	a mesquita	mes-**kee**-ta
most *adj*	mais	**ma**-ees
most *noun*	a maioria	ma-yo-**ree**-a
mother	a mãe	**ma**^{n}-ee
motor boat	o barco a motor	**bar**-koo a mo-**tor**
motor cycle	a motocicleta	mo-to-see-**kle**-ta
motor racing	a moto-velocidade	mo-to-ve-lo-see-**da**-je
motorway	a autoestrada	ow-to-es-**tra**-da
mountain	a montanha	mo^n-**ta**-nya
mouthwash	o enxaguante bucal	e^n-sha-**gwa**^{n}-te boo-**kow**
Mr	Senhor	se-**nyor**
Mrs	Senhora	se-**nyo**-ra
much	muito	**mwee**-too
museum	o museu	moo-**zay**-oo
music	a música	**moo**-zee-ka

muslim	o muçulmano	moo-sool-**ma**-noo
must (to have to)	dever	de-**ver**
my	meu	**may**-oo
myself	eu mesmo	**ay**-oo **mes**-moo

N

nail	a unha	**oo**-nya
nailbrush	a escova de unhas	es-**ko**-va je **oo**-nyas
nailfile	a lixa de unhas	**lee**-sha je **oo**-nyas
nail polish	o esmalte	es-**mal**-te
name	o nome	**no**-me
napkin	o guardanapo	gwar-da-**na**-poo
nappy	a fralda	**frow**-da
narrow	estreito	es-**trey**-too
natural	natural	na-too-**row**
near	perto	**per**-too
nearly	quase	**kwa**-ze
necessary	necessário	ne-se-**sa**-ree-oo
necklace	o colar	ko-**lar**
need (to)	precisar	pre-see-**zar**
needle	a agulha	a-**goo**-lya
nephew	o sobrinho	so-**bree**-nyoo
net	a rede	**he**-je

never	**nunca**	**noo**n-ka
new	**novo**	**no**-voo
news	**a notícia**	no-**tee**-see-a
newspaper	**o jornal**	zhor-**now**
New Zealand	**Nova Zelândia**	**No**-va Ze-la**n**-jee-a
New Zealander	**neo-zelândes**	ne-o-ze-la**n**-**des**
next	**o próximo**	**pro**-see-moo
nice	**simpático/legal**	see**n**-**pa**-tee-koo/le-**gow**
niece	**a sobrinha**	so-**bree**-nya
night	**a noite**	no-**ee**-te
nightclub	**a discoteca/a boate/o clube noturno**	jees-ko-**te**-ka/**bwa**-te/**kloo**-be no-**toor**-noo
nightdress	**camisola**	ka-mee-**zo**-la
nobody	**ninguém**	nee**n**-**ge**n
noisy	**barulhento**	ba-roo-**lye**n-too
none	**nenhum**	ne-**nyoo**n
north	**o norte**	**nor**-te
not	**não**	now**n**
(bank) note	**a nota**	**no**-ta
notebook	**o caderno**	ka-**der**-noo
nothing	**nada**	**na**-da
notice	**o aviso**	a-**vee**-zoo
notice (to)	**notar**	no-**tar**

novel	o romance	ho-**ma**ⁿ-se
now	**agora**	a-**go**-ra
number	o número	**noo**-me-roo
nylon	o náilon	**ny**-loⁿ

O

occasion	a ocasião	o-ka-zee-**ow**ⁿ
occupation	a ocupação	o-koo-pa-**sow**ⁿ
occupied	ocupado	o-koo-**pa**-doo
ocean	o oceano	o-see-**a**-noo
odd *not even*	ímpar	**ee**ⁿ-par
strange	estranho	es-**tra**-nyoo
of	de	je
off	fora	**fo**-ra
offer	a oferta	o-**fer**-ta
offer (to)	oferecer	o-fe-re-**ser**
office	o escritório	es-kree-**to**-ree-oo
official *noun*	o oficial/o funcionário	o-fee-see-**ow**/fooⁿ-see-o-**na**-ree-oo
official *adj.*	oficial	o-fee-see-**ow**
often	frequentemente	fre-kweⁿ-te-**me**ⁿ-te
oily	oleoso	o-le-**o**-zoo
ointment	a pomada	po-**ma**-da

OK	**ok**	ok
old	**velho**	**ve**-lyoo
on	**em**	e^n
on *opp.off*	**ligado**	lee-**ga**-doo
once	**uma vez**	**oo**-ma vez
online	**online**	online
only	**somente**	so-**me**^{n}-te
open (to)	**abrir**	a-**breer**
open(ed)	**aberto**	a-**her**-too
opening	**a abertura**	a-ber-**too**-ra
opera	**a ópera**	**oh**-pe-ra
opportunity	**a oportunidade**	o-por-too-nee-**da**-je
opposite	**o oposto**	o-**pos**-too
or	**ou**	o
orchestra	**a orquestra**	or-**kes**-tra
order (to)	**pedir** *request/* **ordenar** *command*	pe-**jeer**/or-de-**nar**
ordinary	**comum/ ordinário**	ko-**moo**^{n}/ or-jee-na-**ree**-oo
other	**outro**	**o**-troo
otherwise	**senão**	se **now**^{n}
our/ours	**nosso/nossos**	**nos**-soo/**nos**-sos
out	**fora**	**fo**-ra
out of order	**avariado**	a-va-**rya**-doo

outside	**para fora**	pa-ra **fo**-ra
over *above, across*	**sobre/até**	so-bre/a-**teh**
finished	**acabado/terminado**	a-ka-**ba**-doo/ter-mee-na-doo
over there	**lá**	lah
overcoat	**o sobretudo**	so-bre-**too**-doo
overnight	**durante a noite**	du-raⁿ-te a no-**ee**-te
owe (to)	**dever**	de-**ver**
owner	**o dono/ o proprietário**	**do**-noo/pro-pree-e-**ta**-ree-oo

P

pack (to)	**empacotar**	eⁿ-pa-ko-**tar**
packet	**o pacote**	pa-**ko**-te
page	**a página**	**pa**-zhee-na
pain	**a dor**	dor
paint (to)	**pintar**	peeⁿ-**tar**
painting	**a pintura**	peeⁿ-**too**-ra
pair	**o par**	par
palace	**o palácio**	pa-**la**-see-oo
pale	**pálido**	**pa**-lee-doo
panties	**as calcinhas**	kal-**see**-nyas
paper	**o papel**	pa-**pew**

parcel	o pacote/a encomenda	pa-**ko**-te/eⁿ-ko-**meⁿ**-da
park	o parque	**par**-ke
park (to)	estacionar	es-ta-see-o-**nar**
parking meter	o parquímetro	pre-**kee**-me-troo
parking ticket	a multa	**mool**-ta
parliament	o parlamento	par-la-**meⁿ**-too
part	a parte	**par**-te
party	a festa	**fes**-ta
pass (to)	passar	pas-**sar**
passenger	o passageiro	pas-sa-**zhey**-roo
passport	o passaporte	pas-sa-**por**-te
past *noun*	o passado	pas-sa doo
path	a trilha	tree-lya
patient (*n*)	o paciente	pa-see-eⁿ-te
pavement	a calçada	kal-sa-da
pay (to)	pagar	pa-**gar**
peak	o pico	pee-koo
peace	a paz	paz
pearl	a pérola	pe-ro-la
pebble	o pedregulho	pe-dre **goo**-lyoo
pedal	o pedal	pe-dow
pedestrian	pedestre	pe-**des**-tre

pedestrian crossing	a faixa de pedestres	**fay**-sha je pe-**des**-tres
pedestrian precinct	a área de pedestres	a-re-a je pe-**des**-tres
pen	a caneta	ka-**ne**-ta
pencil	o lápis	**la**-pees
penknife	o canivete	ka-nee-**ve**-te
pensioner	o pensionista	pe^n-see-o-**nees**-ta
people	as pessoas	pes-**so**-as
perfect	perfeito	per-**fey**-too
per (person)	por (pessoa)	poor (pes-**so**-a)
performance	a apresentação	a-pre-ze^n-ta-**sow**^{n}
perfume	o perfume	per-**foo**-me
perhaps	talvez	tal-**vez**
perishable	perecível	pe-re-**see**-vew
permit	a permissão	per-mees-**sow**^{n}
permit (to)	permitir	per-mee-**teer**
person	a pessoa	pes-**so**-a
personal	pessoal	pes-so-**ow**
petrol	a gasolina	ga-zo-**lee**-na
petrol station	o posto de gasolina	**pos**-too je ga-zo-**lee**-na
photograph	a fotografia	fo-to-gra-**fee**-a
photographer	o fotógrafo	fo-**to**-gra-foo
piano	o piano	pee-**a**-noo
pick (to) *choose*	escolher	es-ko-**lyer**
gather	colher	ko-**lyer**

picnic	o piquenique	pee-ke-**nee**-ke
piece	o pedaço	pe-**da**-soo
pier	o cais/o pier	**ka**-ees/**pee**-er
pillow	o travesseiro	tra-ves-**sey**-roo
pin	o alfinete	al-fee-ne-te
(safety) pin	o alfinete de fralda	al-fee-ne-te je **fral**-da
pipe *smoking/ music instrument*	o cachimbo /a flauta	ka-**shee**n-boo/**flow**-ta
place	o lugar	loo-**gar**
plain	simples	**see**n-ples
plan	o plano	**pla**-noo
plant	a planta	**pla**n-ta
plastic	o plástico	plas-tee-koo
plate	o prato	**pra**-too
platform	a plataforma	pla-ta-**for**-ma
play	a jogada	**zho**-ga-da
play (to)	jogar	zho-**gar**
player	o jogador	zho-ga-**dor**
please	por favor	poor fa-**vor**
plenty	de sobra	je **so**-bra
plug	o plugue	**ploo**-ghe
pocket	o bolso	**bol**-soo
point	o ponto	**po**n-too
poisonous	venenoso	ve-ne-**no**-zoo

policeman	o policial	po-lee-see-ow
police station	a delegacia de polícia	de-le-ga-see-a je po-lee-see-a
political	político	po-lee-tee-koo
politician	o político	po-lee-tee-koo
politics	a política	po-lee-tee-ka
pollution	a poluição	po-loo-ee-sow[n]
poor	pobre	po-bre
popular	popular	po-poo-lar
porcelain	a porcelana	por-se-la-na
port	o porto	por-too
possible	possível	pos-see-vew
post (to)	postar	pos-tar
post box	a caixa de correio	kay-sha je ko-hey-oo
postcard	o postal	pos-tow
postman	o carteiro	kar-tey-roo
post office	o correio	ko-hey-oo
postpone (to)	adiar	a-jee-ar
pound	a libra/a libra esterlina *money*	lee-bra/es-ter-lee-na
powder	o pó	poh
prefer (to)	preferir	pre-fe-reer
pregnant	grávida	gra-vee-da
prepare (to)	preparar	pre-pa-rar

present *gift*/tense	o presente	pre-ze^n-te
press (to)	pressionar	pres-see-o-**nar**
pretty *adj*	bonito	bo **nee**-too
adv	bastante	bas-**ta**^n-te
price	o preço	**pre**-soo
priest	o padre	**pa**-dre
print	o impresso	ee^n-**pres**-soo
print (to)	imprimir	ee^n-pree-**meer**
private	privado/ particular	pree-**va**-doo/par-tee-koo-**lar**
problem	o problema	pro-**ble**-ma
profession	a profissão	pro-fees-**sow**^n
programme	o programa	pro-**gra**-ma
promise	a promessa	pro-**mes**-sa
promise (to)	prometer	pro-me-**ter**
prompt	ligeiro/rápido	lee-**zhey**-roo/ha-pee-doo
Protestant	Protestante	Pro-tes-**ta**^n-te
provide (to)	fornecer	for-ne-**ser**
public	público	**poo**-blee-koo
public holiday	o feriado	fe-ree-a-doo
pull (to)	puxar	poo-**shar**
pump	a bomba	**bo**^n-ba
pure	puro	**poo**-roo
purse	a bolsa	**bol**-sa

push (to)/ press against	apertar/empurrar	a-per-tar /e^n-poo-har
put (to)	pôr	por
pyjamas	o pijama	pee-zha-ma

Q

quality	a qualidade	ha-lee-da-je
quantity	a quantidade	ka^n-tee-da-je
quarter	um quarto	kwar-too
queen	a rainha	ha-ee-nya
question	a questão	kes-tow^n
queue	a fila	fee-la
queue (to)	fazer fila	fa-zer fee-la
quick(ly)	rápido (rapidamente)	ha-pee-doo (ha-pee-da me^n-te)
quiet(ly)	quieto (quietamente)	kee-e-too (kee-e-ta-me^n-te)
quilt	a colcha	kol-sha
quite	completamente/ consideravelmente	ko^n-ple-ta-me^n-te/ko^n-see-de-ra-vew-me^n-te)

R

race	a corrida	ko-**hee**-da
race course	o hipódromo	ee-**po**-dro-moo
radiator	o radiador	ha-jee-a-**dor**
radio	o radio	**ha**-jee-oo
railway	a estrada de ferro	es-**tra**-da je **fe**-ho
rain	a chuva	**shoo**-va
rain (to)	chover	**shoo**-ver
rainbow	o arco-íris	**ar**-koo-**ee**-rees
raincoat	a capa de chuva	**ka**-pa je **shoo**-va
rare	raro	**ha**-ro
rate *price*	a taxa	**ta**-sha
rather (than)	em vez de	ay^n vez je
raw	crú	kroo
razor	o barbeador	bar-be-a-**dor**
razor blade	a lâmina de barbear	la-**mee**-na je bar-be-**ar**
reach (to)	alcançar	ow-ka^n-**sar**
read (to)	ler	ler
ready	pronto	**pro**^{n}-too
real	real	he-**ow**
really	realmente	he-ow-**me**^{n}-te
reason	a razão	ha-**zow**^{n}
receipt	a nota fiscal	**no**-ta fees-**kow**

receive (to)	receber	he-se-**ber**
recent	recente	he-**se**n-te
recipe	a receita	he-**say**-ta
recognize (to)	reconhecer	he-ko-nye-**ser**
recommend (to)	recomendar	he-ko-men-**dar**
record *written/ sports*	o registro /o recorde	he-**zhees**-tro/ he-**kor**-je
refill	o refil	he-**feew**
refrigerator	a geladeira	zhe-la-**day**-ra
regards	os cumprimentos	koon-**pree**-men-toos
register (to)	inscrever-se/ matricular-se	een-skre-**ver**-se/ma-tree-koo-**lar**-se
relative	o parente	pa-**re**n-te
religion	a religião	re-lee-zhee-**ow**n
remember (to)	lembrar	len-**brar**
rent	o aluguel	a-loo-**ghew**
rent (to)	alugar	a-**loo**-gar
repair (to)	consertar	kon-ser-**tar**
repeat (to)	repetir	he-**pe**-teer
reply (to)	responder	he-spon-**der**
reservation	a reserva	he-**zer**-va
reserve (to)	reservar	he-zer-**var**
restaurant	o restaurante	hes-tow-**ra**n-te
return (to) *go back*	voltar (para)	vol-**tar** (pa-ra)
give back	devolver	de-vol-**vayr**

reward	a recompensa	he-koⁿ-**pe**ⁿ-sa
ribbon	laço	la-soo
rich	rico	hee-koo
ride *lift*	a carona	ka-**ro**-na
ride (to)	andar/montar	an-**dar**/moⁿ-**tar**
right *opp. left*	direita	jee-ray-**ta**
opp. wrong	correto/certo	ko-**he**-too/ **sair**-too
ring	o anel	a-**new**
ripe	maduro	ma-**doo**-roo
rise (to) *increase*	aumentar	ow-meⁿ-**tar**
get up	levantar	le-vaⁿ-**tar**
river	o rio	hee-oo
road	a rua *street/* a estrada *highway*	hoo-a/ es-tra-da
rock	a pedra	**pe**-dra
roll (to)	rolar	ho-lar
roof	o teto	**te**-too
room	o quarto	**kwar**-too
rope	a corda	**kor**-da
rotten	podre	**po**-dre
rough	áspero	**as**-pe-roo
round	redondo	he-**don**-doo
rowing boat	o barco a remo	**bar**-koo a **he**-moo
rubber	a borracha	bo-**ha**-sha

rubbish	a bobagem *talk*/ o lixo *trash*	bo-**ba**-ge^n /**lee**-shoo
rude	rude	**hoo**-je
ruins	as ruínas	hoo-**ee**-nas
rule (to)	reger/governar	he-**zher**/go-ver-**nar**
rule	a regra	**he**-gra
run (to)	correr	**ko**-her
rush hour	a hora do rush	**o**-ra doo rush

S

sad	triste	**tree**-ste
saddle	a sela	**se**-la
safe	seguro	se-**goo**-roo
sailor	o marinheiro	mar-ee-**nye**-roo
sale *clearance*	a liquidação	lee-kee-da-**sow**^{n}
(on) sale	em promoção	e^n pro-mo-**sow**^{n}
(for) sale	à venda	ah **ve**^{n}-da
salesman	o vendedor	ve^n-je-**dor**
saleswoman	a vendedora	ve^n-je-**do**-ra
salt water	a água salgada	**a**-gwa sow-**ga**-da
same	o mesmo	**mes**-moo
sand	a areia	a-**rey**-a
sandal	a sandália	sa^n-**da**-lee-a

sanitary towel	o absorvente feminino	ab-sor-**ve**^{n}-te fe-mee-nee-noo
satisfactory	**satisfatório**	sa-tees-fa-**to**-ree-oo
save (to)	**salvar**	sow-**var**
say (to)	**dizer**	jee-**zer**
scald (to)	**escaldar**	es-kow-**dar**
scarf	o cachecol	ka-she-**kow**
scenery	o cenário	se-na-ree-oo
school	a escola	es-**ko**-la
scissors	a tesoura	te-**zo**-ra
Scot	o escocês	es-ko-**ses**
Scotland	Escócia	Es-ko-see-a
Scottish	escocês	es-ko-**ses**
scratch (to)	coçar/arranhar	ko-sar/a-ha-**nyar**
screw	o parafuso	pa-ra-**foo**-zoo
screwdriver	a chave de fenda	sha-ve je fe^n-da
sculpture	a escultura	es-kool-**too**-ra
sea	o mar	mar
sea food	os frutos do mar	froo-tos doo mar
seasickness	o enjôo/a náusea	e^n-**zho**-oo/**now**-ze-a
season	a estação	es-ta-**sow**^{n}
seat	o banco/o assento	ba^n-koo/as-**se**^{n}-too
seat belt	o cinto de segurança	**see**^{n}-too je se-goo-ra^n-sa
second	segundo	se-**goo**^{n}-doo

second-hand	**segunda-mão**	se-**goo**ⁿ-da mowⁿ
see (to)	**ver**	ver
seem (to)	**parecer**	pa-re-**ser**
sell (to)	**vender**	veⁿ-**der**
send (to)	**mandar**	maⁿ-**dar**
separate *adj.*	**separado**	se-pa-**ra**-doo
serious	**sério**	**se**-ree-oo
serve (to)	**servir**	ser-**veer**
service *in a shop*	**o atendimento**	a-teⁿ-jee-**me**ⁿ-too
church	**a cerimônia religiosa**	se-ree-**mo**-nee-a he-lee-zhee-**o**-za
several	**vários**	**va**-ree-oos
sew (to)	**costurar**	kos-too-**rar**
shade *colour*	**o tom**	toⁿ
shade/shadow	**a sombra**	**so**ⁿ-bra
shallow	**raso**	**ha**-zoo
shampoo	**o shampoo**	**sha**ⁿ-poo
shape	**a forma**	**for**-ma
share (to)	**dividir/ compartilhar**	jee-vee-**jeer**/ koⁿ-par-tee-**lyar**
sharp	**afiado**	a-fee-**a**-doo
shave (to)	**raspar**	has-**par**
shaving brush	**o pincel de barba**	peeⁿ-**sew** je **bar**-ba
shaving cream	**o creme de barbear**	**kre**-me je bar-be-**ar**

she	ela	e-la
sheet	o lençol	len-**sow**
shell	a concha	kon-sha
shelter	o abrigo	a-**bree**-goo
shine (to)	brilhar	bree-**lyar**
shingle *beach*	as pedrinhas	pe-**dree**-nyas
ship	o navio	na-**vee**-oo
shirt	a camisa	ka-**mee**-za
shock	o choque	**sho**-ke
shoe	o sapato	sa-**pa**-too
shoelace	o cadarço	ka-**dar**-soo
shoe polish	a graxa de sapato	gra-sha je sa-**pa**-too
shop	a loja	**lo**-zha
shore	o litoral	lee-to-**row**
short	curto	**koor**-too
shorts	os shorts	shorts
show	o show	show
show (to)	mostrar	mos-**trar**
shower	o chuveiro	shoo-**vey**-roo
shut (to)	fechar	fe-**shar**
closed	fechado	fe-**sha**-doo
side	o lado	**la**-doo
sights	os pontos turísticos	pon-toos too-**rees**-tee-koos

sightseeing	a excursão/a visita a lugares turísticos	es-koor-**sow**ⁿ/vee-**zee**-ta a loo-**gar**-es too-**rees**-tee-koos
sign	o sinal	see-**now**
sign (to)	assinar	as-see-**nar**
signpost	a placa de sinalização	**pla**-ka je see-na-lee-za-**sow**ⁿ
silver	a prata	**pra**-ta
simple	simples	**see**ⁿ-ples
since	desde	**des**-je
sing (to)	cantar	kaⁿ-**tar**
single	solteiro	sol-**tey**-roo
single room	o quarto de solteiro	**kwar**-too je sol-**tey**-roo
sister	a irmã	**eer**-maⁿ
sit (to)	sentar	seⁿ-**tar**
sit down (to)	sentar-se	seⁿ-**tar**-se
size	o tamanho	ta-**ma**-nyoo
skating	a patinação	pa-tee-na-**sow**ⁿ
skid (to)	derrapar	de-ha-**par**
skiing	o esqui	es-**kee**
skirt	a saia	**sa**-ya
sky	o céu	**se**-oo
sleep (to)	dormir	dor-**meer**

sleeping bag	o saco de dormir	sa-koo je dor-meer
sleeve	a manga	ma^n-ga
slice	a fatia	fa-tee-a
slip (to)	escorregar	es-ko-he-gar
slipper	o chinelo	shee-ne-loo
slowly	lentamente/ devagar	le^n-ta-me^n-te/je-va-gar
small	pequeno	pe-ke-noo
smart	esperto	es-per-too
smell	o cheiro	shay-roo
smell (to)	cheirar	shay-rar
smile	o sorriso	so-hee-zoo
smile (to)	sorrir	so-heer
smoke (to)	fumar	foo-mar
smoking area	área para fumantes	ah ree-a pa-ra foo-ma^n-tes
snack	o lanche	la^n-she
snow	a neve	ne-ve
snow (to)	nevar	he-var
so	então	e^n-tow^n
soap	o sabonete	sa-bo-ne-te
soap powder	o sabão em pó	sa-bow^n e^n poh
sober	sóbrio	so-bree-oo
sock	a meia	mey-a
socket electrical	a tomada	to-ma-da

soft	macio	ma-**see**-oo
sold	vendido	ve^n-**jee**-doo
sole *shoe*	a sola	**so**-la
solid	sólido	**so**-lee-doo
some	alguns	ow-**goo**^ns
somebody	alguém	ow-**ghe**^n
somehow	de algum modo	je ow-**goo**^n **mo**-doo
something	alguma coisa	ow-**goo**-ma **ko**-ee-za
sometimes	às vezes	as **ve**-zes
somewhere	em algum lugar	e^n al-**goo**^n loo-**gar**
son	o filho	**fee**-lyoo
song	a canção/ a música	ka^n-**sow**^n/**moo**-zee-ka
soon	logo/em breve	lo-goo/e^n **bre**-ve
sort	o tipo	**tee**-poo
sound	o som	so^n
sour	azedo	a-**ze**-doo
south	o sul	sool
souvenir	o suvenir/a lembrancinha de viagem	soo-ve-**neer**/le^n-bra^n-**see**-nya je vee-a-**zhe**^n
space	o espaço	es-**pa**-soo
spanner	a chave inglesa	**sha**-ve ee^n-**gle**-sa
spare	sobresselente	sos-bres-se-**le**^n-te
speak (to)	falar	fa-**lar**

speciality	a especialidade	es-pe-see-a-lee-**da**-je
spectacles	óculos	**oh**-koo-loos
speed	a velocidade	ve-lo-see-**da**-je
speed limit	o limite de velocidade	lee-**mee**-te je ve-lo-see-**da**-je
spend (to)	gastar	gas-**tar**
spoon	a colher	ko-**lyer**
sport	o esporte	es-**por**-te
sprain (to)	torcer	tor-**ser**
spring *water*	a água da fonte/a nascente	**a**-gwa da fon-te/na-sen-te
square *shape*	o quadrado	kwa-**dra** doo
in a town	a praça	**pra**-sa
square metre	o metro quadrado	**me**-troo kwa-**dra**-doo
stable	estável	es-ta-vew
stage	o palco *theatre*/ estágio *in a process*	**pow**-koo/es-a-ta-zhee-oo
stain	a mancha	**man**-sha
stained	manchado	man-sha-doo
stairs	a escada	es-**ka**-da
stale	velho	**ve**-lyoo
stall *market*	a barraca	ba-ħa-ka
stalls *theatre*	a platéia	pla-**te**-ya
stamp	o selo *letter*/ o carimbo *ink stamp*	se-loo/ka-**reen**-boo

stand (to)	**levantar-se**	le-va^n-**tar**-se
star	**a estrela**	es-**tre**-la
start (to)	**começar**	ko-me-**sar**
(main) station	**a estação (principal)**	es-ta-**sow**^{n} (pree^n-see-**pow**)
stay (to)	**ficar**	fee-**kar**
step	**o passo**	**pas**-soo
steward	**o comissário de bordo** *aeroplane*	ko-mees-**sa**-ree-oo je **bor**-doo
stewardess	**a aero-moça**	ae-ro-**mo**-sa
stick	**o taco/o bastão**	**ta**-koo/bas-**tow**^{n}
stiff	**duro**	**doo**-roo
still *not moving*	**parado**	pa-**ra**-doo
time	**ainda**	ah-**ee**^{n}-da
sting	**a picada**	pee-**ka**-da
stolen	**roubado**	ho-**ba**-doo
stone	**a pedra**	**pe**-dra
stool	**o banquinho**	ba^n-**kee**-nyoo
stop (to)	**parar**	pa-**rar**
storm	**a tempestade**	te^n-pes-**ta**-je
stove	**o fogão**	fo-**gow**^{n}
straight *line*	**a reta**	**he**-ta
heterosexual	**heterosexual**	e-te-ros-sex-soo-**ow**
straight on	**seguir direto/seguir adiante**	se-**gheer** jee-re-too/se-**gheer** a-jee-a^n-te

strange	estranho	es-**tra**-nyoo
strap	a tira	**tee**-ra
stream	o riacho	hee-a-shoo
street	a rua	**hoo**-a
stretch (to)	esticar	es-tee-**kar**
string	o barbante/o cordão	bar-**ba**^{n}-te/kor-**dow**^{n}
strong	forte	**for**-te
student	o estudante	es-too-**da**^{n}-te
stung (to be)	ser picado	ser pee-**ka**-doo
style	o estilo	es-**tee**-loo
suburb	o subúrbio	soo-**boor**-bee-oo
subway	o metrô	me **tro**
such	tal qual	tow kwaw
suede	a camurça	ka-**moor**-sa
sugar	o açúcar	a-**soo**-kar
suggestion	a sugestão	soo-zhes-**tow**^{n}
suit *men*	o terno	**ter**-noo
suitcase	a mala/a maleta	**ma**-la/ma-**le**-ta
sun	o sol	sow
sunbathe (to)	tomar sol	to mar sow
sunburn	a queimadura de sol	key-ma-**doo**-ra je sow
sunglasses	os óculos escuros	o-koo-loos es-**koo**-roos
sunhat	o chapéu de sol	sha-pe-oo je sow

sunny	ensolarado	e^n-so-la-**ra**-doo
sunshade	o guarda-sol	**gwar**-da-sow
supermarket	o supermercado	soo-per-mer-**ka**-doo
supper	o jantar	zha^n-**tar**
sure	certo	**sair**-too
surf board	a prancha de surf	**pra**-sha je surf
surgery	a cirurgia	see-roor-**zhee**-a
surgery hours	o horário de consulta médica	o-**ra**-ree-oo je ko^n-**sool**-ta **meh**-jee-ka
surprise	a surpresa	soor-**pre**-za
surprise (to)	surpreender	soor-pree-e^n-**der**
sweater	o suéter	**swe**-ter
sweet	doce	**do**-se
sweets	os doces/as balas	**do**-ses/**ba**-las
swell (to)	inchar	ee^n-**shar**
swim (to)	nadar	na-**dar**
swimming pool	a piscina	pee-**see**-na
swing	o balanço	ba-**la**^n-soo
switch *electrical*	o interruptor	ee^n-te-hoop-**tor**
swollen	inchado	ee^n-**sha**-doo
synagogue	a sinagoga	see-na-**go**-ga

T

table	a mesa	me-za
tablecloth	a toalha de mesa	to-a-lya je me-za
tablet *medicine*	o tablete/o comprimido	ta-**ble**-te/ ko^n-pree-**mee**-doo
tailor	o alfaiate	ow-fa-ee-a-te
take (to)	levar/pegar	le-**var**/pe-**gar**
talk (to)	falar	fa-**lar**
tall	alto	ow-too
tampon	o tampão	ta^n pow^n
tank	o tanque	ta^n-ke
tap	a torneira	tor-**ney**-ra
taste	o gosto	gos-too
taste (to)	experimentar	es-pe-ree-me^n-**tar**
tax	a taxa	**ta**-sha
taxi	o táxi	tak-see
taxi rank	o ponto de táxi	po^n-too je tak-see
teach (to)	ensinar	e^n see-**nar**
tear	a lágrima	la-gree-ma
tear (to)	rasgar	has-**gar**
telephone	o telefone	te-le-fo-ne
telephone (to)	telefonar	te-le-fo nar

telephone call	a chamada telefônica	sha-**ma**-da te-le-**fo**-nee-ka
telephone directory	a lista telefônica	**lees**-ta te-le-**fo**-nee-ka
telephone number	o número de telefone	**noo**-me-roo je te-le-**fo**-ne
telephone operator	o telefonista	te-le-fo-**nees**-ta
television	a televisão	te-le-vee-**zow**ⁿ
tell (to)	dizer	jee-**zer**
temperature	a temperatura	teⁿ-pe-ra-**too**-ra
temple	o templo	teⁿ-ploo
temporary	temporário	teⁿ-po-**ra**-ree-oo
tennis	o tênis	**te**-nees
tent	a barraca/a tenda	ba-**ha**-ka/**te**ⁿ-da
terrace	o terraço	te-**ha**-soo
than	do que	doo ke
that	esse/isso	**es**-se/ **ees**-soo
the	o, a/os, as	oo, a/oos, as
theatre	o teatro	te-**a**-troo
their(s)	deles/delas	**de**-les/**de**-las
them	eles, elas	**e**-les, **e**-las
then	depois/então	**de**-poys/e**ⁿ-tow**ⁿ
there	lá/ali/aí	lah/**a-lee**/a-**ee**
there is/are	há/tem	ah/**te**ⁿ
thermometer	o termômetro	ter-**mo**-me-troo

these	estes/estas	es-tes/es-tas
they	eles/elas	e-les/ e-las
thick	grosso	gros-soo
thief	o ladrão	la-drow^n
thin	magro	ma-groo
thing	a coisa	ko-ee-sa
think (to)	pensar	pe^n-sar
thirsty	com sede	ko^n se-de
this	isto/este/esta	ees-too/es-te/es-ta
those	aqueles/aquelas	a-ke-les/a-ke-las
though	embora	e^n-bo-ra
thread	o fio/o barbante	fee-oo/bar-ba^n-te
through	através/por	a-tra-ves/poor
throughout	por todo	poor to-doo
throw (to)	jogar/atirar	zho-gar/a-tee-rar
thunderstorm	a tempestade	te^n-pes-ta-je
ticket	a multa for violations/ o ingresso/o bilhete	mool-ta/ee^n-gres-soo/ bee-lye-te
tide	a maré	ma-reh
tie clothing	a gravata	gra-va-ta
sport	o empate	e^n-pa-te
tight	apertado	a-per-ta-doo
tights	a meia-calça	mey-a -kal-sa

time	o tempo	te^n-poo
timetable	o horário	o-**ra**-ree-oo
tin	a lata	**la**-ta
tin opener	o abridor de latas	a-bree-**dor** je **la**-tas
tip	a gorgeta	gor-**zhe**-ta
tip (to)	dar gorgeta	dar gor-**zhe**-ta
tired	cansado	ka^n-**sa**-doo
tissue	o tecido *body/* o lenço de papel	te-**see**-doo/le^n-soo je pa-**pew**
to	a/para	a/**pa**-ra
tobacco	o tabaco	ta-**ba**-koo
together	junto	**zhoo**^{n}-too
toilet	o banheiro	ba-**nyer**-oo
toilet paper	o papel higiênico	pa-**pew** ee-zhee-**e**-nee-koo
toll *road fee*	o pedágio	pe-**da**-zhee-oo
too *also*	também	ta^n-**be**^{n}
too (much, many)	demais	je-**ma**-ees
toothbrush	a escova de dentes	es-**ko**-va je **de**^{n}-tes
toothpaste	a pasta de dentes	**pas**-ta je **de**^{n}-tes
toothpick	o palito de dentes	pa-**lee**-too je **de**^{n}-tes
top	o topo	**to**-poo
torch	a lanterna	la^n-**ter**-na
torn	rasgado	has-**ga**-doo

touch (to)	**tocar**	to-**kar**
tough	**duro**	**doo**-roo
tour (to)	**viajar**	vee-a-**zhar**
tourist	**o turista**	too-**rees**-ta
tourist office	**o posto de informações turísticas**	**pos**-too je ee^n-for-ma-**soy**^{n}s too-**rees**-tee-kas
towards	**em direção a**	e^n jee-re-**sow**^{n} a
towel	**a toalha**	to-**a**-lya
tower	**a torre**	**to**-he
town	**a cidadezinha**	see-da-je-**zee**-nya
town hall	**a prefeitura**	pre-fey-**too**-ra
toy	**o brinquedo**	bree^n-**ke**-doo
traffic	**o tráfego**	**tra**-fe-goo
traffic jam	**o engarrafamento**	e^n-ga-ha-fa-**me**^{n}-too
traffic lights	**o sinal de trânsito/o semáforo**	see-**now** je tra^n-zee-too/ se-**ma**-fo-roo
trailer	**o trailer**	traller
train	**o trem**	tre^n
trainers	**os tênis**	te-nees
tram	**o bonde**	bo^n-je
transfer (to)	**transferir**	tra^n-s-fe-reer
travel	**baldear**	bow-je-**ar**
transit	**o trânsito**	**tra**^{n}-zee-too

translate (to)	**traduzir**	tra-doo-**zeer**
travel (to)	**viajar**	vee-a-**zhar**
travel agency	**a agência de viagem**	a-**zhe**ⁿ-see-a je vee-a-**zhe**ⁿ
treat (to)	**tratar**	tra-**tar**
treatment	**o tratamento**	tra-ta-**me**ⁿ-too
tree	**a árvore**	**ar**-vo-re
trip	**a viagem**	vee-a-**zhe**ⁿ
trouble	**a dificuldade/o problema**	jee-fee-kool-**da**-je/pro-ble-ma
trousers	**as calças**	**kal**-sas
true	**verdadeiro**	ver-da-**dey**-roo
trunk	**o tronco**	**tro**ⁿ-koo
trunks *swimming*	**a sunga**	**soo**ⁿ-ga
truth	**a verdade**	ver-**da**-je
try (to)	**tentar**	te**ⁿ**-**tar**
try on (to)	**experimentar**	es-pe-ree-me**ⁿ**-**tar**
tunnel	**o túnel**	**too**-new
turn (to)	**virar**	vee-**rar**
turning	**a volta/a esquina**	**vow**-ta/es-**kee**-na
tweezers	**a pinça**	**pee**ⁿ-sa
twin-bedded room	**o quarto com duas camas**	**kwar**-too ko**ⁿ** **doo**-as **ka**-mas
twisted	**torcido/distorcido**	tor-**see**-doo/jees-tor-**see**-doo

U

ugly	feio	fey-oo
UK	Reino Unido	He-ee-noo Oo-nee-doo
umbrella	o guarda-chuva	gwar-da shoo-va
(beach) umbrella	o guarda-sol	gwar-da-sow
uncle	o tio	tee-o
uncomfortable	inconfortável	een-kon-for-ta-vew
unconscious	inconsciente	een-kon-see-en-te
under(neath)	debaixo	de-bay-shoo
underground	o metrô	me-tro
underpants	a cueca *male*/a calcinha *female*	kwe-ka/kal-see-nya
understand (to)	entender	en-ten-der
underwater fishing	a pesca submarina	pes-ka soob-ma-ree-na
underwear	a roupa de baixo	ho-pa je bay-shoo
university	a universidade	oo-nee-ver-see-da-je
unpack (to)	desembrulhar/ desembalar	de-zen-broo-lyar/de-zen-ba-lar
until	até	a-teh
unusual	incomum	een-ko-moon
up	para cima	pa-ra see-ma
upstairs	o andar superior	an-dar soo-pay-ree-or
urgent	urgente	oor-zhayn-te

us	nós	nohs
USA (United States of America)	EUA (Estados Unidos da América)	eh-oo-ah (es-**ta**-doos oo-**nee**-doos da a-**me**-ree-ka)
use (to)	usar	oo-zar
useful	útil	**oo**-teew
useless	inútil	ee-**noo**-teew
usual	usual	oo-zoo-**wow**

V

vacancies	as vagas	**va**-gas
vacant	vago/vazio	**va**-go/va-**zee**-oo
vacation	as férias	**fe**-ryas
valid	válido	**va**-lee-do
valley	o vale	**va**-le
valuable	valioso	va-lee-o-zoo
value	o valor	va-**lor**
vase	o vaso	**va**-zo
VAT	IVA (imposto sobre valor agregado)	**ee**-va
vegetable	o vegetal	ve-zhe-**tow**
vegetarian	o vegetariano	ve-zhe-ta-ree-a-noo
ventilation	a ventilação	ve^{n}-tee-la-**sow**^{n}
very	muito	**mwee**-too

vest	o colete	ko-**le**-te
view	a vista	**vees**-ta
village	a aldéia	ow-**dey**-ya
violin	o violino	vee-o-**lee**-noo
visa	o visto	**vees**-too
visibility	a visibilidade	vee-zee-bee-lee-**da**-je
visit	a visita	vee-zee-**ta**
visit (to)	visitar	vee-zee-**tar**
voice	a voz	voz
voltage	a voltagem	vol-ta-zhe^n
voucher	o voucher	voucher

W

wait (to)	esperar	es-pe-**rar**
waiter	o garçon	**gar**-so^n
waiting room	a sala de espera	**sa**-la je es-**pe**-ra
waitress	a garçonete	gar-so-**ne**-te
wake (to)	acordar/despertar	a-kor-**dar**/jes-per-**tar**
Wales	País de Gales	pa-**ees** je **ga**-les
walk	a caminhada	ka-mee-**nya**-da
walk (to)	andar	a^n-**dar**
wall *inside*	a parede	pa-**ray**-je

outside	o muro	moo-roo
wallet	a carteira	kar-**tey**-ra
want (to)	querer	ke-**rer**
wardrobe	o guarda-roupa	**gwar**-da-**ho**-pa
warm	morno	**mor**-noo
warranty	a garantia	ga-ra^n-**tee**-a
wash (to)	lavar	la-**var**
washbasin	a pia/ o lavatório	**pee**-a/la-va-**to**-ree-oo
waste	o desperdício	des-per-**jee**-see-oo
waste (to)	desperdiçar	des-per-jee-**sar**
watch *timepiece*	o relógio	he-**lo**-zhee-oo
water	a água	**a**-gwa
waterfall	a cachoeira	ka-shoo-**ey**-ra
water skiing	o esqui aquático	es-**kee** a-**kwa**-tee-koo
waterproof	à prova d'água	ah pro-**va da**-gwa
wave	a onda	o^n-da
way	o caminho	ka-**mee**-nyo
we	nós	nohs
wear (to)	vestir	ves-**teer**
weather	o tempo	**tay**^{n}-poo
weather forecast	a previsão do tempo	pre-vee-**zow**^{n} doo **tay**^{n}-poo
website	o website	website
wedding ring	a aliança	a-lee-**a**^{n}-sa

week	a semana	se-**ma**-na
weekend	o fim de semana	fee^n je se-**ma**-na
weigh (to)	pesar	pe-**zar**
weight	o peso	**pe**-zoo
welcome	bem-vindo	be^n **vee**^{n}-doo
well	bem	be^n
Welsh	galês	ga-**les**
Welsh man/woman	galês/galesa	ga-**les**/ga-**le**-sa
west	oeste/ocidente	o-**es**-te/o-see-**de**^{n}-te
wet	molhado	mo-**lya**-doo
what	o quê	oo ke
wheel	a roda	**ho**-da
when	quando	**kwa**^{n}-doo
where	onde	**o**^{n}-je
whether	se	se
which	qual	kwal
while	enquanto	e^n **kwa**^{n}-too
who	quem	kay^n
whole	inteiro	ee^n **tay** roo
whose	de quem	je kay^n
why	porquê	poor-**kay**
wide	largo/amplo	**lar**-goo/a^n-ploo
widow	a viúva	vee-**oo**-va

widower	o viúvo	vee-**oo**-voo
wife	a esposa/a mulher	es-**po**-za/ moo-**lyer**
wild	selvagem	sew-va-**zhe**ⁿ
win (to)	ganhar	ga-**nyar**
wind	o vento	**ve**ⁿ-too
window	a janela	zha-**ne**-la
wing	a asa	**a**-za
wire	o fio	**fee**-oo
wish (to)	desejar	de-ze-**zhar**
with	com	koⁿ
without	sem	seⁿ
woman	a mulher	moo-**lyer**
wood *timber*	a madeira	ma-**day**-ra
forest	a floresta	flo-**res**-ta
wool	a lã	laⁿ
word	a palavra	pa-**la**-vra
work	o trabalho	tra-ba-**lyo**
work (to)	trabalhar	tra-ba-**lyar**
worry (to)	preocupar	pray-o-koo-**par**
worse	pior	pee-**or**
worth (to be)	valer a pena	va-**ler** a **pe**-na
wrap (to)	embrulhar	eⁿ-broo-**lyar**
write (to)	escrever	es-kre-**ver**
wrong	errado	e-**ha**-doo

Y

yacht	o iate	ya-te
year	o ano	a-noo
yet	já/ainda	zhah/a-een-da
you	você	vo-seh
young	jovem	zho-vayn
your	teu/seu	tay-oo /say-oo
youth hostel	o albergue da juventude	al-ber-ghe da zhoo-ven-too-je

Z

| zip | o zíper | zi-per |
| zoo | o zoológico | zoo-o-lo-zhee-koo |

INDEX